Doing Qualitative Research

A Practical Handbook

David Silverman

SAGE Publications

London · Thousand Oaks · New Delhi

SAGE Publications Ltd
6 Bonhill Street
London EC2A 4PU

SAGE Publications Inc
2455 Teller Road
Thousand Oaks, California 91320

SAGE Publications India Pvt Ltd
32, M-Block Market
Greater Kailash - I
New Delhi 110 048

British Library Cataloguing in Publication data

A catalogue record for this book is available from the British Library

ISBN 0 7619 5822 3
ISBN 0 7619 5823 1 (pbk)

Library of Congress catalog card number 99-72804

Typeset by Type Study, Scarborough, North Yorkshire
Printed in Great Britain by The Cromwell Press Ltd, Trowbridge, Wiltshire

For my students

Contents

CONTENTS

CONTENTS

Preface

This is the fourth textbook on methodology which I have written or edited since 1985. Everyone knows that research methods texts often sell well but that is hardly an excuse to write yet another one. So you may properly ask: why have I written this book?

The brief answer is that, in my view, research students still lack a singly authored, 'hands-on', practical guide to the business of doing qualitative research, writing it up and making use of it. This is what this book sets out to do.

Much more than other methodology texts, it aims to teach the skills of qualitative research in the context of the practical problems that face the novice researcher. To this end it combines telling examples of students' experiences 'in the field', case studies of relevant qualitative research, summaries of key skills and exercises to test your knowledge.

The content of this book derives from my experience over fifteen years of teaching introductory workshops for research students, a course in Concepts and Methods of Qualitative Research for MA students and an undergraduate qualitative research course. These courses have convinced me that the only way to learn the craft skills of qualitative research is to apply classroom knowledge about different methodologies to actual data. The examples and exercises in this book are designed to allow the novice to emerge with practical skills rather than simply the ability to write good examination answers.

However, my readers should be aware that even textbooks cannot offer purely 'neutral' treatment of the topics they cover. Much will depend upon the material included (and excluded) and upon the particular position of the author: we all have our own 'axes to grind'.

In this book, I argue that doing qualitative research is always a theoretically driven undertaking. This means that 'practical skills' are not the whole of the story, particularly if such skills are (wrongly) seen as sets of arbitrary 'recipes'.

Second, I have long argued that most dichotomies or polarities in social science are highly dangerous. At best, they are pedagogic devices for students to obtain a first grip on a difficult field: they help us to learn the jargon. At worst, they are excuses for not thinking, which assemble groups of researchers into 'armed camps', unwilling to learn from one another.

For instance, unlike some qualitative researchers, I have used quantitative measures where appropriate. This is because I share quantitative researchers' aim to do a 'science' (loosely defined as critical sifting of data, leading to cumulative generalizations which can always be later refuted).

Because I despise 'armed camps', I hope this book will be equally accessible to students of qualitative method across a wide range of disciplines. Although I cannot escape my own sociological background, I have tried throughout to provide helpful resources for students across the social sciences and throughout the world.

I hope that this book will become a basic primer for PhD students, combining 'hands-on' guidance on completing a good qualitative research project with practical advice on the criteria used in oral examinations and in publication. I have also attempted to make the book useful and accessible to the many MA and BA students who now prepare qualitative research dissertations. Although such students will normally be expected to complete their research in months rather than years, they confront the same problems of research design, execution and writing up discussed in this book. Even if they do not face an oral examination on their research, the best MA students should be thinking about publishing their work and both BA and MA students should be interested in how higher-level work is evaluated and the significance of 'originality'.

This book is organized into seven parts. Part One provides a context for thinking about doing qualitative research. Chapter 1 compares qualitative and quantitative research and demonstrates what they have in common. Chapters 2 and 3 offer examples of early and late stages of research students' work and show what we can learn from these experiences and ideas. Finally, in Chapter 4, I address (and seek to demystify) the troubling concept of 'originality' in research.

In Part Two, I review some major issues that arise when you start to design a research study. Chapter 5 discusses how to select a topic. Chapters 6 and 7 deal with using theories and choosing a methodology. The tricky question of selecting which case(s) to study is discussed in Chapter 8. The final chapter in Part Two considers how to write a research proposal.

Part Three moves you on to issues in data analysis. In Chapter 10, I outline what is to be gained by working early with datasets. Chapter 11 discusses how to develop your early analysis. The two final chapters in this part of the book consider the use of computer-aided qualitative data analysis, and validity and reliability.

In Part Four, I address ways of keeping in touch both with your data and with subjects 'in the field'. In three chapters, I discuss record-keeping (including a research diary), relations in the field (including ethical issues) and how to get feedback about your research.

Part Five is concerned with the 'writing-up' stage of research. Its five chapters address the following topics: how to begin your research report; how to write effective literature review, methodology and data chapters; and what to put in your concluding chapter.

The four chapters in Part Six consider the aftermath of a finished piece of research. Depending on the level of your work, this may involve an oral examination, the possibility of getting your research published and, perhaps, getting a job. Whatever its level, a good research report is always designed for a particular audience (Chapter 24).

I conclude with Part Seven, which consists of just one chapter on the contested character of qualitative research. This chapter is written in a much more polemical tone than the rest of the book and serves as its epilogue.

Chapter 12 of this book was written by my colleague Clive Seale and I am most grateful for his skilful exposition of computer-aided data analysis.

Many people have helped in successive drafts of this book. In particular, I would like to mention Jay Gubrium, Clive Seale and Kathy Charmaz who gave their time and efforts freely and well beyond the call of duty. I also want to thank all the students whose work is referred to in Chapter 3; Georgia Lepper, Seta Waller and Vicki Taylor for allowing me to quote from their research diaries; and Greer Rafferty for printing successive drafts with barely a complaint. Anne Murcott kindly allowed me to quote from her unpublished paper on writing a student dissertation.

The first and last chapters of this book are revised versions of some of my recently published work. Chapter 1 draws, in part, on my chapter 'Qualitative/quantitative', in C. Jenks (ed.), *Core Sociological Dichotomies*, London: Sage, 1998. Chapter 26 is a revised version of my paper 'The quality of qualitative health research', *Social Sciences in Health*, 1998, 4(2): 104–18.

1

What is Qualitative Research?

In the Sociology Department where I work, we offer a graduate degree in Qualitative Research. This title was chosen to give a flavour of a course largely taught by ethnographers who themselves mainly use qualitative methods. However, I feel that such a title may attract students more in terms of what it promises to avoid rather than by reason of what it offers.

'Qualitative research' seems to promise that we will avoid or downplay statistical techniques and the mechanics of the kinds of quantitative methods used in, say, survey research or epidemiology. In fact, this is indeed the case – although we expect students to take a course in survey methods and to be aware of how the issues of validity and reliability so often posed by quantitative researchers are relevant to any kind of research (albeit in varying ways).

The danger in the title, however, is that it seems to assume a fixed preference or pre-defined evaluation of what is 'good' (i.e. qualitative) and 'bad' (i.e. quantitative) research. In fact, the choice between different research methods should depend upon what you are trying to find out.

For instance, if you want to discover how people intend to vote, then a quantitative method, like a social survey, may seem the most appropriate choice. On the other hand, if you are concerned with exploring people's life histories or everyday behaviour, then qualitative methods may be favoured. However, other, less practical questions arise when you choose between 'qualitative' and 'quantitative' methods. The researcher has to bear in mind that these methods are often evaluated differently. This is shown in Table 1.1, which is drawn from the terms used by speakers at a conference on research methods.

Table 1.1 shows how imprecise, evaluative considerations come into play when researchers describe qualitative and quantitative methods. Depending on your point of view, Table 1.1 might suggest that quantitative research is superior because, for example, it is value-free. The implication here is that

TABLE 1.1   Claimed features of qualitative and quantitative methods

Qualitative	Quantitative
Soft	Hard
Flexible	Fixed
Subjective	Objective
Political	Value-free
Case study	Survey
Speculative	Hypothesis testing
Grounded	Abstract

Source: Halfpenny, 1979: 799

quantitative research simply objectively reports reality, whereas qualitative research is influenced by the researcher's political values. Conversely, other people might argue that such value freedom in social science is either undesirable or impossible.

The same sort of argument can arise about 'flexibility'. For some people, this flexibility encourages qualitative researchers to be innovative. For others, flexibility might be criticized as meaning lack of structure. Conversely, being 'fixed' gives such a structure to research but without flexibility.

However, this is by no means a balanced argument. Outside the social science community, there is little doubt that quantitative data rule the roost. Governments favour quantitative research because it mimics the research of its own agencies (Cicourel, 1964: 36). They want quick answers based on 'reliable' variables.

Similarly, many research funding agencies call qualitative researchers 'journalists or soft scientists. Their work is termed unscientific, or only exploratory, or entirely personal and full of bias' (Denzin and Lincoln, 1994: 4).

For the general public, there is a mixture of respect and suspicion of quantitative data ('you can say anything you like with figures'; 'lies, damn lies and statistics'). This is reflected by the media. On the one hand, public opinion polls are treated as newsworthy – particularly immediately before elections. On the other hand, unemployment and inflation statistics are often viewed with suspicion – particularly when they appear to contradict your own experience (statistics which show that inflation has fallen may not be credible if you see prices going up for the goods you buy!).

By the 1990s, in many Western countries, the assumed reliability of quantitative research was beginning to be under significant threat. In Britain, for instance, the ways in which inflation and unemployment were calculated during the Thatcher era were regularly changed. This suggested to some that such indexes might be being 'fixed' in order to cast a favourable light upon these matters. Similarly, the failure of surveys of voting intention in the British general election of 1992 (almost comparable to the similar failure of US polling studies in the 1948 Truman–Dewey presidential race) made the public a little sceptical about such statistics – even though the companies involved insisted they were providing only statements of current voting intentions and not predictions of the actual result.

But such concerns may constitute only a 'blip' in the ongoing history of the dominance of quantitative research. Qualitative researchers still largely feel themselves to be second-class citizens whose work typically evokes suspicion, where the 'gold standard' is quantitative research.

However, so far we have been dealing with little more than empty terms, apparently related to whether or not researchers use statistics of some kind. In the next two sections, I address in rather more detail what social scientists mean by quantitative and qualitative research.

VARIETIES OF QUANTITATIVE RESEARCH

Bryman (1988) has discussed the five main methods of quantitative social science research and these are set out in Table 1.2.

To flesh out the bare bones of Table 1.2, I will use one example based on the quantitative analysis of official statistics. The example relates to data taken from the General Social Survey (GSS) carried out every year by the US National Opinion Research Center (NORC) and discussed by Procter (1993).

Procter shows how you can use these data to calculate the relationship between two or more variables. Sociologists have long been interested in 'social mobility' – the movement between different statuses in society either within one lifetime or between generations. The GSS data can be used to calculate the latter, as Table 1.3 shows.

In Table 1.3, we are shown the relationship between father's and son's occupations. In this case, the father's occupation is the 'independent' variable because it is treated as the possible cause of the son's occupation (the 'dependent' variable).

TABLE 1.2 **Methods of quantitative research**

Method	Features	Advantages
Social survey	Random samples Measured variables	Representative Tests hypotheses
Experiment	Experimental stimulus 'Control group' not exposed to stimulus	Precise measurement
Official statistics	Analysis of previously collected data	Large datasets
'Structured' observation	Observations recorded on pre-determined 'schedule'	Reliability of observations
Content analysis	Pre-determined categories used to count content of mass media products	Reliability of measures

Source: adapted from Bryman, 1988: 11–12

TABLE 1.3   Respondent's occupation by father's occupation

| | | Father's occupation | |
		Non-manual	Manual
Son's occupation	Non-manual	63.4%	27.4%
	Manual	36.6%	72.6%

Source: adapted from Procter, 1993: 246

Table 1.3 appears to show a strong association (or 'correlation') between father's and son's occupations. For instance, of the group with non-manual fathers, 63.4 per cent were themselves in non-manual jobs. However, among sons with fathers in manual occupations, only 27.4 per cent had obtained non-manual work. Because the sample of over 1000 people was randomly recruited, we can be confident, within specifiable limits, that this correlation is unlikely to be obtained by chance.

However, quantitative researchers are reluctant to move from statements of correlation to causal statements. For instance, both father's and son's occupations may be associated with another variable (say inherited wealth) which lies behind the apparent link between occupations of father and son. Because of such an 'antecedent' variable, we cannot confidently state that father's occupation is a significant *cause* of son's occupation. Indeed, because this antecedent variable causes both of the others to vary together, the association between the occupations of fathers and sons is misleading or 'spurious'.

Along these lines Procter (1993: 248–9) makes the interesting observation that there appears to be a marked correlation between the price of rum in Barbados and the level of Methodist ministers' salaries, i.e. in any given year, both go up or down together. However, we should not jump to the conclusion that this means that rum distillers fund the Methodist Church. As Procter points out, both the price of rum and ministers' salaries may simply be responding to inflationary pressures. Hence the initial correlation is 'spurious'.

While looking at Tables 1.2 and 1.3, you may have been struck by the extent to which quantitative social research uses the same language that you may have been taught in say physics, chemistry or biology. As Bryman notes:

> Quantitative research is . . . a genre which uses a special language . . . [similar] to the ways in which scientists talk about how they investigate the natural order – variables, control, measurement, experiment. (1988: 12)

Sometimes, this has led critics to claim that quantitative research ignores the differences between the natural and social world by failing to understand the 'meanings' that are brought to social life. This charge is often associated with critics who label quantitative research as 'positivistic' (e.g. Filmer et al., 1972).

Unfortunately, 'positivism' is a very slippery and emotive term. Not only is it difficult to define but there are very few quantitative researchers who would accept it (see Marsh, 1982: Ch. 3). Instead, most quantitative researchers would argue that they do not aim to produce a science of laws (like physics) but aim simply to produce a set of cumulative generalizations based on the critical sifting of data, i.e. a 'science' as defined above.

As I argue, at this level, many of the apparent differences between quantitative and qualitative research should disappear – although some qualitative researchers remain insistent that they want nothing to do with even such a limited version of science (see Phillips, 1973). It follows that, when we compare the two kinds of research, the most we should be looking for are different *emphases* between 'schools' who themselves contain many internal differences.

CRITICISMS OF QUANTITATIVE RESEARCH

Qualitative researchers often assume that a dependence on purely quantitative methods may neglect the social and cultural construction of the 'variables' which quantitative research seeks to correlate. As Kirk and Miller (1986) argue, 'attitudes', for instance, do not simply attach to the inside of people's heads and researching them depends on making a whole series of analytical assumptions. They conclude:

> The survey researcher who discusses is not wrong to do so. Rather, the researcher is wrong if he or she fails to acknowledge the theoretical basis on which it is meaningful to make measurements of such entities and to do so with survey questions. (1986: 15)

According to its critics, much quantitative research leads to the use of a set of *ad hoc* procedures to define, count and analyse its variables (Blumer, 1956; Cicourel, 1964; Silverman, 1975). On the basis of this critique, qualitative researchers have preferred to describe how, in everyday life, we actually go about defining, counting and analysing. The implication is that quantitative researchers unknowingly use the methods of everyday life, even as they claim scientific objectivity (Cicourel, 1964; Garfinkel, 1967).

Let me try to concretize this critique by means of a single example. More than twenty years ago, two American sociologists, Peter Blau and Richard Schoenherr, conducted a study of several large organizations. The study is interesting for our present purposes because it is explicitly based on a critique of qualitative methods. In these authors' view, too much research in the 1960s had used qualitative methods to describe 'informal' aspects of organization – like how employees perceive their organization and act according to these perceptions rather than according to the organizational 'rulebook'.

Blau and Schoenherr (1971) suggested that the time was ripe to switch the balance and to concentrate on 'formal' organization, like how jobs are officially defined and how many 'levels' exist in the organizational hierarchy. Such features can then be seen as 'variables' and statistical correlations can be produced which are both reliable and valid.

Let us see how such an apparently simple, quantitative logic worked out in practice. Blau and Schoenherr used as their data organizational wallcharts which show hierarchies and job functions. Unfortunately, from their point of view, as a revealing early chapter acknowledges, these wallcharts are often ambiguous and vary in structure from one organization to another. Consequently, it was necessary to discuss their meaning in interviews with 'key informants' in each organization. Using this information, Blau and Schoenherr constructed standardized measures of various aspects of organizational structure such as 'hierarchy' and 'job specificity'. The result of all this was a set of statistical correlations which convincingly show the relationship between the variables that Blau and Schoenherr constructed.

Unfortunately, given the indeterminancy of the data they were working with, the authors engaged in a series of sensible but undoubtedly *ad hoc* decisions in order to standardize the different forms in which people talk about their own organization. For instance, they decided to integrate into one category the two grades of 'clerk' that appear on one organization's wallchart of authority.

This decision was guided by a statistical logic that demanded clearly defined, 'reliable' measures. However, the researchers' decision has an unknown relationship to how participants in the organization concerned actually relate to this wallchart and how or when they invoke it. Indeed, Blau and Schoenherr are prevented from examining such matters by their decision to stay at a purely 'structural' level and to avoid 'informal' behaviour. This means that their own interpretation of the meaning of the statistical correlations so obtained, while no doubt statistically rigorous, is equally *ad hoc*.

What we have here is a nice case of 'the cart leading the horse'. Blau and Schoenherr adopt a purely statistical logic precisely in order to replace common-sense understandings by scientific explanations. However, despite themselves, they inevitably appeal to common-sense knowledge both in defining their 'variables' and in interpreting their correlations. So the quantitative desire to establish 'operational' definitions at an early stage of social research can be an arbitrary process which deflects attention away from the everyday sense-making procedures of people in specific milieux. As a consequence, the 'hard' data on social structures which quantitative researchers claim to provide can turn out to be a mirage (see also Cicourel, 1964).

This brief (non-random!) example should allow you to understand the kind of criticisms that are often directed at purely quantitative research by more qualitative 'types'. Because space is short, Table 1.4 attempts to summarize these criticisms.

It should be noted that Table 1.4 contains simply some complaints made about *some* quantitative research. Moreover, because quantitative researchers

TABLE 1.4 **Some criticisms of quantitative research**

1 Quantitative research can amount to a 'quick fix', involving little or no contact with people or the 'field'
2 Statistical correlations may be based upon 'variables' that, in the context of naturally occurring interaction, are arbitrarily defined
3 After-the-fact speculation about the meaning of correlations can involve the very common-sense processes of reasoning that science tries to avoid (see Cicourel, 1964: 14, 21)
4 The pursuit of 'measurable' phenomena can mean that unperceived values creep into research by simply taking on board highly problematic and unreliable concepts such as 'delinquency' or 'intelligence'
5 While it is important to test hypotheses, a purely statistical logic can make the development of hypotheses a trivial matter and fail to help in generating hypotheses from data (see Glaser and Strauss, 1967)

are rarely 'dopes', many treat such matters seriously and try to overcome them. So, for instance, epidemiologists, who study official statistics about disease, and criminologists are only too aware of the problematic character of what gets recorded as, say, 'cause of death' or a 'criminal offence' (see Hindess, 1973). Equally, good quantitative researchers are only too aware of the problems involved in interpreting statistical correlations in relation to what the variables involved 'mean' to the participants (see Marsh, 1982: Ch. 5).

In the light of this qualification, I conclude this section by observing that an insistence that any research worth its salt should follow a purely quantitative logic would simply rule out the study of many interesting phenomena relating to what people actually do in their day-to-day lives, whether in homes, offices or other public and private places. But, as the next section shows, a balanced view should accept the strengths, as well as the limitations, of quantitative research.

VARIETIES OF QUALITATIVE RESEARCH

Qualitative researchers suggest that we should not assume that techniques used in quantitative research are the *only* way of establishing the validity of findings from qualitative or field research. This means that a number of practices which originate from quantitative studies may be *inappropriate* to qualitative research. These include the assumptions that social science research can only be valid if based on experimental data, official statistics or the random sampling of populations and that quantified data are the only valid or generalizable social facts.

Critics of quantitative research argue that these assumptions have a number of defects (see Cicourel, 1964; Denzin, 1970; Schwartz and Jacobs, 1979; Hammersley and Atkinson, 1983; Gubrium, 1988). These critics note that experiments, official statistics and survey data may simply be inappropriate to some of the tasks of social science. For instance, they exclude the observation of behaviour in everyday situations. Hence, while quantification may *sometimes* be useful, it can conceal as well as reveal basic social processes.

Consider the problem of counting attitudes in surveys. Do we all have coherent attitudes on any topics which await the researcher's questions? And how do 'attitudes' relate to what we actually do – our practices? Or think of official statistics on cause of death compared with studies of how hospital staff (Sudnow, 1968a), pathologists and statistical clerks (Prior, 1987) attend to deaths (see Chapter 6). Note that this is *not* to argue that such statistics may be biased. Instead, it is to suggest that there are areas of social reality which such statistics cannot measure.

The methods used by qualitative researchers exemplify a common belief that they can provide a 'deeper' understanding of social phenomena than would be obtained from purely quantitative data. However, just as quantitative researchers would resist the charge that they are all 'positivists' (Marsh, 1982), there is no agreed doctrine underlying all qualitative social research. Instead, there are many 'isms' that appear to lie behind qualitative methods – for example interactionism, feminism, postmodernism and ethnomethodology (see Chapter 6).

In spite of this diversity, qualitative researchers are seen by Hammersley (1992) to share a set of preferences which are set out in Table 1.5.

Unfortunately, as Hammersley himself recognizes, such a simple list is a huge over-generalization. For instance, to take just item 5 in Table 1.5, qualitative research would look a little odd, after a history of over 100 years, if it had no hypotheses to test!

Nonetheless, if we take the list in Table 1.5 as a reasonable approximation of the main features of qualitative research, we can start to see why it can be criticized. As already noted, in a world where numbers talk and people use the term 'hard' science, a failure to test hypotheses, coupled with a rejection of natural science methods, certainly leaves qualitative researchers open to criticism.

Of course, many scientists themselves reject the wilder dreams of positivism, for instance the search for laws based on laboratory experiment as the 'gold standard' of good science. Nonetheless, we are still left with this

TABLE 1.5   **The preferences of qualitative researchers**

1   A preference for qualitative data – understood simply as the analysis of words and images rather than numbers
2   A preference for naturally occurring data – observation rather than experiment, unstructured rather than structured interviews
3   A preference for meanings rather than behaviour – attempting 'to document the world from the point of view of the people studied' (Hammersley, 1992: 165)
4   A rejection of natural science as a model
5   A preference for inductive, hypothesis-generating research rather than hypothesis testing (cf. Glaser and Strauss, 1967)

Source: adapted from Hammersley, 1992: 160–72

troubling question: why should we *believe* what qualitative researchers tell us? How can they demonstrate that their descriptions are accurate and that their explanations hold water? It is to these questions which I now turn.

CRITICISMS OF QUALITATIVE RESEARCH

In many, quantitatively oriented social science methodology textbooks, qualitative research is often treated as a relatively minor methodology. As such, it is suggested that it should only be contemplated at early or 'exploratory' stages of a study. Viewed from this perspective, qualitative research can be used to familiarize oneself with a setting before the serious sampling and counting begins.

This view is expressed in the following extract from an early text. Note how the authors refer to 'nonquantified data' – implying that quantitative data are the standard form:

> The inspection of *nonquantified* data may be particularly helpful if it is done periodically throughout a study rather than postponed to the end of the statistical analysis. Frequently, a single incident noted by a perceptive observer contains the clue to an understanding of a phenomenon. If the social scientist becomes aware of this implication at a moment when he can still add to his material or exploit further the data he has already collected, he may considerably enrich the quality of his conclusions. (Selltiz et al., 1964: 435, my emphasis)

Despite these authors' 'friendly' view of the uses of 'nonquantified' data, they assume that 'statistical analysis' is the bedrock of research. A similar focus is to be found, a quarter of a century later, in another mainly quantitative text:

> Field research is essentially a matter of immersing oneself in a naturally occurring ... set of events in order to gain firsthand knowledge of the situation. (Singleton et al., 1988: 11)

Note the emphasis on 'immersion' and its implicit contrast with later, more focused research. This is underlined in the authors' subsequent identification of qualitative or field research with 'exploration' and 'description' (1988: 296) and their approval of the use of field research 'when one knows relatively little about the subject under investigation' (1988: 298–9).

These reservations have some basis given the fact that qualitative research is, by definition, stronger on long descriptive narratives than on statistical tables. The problem that then arises is how such a researcher goes about categorizing the events or activities described.

This is sometimes known as the problem of *reliability*. As Hammersley puts it, reliability

> refers to the degree of consistency with which instances are assigned to the same category by different observers or by the same observer on different occasions. (1992: 67)

The issue of consistency particularly arises because shortage of space means that many qualitative studies provide readers with little more than brief, persuasive, data extracts. As Bryman notes about the typical observational study:

> field notes or extended transcripts are rarely available; these would be very helpful in order to allow the reader to formulate his or her own hunches about the perspective of the people who have been studied. (1988: 77)

Moreover, even when people's activities are tape-recorded and transcribed, the reliability of the interpretation of transcripts may be gravely weakened by a failure to record apparently trivial, but often crucial, pauses and overlaps. For instance, a recent study of medical consultations was concerned to establish whether cancer patients had understood that their condition was fatal. When researchers first listened to tapes of relevant hospital consultations, they sometimes felt that there was no evidence that the patients had picked up their doctors' often guarded statements about their prognosis. However, when the tapes were retranscribed, it was demonstrated that patients used very soft utterances (like 'yes' or, more usually 'mm') to mark that they were taking up this information. Equally, doctors would monitor patients' silences and rephrase their prognosis statements (see Clavarino et al., 1995).

Some qualitative researchers argue that a concern for the reliability of observations arises only within the quantitative research tradition. Because what they call the 'positivist' position sees no difference between the natural and social worlds, reliable measures of social life are only needed by such 'positivists'. Conversely, it is argued, once we treat social reality as always in flux, then it makes no sense to worry about whether our research instruments measure accurately (e.g. Marshall and Rossman, 1989).

Such a position would rule out any systematic research since it implies that we cannot assume any stable properties in the social world. However, if we concede the possible existence of such properties, why shouldn't other work replicate these properties? As Kirk and Miller argue:

> Qualitative researchers can no longer afford to beg the issue of reliability. While the forte of field research will always lie in its capability to sort out the validity of propositions, its results will (reasonably) go ignored minus attention to reliability. For reliability to be calculated, it is incumbent on the scientific investigator to document his or her procedure. (1986: 72)

A second criticism of qualitative research relates to how sound are the explanations it offers. This is sometimes known as the problem of 'anecdotalism', revealed in the way in which research reports sometimes appeal to a few, telling 'examples' of some apparent phenomenon, without any attempt to analyse less clear (or even contradictory) data (Silverman, 1989).

This problem is expressed very clearly by Bryman:

> There is a tendency towards an anecdotal approach to the use of data in relation to conclusions or explanations in qualitative research. Brief conversations, snippets from unstructured interviews ... are used to provide evidence of a particular contention. There are grounds for disquiet in that the representativeness or generality of these fragments is rarely addressed. (1988: 77)

This complaint of 'anecdotalism' questions the *validity* of much qualitative research. 'Validity' is another word for truth (see Chapter 13). Sometimes one doubts the validity of an explanation because the researcher has clearly made no attempt to deal with contrary cases. Sometimes, the extended immersion in the 'field', so typical of qualitative research, leads to a certain preciousness about the validity of the researcher's own interpretation of 'their' tribe or organization. Or sometimes, the demand by journal editors for shorter and shorter articles simply means that the researcher is reluctantly led only to use 'telling' examples – something that can happen in much the same way in the natural sciences where, for instance, laboratory assistants have been shown to select 'perfect' slides for their professor's important lecture (see Lynch, 1984).

Despite these common problems, doubts about the reliability and validity of qualitative research have led many quantitative researchers to downplay its value. However, as we have seen, this kind of 'damning by faint praise' has been more than balanced by criticisms of quantitative research offered by many qualitative researchers.

CONCLUSION

The fact that simple quantitative measures are a feature of some good qualitative research shows that the whole 'qualitative/quantitative' dichotomy is open to question. In the context of this book, as I stated in the Preface, I view most such dichotomies or polarities in social science as highly dangerous. At best, they are pedagogic devices for students to obtain a first grip on a difficult field: they help us to learn the jargon. At worst, they are excuses for not thinking, which assemble groups of sociologists into 'armed camps', unwilling to learn from one another.

Ultimately, objectivity should be the common aim of all social science (see Kirk and Miller, 1986: 10–11). As Hammersley argues:

> the process of inquiry in science is the same whatever method is used, and the retreat into paradigms effectively stultifies debate and hampers progress. (1992: 182)

This means that, if we wish to establish criteria for distinguishing qualitative research, we will need to understand the similar issues faced by any systematic attempt at description and explanation, whether quantitative or qualitative (see Table 1.6).

Although Table 1.6 was prepared as a set of criteria for the evaluation of *qualitative* research papers, I believe that the criteria I have selected are

TABLE 1.6 **Criteria for the evaluation of research**

1	Are the methods of research appropriate to the nature of the question being asked?
2	Is the connection to an existing body of knowledge or theory clear?
3	Are there clear accounts of the criteria used for the selection of cases for study, and of the data collection and analysis?
4	Does the sensitivity of the methods match the needs of the research question?
5	Was the data collection and record-keeping systematic?
6	Is reference made to accepted procedures for analysis?
7	How systematic is the analysis?
8	Is there adequate discussion of how themes, concepts and categories were derived from the data?
9	Is there adequate discussion of the evidence for and against the researcher's arguments?
10	Is a clear distinction made between the data and their interpretation?

Source: adapted from criteria agreed and adopted by the British Sociological Association Medical Sociology Group, September 1996

equally appropriate for quantitative studies. This shows that, in principle, there is no reason to prefer any form of data.

I conclude, therefore, with a statement which shows the absurdity of pushing too far the qualitative/quantitative distinction:

> We are not faced, then, with a stark choice between words and numbers, or even between precise and imprecise data; but rather with a range from more to less precise data. Furthermore, our decisions about what level of precision is appropriate in relation to any particular claim should depend on the nature of what we are trying to describe, on the likely accuracy of our descriptions, on our purposes, and on the resources available to us; not on ideological commitment to one methodological paradigm or another. (Hammersley, 1992: 163)

SUMMARY

In this chapter, I have made four basic points. First, 'qualitative' research involves a variety of quite different approaches. Second, although some 'quantitative' research can be properly criticized or found insufficient, the same may be said about some 'qualitative' research. Third, in these circumstances it is sensible to make pragmatic choices between research methodologies according to your research problem. Finally, doing 'qualitative' research should offer no protection from the rigorous, critical standards that should be applied to any enterprise concerned to sort 'fact' from 'fancy'.

Further reading

The most useful introductory texts are Alan Bryman's *Quantity and Quality in Social Research* (Unwin Hyman, 1988), Nigel Gilbert's (ed.), *Researching Social Life* (Sage, 1993) and Clive Seale's (ed.), *Researching Society and Culture* (Sage, 1998). More advanced qualitative analysis is offered by Silverman's *Interpreting Qualitative Data: Methods for Analysing Talk, Text and Interaction* (Sage, 1993), Miles and Huberman's *Qualitative Data Analysis* (Sage, 1984), Hammersley and Atkinson's *Ethnography: Principles in Practice* (Tavistock, 1983) and Denzin and Lincoln's (eds), *Handbook of Qualitative Research* (Sage, 1994). Sensible statements about the quantitative position are to be found in Marsh (1982) (on survey research) and Hindess (1973) (on official statistics).

In addition to these general texts, readers are urged to familiarize themselves with examples of qualitative and quantitative research. Strong (1979) and Lipset et al. (1962) are good examples of each.

Exercise 1.1

Review any research study with which you are familiar. Then answer the following questions:

1 To what extent are its methods of research (qualitative, quantitative or a combination of both) appropriate to the nature of the research question(s) being asked?
2 How far does its use of these methods meet the criticisms of both qualitative and quantitative research discussed in this chapter?
3 How fully does this study satisfy the criteria for the evaluation of research set out in Table 1.6?
4 In your view, how could this study have been improved methodologically and conceptually?

2
The Research Experience I

Switch on your television and graze through the channels. You will un-doubtedly come across a chat show in which people are talking about their rise and fall from grace. Or maybe you will find a sports channel where, more often than not, you will see not a game but interviews with players about their hopes and feelings.

We live in a world in which our yearning for people's 'experiences' is more than satisfied by the popular media. Indeed, very often this pursuit of the 'personal' becomes repetitive and we should resist it (see Atkinson and Silverman, 1997).

However, this is not always the case. Any book which sets out to offer information and advice about doing a piece of research without telling a few personal 'stories' would be in danger of being received as empty and unhelpful. If we can draw out appropriate implications from these stories, moving from the personal to the practical, then we will have achieved some-thing more substantial than merely providing some kind of experiential comfort blanket.

In this spirit, this chapter is devoted to telling the stories of three of my research students. The three students have much in common apart from the fact that I supervised them for a PhD in sociology. Georgia Lepper, Seta Waller and Vicki Taylor began their research many years after their first degrees (none of which were in sociology) and held down demanding jobs while doing their research. Georgia was a freelance ana-lytical psychologist, Seta a research sociologist and Vicki a health promotion administrator.

All three came to share what might be regarded as a very 'narrow' research perspective deriving from the approach to talk-in-interaction of Harvey Sacks (see Silverman, 1998a). They applied this approach to documents (Georgia), to documents and interviews (Seta) and to audio recordings (Vicki).

I realize that many of my readers will have different interests and backgrounds. Let me assure you at once that you will not need any special knowledge to understand what follows. The approach that they used is, for my present purposes, of far less significance than the trajectory of their projects. Moreover, as I argue below, there are lessons here to be drawn for anybody who is contemplating writing a research dissertation at any level.

Perhaps more relevant than their common theoretical perspective was the different amount of time that their research took: Georgia completed her PhD in three years and Seta in ten; as I write, Vicki is in her sixth, and hopefully final, year. As you will see below, these different timespans were strongly associated with practical contingencies, more or less unrelated to technical issues of research design. Their stories of hope, setbacks, persistence and sheer blood, sweat and tears should strike a chord with any researcher.

In what follows, the three tell their stories largely in their own words drawn from their research diaries. I have limited myself merely to adding some headings and asides (the latter are indicated by square brackets). After each story, I suggest some more general implications. The chapter concludes with a summary in the form of a twelve-point guide to completing a successful research study.

GEORGIA'S RESEARCH DIARY

1 THE WORK SETTING
Like most human activities, this research started in the midst of experiences and events which make more sense in retrospect than they did at the time. As a practising analytical psychologist, I supervise counsellors working in institutional settings. I had observed how the practices of counsellors are affected by the setting they are working in.

2 TRYING OUT STUDYING IT
I became interested in (and, in an *ad hoc* way, began to study) how institutions work from the perspective of 'group relations' (the psychoanalytically oriented study of institutions that developed at the Tavistock Institute of Human Relations in London in the 1960s).

I was interested in what I was learning, but became dissatisfied with some of its assumptions. In particular, I found that 'group relations' theory, borrowing as it does from the psychoanalytic model, made assumptions about 'boundaries' which, to me, seemed crude, and to lend themselves to rather authoritarian practices with which I felt ill at ease.

3 LOOKING FOR A NEW PERSPECTIVE
I decided to return, once again, to formal study, and I began to search for a discipline appropriate to my concerns, without a really clear idea of what I would encounter, or, indeed, even quite what I was looking for. It was in this way [via a meeting with DS to explore the possibility of registering for a PhD at Goldsmiths College] that I encountered conversation analysis (CA).

4 FINDING AN INTELLECTUAL HOME: SERENDIPITY
As soon as CA was explained to me, though briefly, I recognized that [a study based upon it] would complement my current interests and existing analytic skills. Later, as I began reading, I was to discover that its origins lay in intellectual traditions which informed my own undergraduate education in the late 1950s and early 1960s. This was grounded in literature, in linguistics (Whorf and Benjamin) and in the (then new) analytic philosophy of Wittgenstein. I had found an intellectual home.

5 GETTING COMFORTABLE IN THE NEW HOME
As I found out more and more about CA, in my first exploratory reading, I found myself alternately excited and exasperated. Excited by my sense of its potential applications; exasperated by its restrictiveness, by its exactitude – by the seemingly *mechanical* analytic style its earliest practitioners espoused. [However] I came to appreciate that methodological discipline, and I believe my research has benefited from it. I also have some substantial objections [which] I hope to develop.

6 SELECTING DATA AND A RESEARCH PROBLEM
[I discussed with my supervisor what data I might use in my research and, at his suggestion,] attempted an initial analysis of some documents which [I had obtained] from some earlier work I had done with counsellors at an inner-city further education college. The documents were simply a collection of routine reports and memos which had accumulated in their files during the year we worked together.

7 INITIAL DISAPPOINTMENTS WITH THE DATA
At first, I was disappointed with what I found. I was to become familiar with dismay: many times, I was to look at a piece of text and feel: 'there's nothing here, I'm on the wrong track'. [The documents in the files] seemed scrappy, and I knew that there were many other, less formal documents, mostly scribbled notes, which had not been deemed worthy of inclusion in the files.

8 TURNING THE 'INADEQUACY' OF THE DATA INTO A 'FINDING'
Drawing on my psychoanalytic experience, I took this absence to be information, and concluded that these memos might, therefore, be presumed to serve a particular 'function'. It seemed that they might be an example of the way 'organizational materials "freeze" objects and events so that sets are created, and a metalanguage [is] generated for 'talking about' (but not checking out systematically) "what happened"' (Cicourel, 1968: 108).

9 REFINING THE RESEARCH PROBLEM AND APPROACH
What I did find were reports of incidents. I had heard other details [of these incidents] in ongoing stories in supervision sessions. I became interested in how these stories were represented in the reports [using what Harvey Sacks, 1992, has called 'membership categorization device' (MCD) analysis].

I concluded with this statement of my research objectives: 'I would be interested in exploring how MCDs might be used to generate and maintain "boundaries" in multi-person settings. How relatively enduring are they? Does the management of MCDs show . . . a tendency to create orderly, relatively enduring "stories" about perceived events, over time?'

With this proposal, I set my task within the contemporary study of situated practices which could be called 'ethnomethodological ethnography' or 'constitutive ethnography' (Silverman: 1985).

Some implications of Georgia's story

What can the aspiring researcher learn from Georgia's tale? First, it shows what you can gain by beginning your research around a topic with which you are already familiar and/or involved. Consider Georgia's reflections on her work as the germ of a thesis topic (item 1).

Note how she also began with a familiar methodology with which she then became dissatisfied (2). Of course, such dissatisfaction is not inevitable but it is more likely when your supervisor comes from a different intellectual background to your own. It is thus very important to find a supervisor who is following an approach that suits you. However, only plodding students blindly follow every whim of their supervisor. Notice how Georgia eventually found a more satisfactory theory/method that made personal sense to her (3, 4) but even then did not accept it totally uncritically (5).

Sensibly, Georgia applied her new approach to readily obtained data (6). However, at the start, like many of us doing qualitative research, she was frustrated with the apparent 'obviousness' of the data (7). Intelligently, she decided to make that 'obviousness' something to be investigated (8).

By now, she had a clear approach (9). This was to lead to a speedy conclusion to her dissertation. Within a year or two, she was to add to her PhD a journal article which developed some of its ideas (Lepper, 1995).

I will now turn to Seta's story. Like Georgia, Seta made use of her work experience in her research. Both women also rebelled against some of their earlier training: Georgia became critical of the psychoanalytical assumptions of what she calls the 'Tavistock' approach; as we see below, Seta progressively distanced herself from the quantitative, epidemiological studies which she had been paid to conduct.

SETA'S RESEARCH DIARY

1 THE WORK SETTING

My interest in developing a research study in the field of alcoholism came about naturally as I had been working in this field for many years. My research experience and training however had been exclusively in quantitative socio-medical studies on alcoholism before I came to Goldsmiths. At first, in the late 1960s to mid 1970s, I was working on an epidemiological study of student drinking habits and attitudes, and then a census study of the residents of a reception centre. Later, I got involved in an evaluation study of an organization providing accommodation to homeless persons and the assessment of outcome in groups of alcoholic patients.

The first study I worked on was at the Institute of Psychiatry, Addiction Research Unit (ARU). Having recently completed a postgraduate diploma in social policy and administration at the London School of Economics and Political Science, I took part in a one-night census of the residents of a large reception centre which provided night shelter for many homeless persons. I was part of a team of researchers conducting the census. The aim of that study was to establish the proportion of people with a history of criminal and psychiatric behaviour, and drug and alcohol misuse. The findings have been published in the *British Journal of Psychiatry* (Edwards et al., 1968).

As a member of staff of the ARU, I presented regular papers in seminars regarding my research work or other published work. This helped me to develop skills in presentation of research material.

The second and main study I was involved in at the ARU was an epidemiological study of drinking behaviour and attitudes among first-year university students in two colleges of an English university. A psychologist and myself were responsible for the design, the data collection and the writing up of the results of this study. Over 1000 students completed a lengthy questionnaire and most of those repeated it in their third year, thus enabling us to look into changes in attitudes and behaviour regarding drinking and other kinds of behaviour such as smoking, fast driving, criminality. The results are published in the American *Quarterly Journal of Studies on Alcohol* (Orford et al., 1974).

I later worked briefly on an evaluation study of St Mungo Community's work, interviewing residents of the houses who were homeless persons, offered short-term accommodation. Contact with these persons was made through the Community's workers who organized a soup-run every night in Central London. Evaluation meant an assessment of the role of the Community in the rehabilitation of homeless persons.

Later I joined the Alcohol Treatment Unit (ATU) of a psychiatric hospital. The ATU was situated in the grounds of the hospital in south-east England, and I worked there for eleven years as a research sociologist. It was set up in 1962 following the publication of a DHSS White Paper. This White Paper recommended that the number of treatment units for alcoholism should be significantly increased to provide at least one per regional health authority.

However, after thirty years of existence, this unit had to close down in 1992, following the National Health Service and Community Care Act of 1990 and its associated White Papers. The legislation emphasized 'community care' of the mentally ill, and planning started for the closure of the psychiatric hospital. The official reason given for the closure of the ATU was its financial non-viability. Treatment evaluation research continued in a small research team, which was part of the Alcohol Research Unit of the ATU, for a further two years until 1994.

2 RESEARCH EXPERIENCE

At the ATU I was involved in further quantitative studies designed to measure treatment outcome in alcoholic patients. Two studies were concerned with the effectiveness of Tiapride, a non-sedative anxiety-reducing drug used in the prevention of relapse and in the long-term management of alcoholics.

Two further studies in which I have been the main researcher consisted of evaluation of the treatment programme, a four-week intensive inpatient course for alcoholic patients, and a short alcohol detoxification treatment. A third evaluation study in the ATU is an eight-year follow-up of the 112 alcoholic patients who took part in the evaluation study of the treatment programme. I worked on this study after I started designing my PhD study.

3 INITIAL RESEARCH PROBLEM

When I decided to develop a PhD study, my initial interest was to find out what patients thought of their drink problem – how they conceptualized it. This would have been a quantitative study but one quite different from the usual measurement of outcome studies. I therefore began designing a quantitative study enquiring into alcoholic patients' concepts of alcoholism. The sample was to be drawn from groups of alcoholics, admitted to a four-week inpatient treatment programme in the ATU where I was employed.

Having developed some rating scales on concepts of alcoholism, following interviews with patients, I carried out a pilot study on a small sample. Patients were asked to complete five-point rating scales consisting of statements, by indicating whether they agreed or not with each statement: responses ranged from 'agree strongly' to 'disagree strongly'.

4 EARLY DOUBTS

This whole process took about eight months. However, I was feeling uncomfortable with the results of my pilot study as I tried to make sense of the data. I felt very uncertain about the attitudes and beliefs expressed in the scales; I began to question how one could consider that all patients who, for instance, stated 'agree strongly' on the rating scales, meant the same thing. I then thought of starting another study using semi-structured questionnaires to find out the social meanings of alcoholism among inpatient alcoholics. Rather than develop this idea further, at this stage, with the encouragement of my supervisor, I decided not to use the traditional ways of looking at reliability and validity of data.

5 DEVELOPING A NEW PERSPECTIVE

I started thinking of a new study with a qualitative methodology which I was introduced to on my [part-time] MA course in sociology [at Goldsmiths] in 1985–6. On this course, I became aware of the relevance of the status of interview data, how naturally occurring data or unstructured interview data can be treated as analysable texts which do not need to be considered as being true or false.

As my main interest in my work had been alcoholism for many years, I decided to look at alcoholic patients' accounts of their experiences by means of open-ended interviews rather than the traditional structured methods. I therefore asked the patients to tell me about their drinking, allowing them to talk with a non-directive approach. I tape-recorded some interviews in the beginning, and, when I looked at my transcripts, I knew this was what I ought to do. The qualitative data resulting from this kind of approach were so rich and rewarding that I decided to proceed in this way and carried out 40 interviews.

6 THEORIZING ABOUT THE DATA

At first my approach to the analysis of the data was to look at 'social meanings', concerned mainly with 'why' certain causes of alcoholism were given as explanations, partly inspired by Mary Douglas's (1975) work. I then tried a 'frame analysis' following Goffman's (1974) methodology. After having applied the frame analysis to some patients' interview data, I still was not satisfied with the results as I had no means of knowing if the staff used similar frames. Patients' hospital notes did not reveal sufficient data to study this. I realized that my interest lay in how patients were formulating and presenting their drinking problem and then in attempting to look at 'why' they were presenting in these particular ways. I was introduced to ethnomethodology and to studies in conversation analysis. Having read Schegloff's (1991) and Sacks's (1992), I became interested in the structure of 'talk' and the way [societal] members make use of categories to describe themselves.

7 DEVELOPING A CLEAR RESEARCH PROBLEM

Adopting a qualitative approach, I was able to look at the narrative structure of patients' accounts to see how the texts were accomplished and organized. The structure of the accounts seemed to have a common chronologically organized pattern. Examination of the narratives made me realize that patients were showing their skills in presenting themselves as morally adequate individuals, as Baruch (1981) had found in his sample of parents of children with congenital illness. I also found that patients were displaying considerable insights into their problems and were emerging as well-informed individuals.

8 NEW SOURCES OF DATA

After discussions with my supervisor, I started to explore another source of data. Most patients were referred to the ATU by their general practitioners, others by probation officers, social workers or hospital registrars. In some cases self-referrals were accepted, particularly when these were former patients of the unit. At the time of a patient's discharge, the unit's senior registrar would write a 'discharge letter' to the patient's general practitioner. The GP would be asked to continue seeing the patient after discharge from hospital and help him/her to maintain sobriety. The unit's social workers would be involved in writing to social services departments, solicitors or directors of 'dry houses', in their attempts to help patients with their problems.

These various referral letters offer a different source of data and enable comparisons to be made between patients' and professionals' discourses on alcohol and alcohol-related problems. I decided to compare patients' accounts with professionals' naturally occurring texts.

9 THE IMPLICATIONS OF THE APPROACH USED

This has proved to be a very interesting analytical experience for me. I found similarities and differences in these texts. Professionals' texts were drawn from hospital notes containing the senior registrar's 'discharge letters' to patients' general practitioners, social workers' letters to various agencies, and referral letters written by GPs and hospital registrars.

These narratives also present displays of the modern medical 'whole person' approach to illness which is the focus in the treatment programme. All patients in this study had nearly completed this programme at the time of their interview.

My current approach is therefore not simply an analytical shift, but another way of looking at interview data to see how they can help our understanding of alcoholic patients' versions and presentations of their problems.

Some implications of Seta's story

Like Georgia, Seta chose a topic which was close to hand for her (item 1). Conveniently, her initial research orientations were drawn from the quantitative tradition in which she had experience (2, 3). However, she revealed independent critical thought in her reservations about a pilot study based on this tradition (4).

Her MA course taught her about qualitative theories and method which, sensibly, she decided to apply to a corpus of data readily available from her work (5). She understood that there are many different qualitative approaches to data and tried out a number of theories and concepts on her data (6) before settling upon one clear approach to data analysis (7).

Finally, Seta broadened the scope of her findings by applying her new approach to a different but accessible dataset (8) and reflecting upon the implications of the approach used for theory and methodology (9).

Both Seta and Georgia followed a research trajectory common in qualitative research: rather than begin with hypotheses and variables, their approach was largely inductive. As Georgia put it:

> It will be apparent by now that my methodology is interpretive and inductive. 'Getting started' did not involve formulating a hypothesis, which could be proved or disproved, or could prove or disprove someone else's. It started ... with an interest in a problem, and an interest in the kinds of thinking I was being introduced to through the teaching I was offered and my reading.

Of course, inductivism and exploratory work are not synonymous with qualitative research. As already noted, both Georgia and Seta came to depend upon a very clearly defined theoretical perspective. As I argue in Chapter 6, without some such theory, even inductive work is rendered meaningless. So their chosen theories provided considerable intellectual sustenance to both women. In Seta's case, this was supplemented by an earlier PhD dissertation I had supervised which had applied the same approach to a different body of data (Baruch, 1982).

My third story relates to work still in progress. Vicki Taylor started with a first degree in biology and education followed by an MSc in health promotion. She is now Assistant Director of Public Health concerned with health strategy and health promotion policy within an inner-city health authority.

To improve her research skills, like Seta, Vicki studied for the Goldsmiths' MA in Qualitative Research part-time over two years. She took my graduate course in Health and Illness and wrote her MA dissertation on counselling interviews sought by women with phobias. Her approach drew on the finding in conversation analysis that speakers use different interactional markers to indicate upcoming acceptance or rejection of prior suggestions, invitations or offers. This activity is described in CA as 'preference organization' (see Heritage, 1984). It relates to how social solidarity is maintained and displayed during interaction.

Vicki performed very well in her MA assessments, obtaining a distinction overall. Part of her MA dissertation was published, in a revised form, in a scholarly journal (Taylor, 1994). In September 1993, she registered for a PhD under my supervision. We decided that she should work on my counselling audiotapes but, this time, attempting to develop my findings on advice giving and advice reception in relation to the 'communication formats' established between counsellors and clients (Silverman, 1997b, Chapter Three).

Unlike many beginning research students, Vicki thus had no difficulty in finding appropriate data or in selecting a theoretical approach that worked for her. However, this did not mean that everything was plain sailing.

The following consists of extracts from Vicki's research diary to which, as before, I have added my own headings.

VICKI'S RESEARCH DIARY

NARROWING DOWN (SEPTEMBER 1993)
I identified the difficulties of narrowing down which extracts to use, which extracts to transcribe. I wanted to look at how advice giving and advice reception were constructed in these interactions. I found that I kept going back to preference organization – an area that I had originally looked at for my MA.

Concurrently, I had discussions with another member of staff in the Sociology Department at Goldsmiths about the theoretical background to my work. My attention was drawn to the work of Alfred Schutz and, in particular, to the relevance of Schutz's account of the 'reciprocity of perspectives'.

TRYING OUT NEW CONCEPTUALIZATIONS (OCTOBER 1993)
Reread a recently completed thesis, under DS's supervision, which looked at data from another counselling centre (see Peräkylä, 1995). I focused on Peräkylä's chapter on how clients' 'experience' is discussed and reanalysed my existing data from the point of view of (a) advice giving, (b) construction of experience.

COMING ACROSS NEW DATA (NOVEMBER 1993)
Through a contact elsewhere, I was offered a new source of data – a counselling interview with a 'manic depressive' client based on a method not seen in either Peräkylä's or Silverman's data (rational-emotive theory).

I refocused on an extract from Silverman's data. Ended up seeing this as minimizing disagreement and maximizing agreement; found it difficult to get beyond this. So back to preference organization (PO) again?

MOVING BACK TO MULTIPLE TOPICS (DECEMBER 1993)
Tried looking at further data from DS's corpus. Initially, I looked at five transcripts, with a view to seeing how clients got into the talk, how they achieved entry *but* also using ideas related to PO, advice giving, advice receipt, communication formats etc. I looked at all of these extracts with an open mind but informed by CA literature.

For each transcript, a range of areas was identified as being of interest:

1   Delicacy; PO; advice giving; information delivery.
2   Information delivery; advice giving; how clients gain entry and counsellor gets back.
3   Delicacy; politeness is all; ambiguous advice; stability of communication format; information delivery.
4   Advice giving/resistance; PO; information delivery; interview formats.
5   Experience; marked/unmarked acknowledgements; generalized form of advice; how client gains entry.

SUPERVISION LEADS TO NARROWING DOWN AGAIN (DECEMBER 1993)
Feedback from DS. We agreed three workable areas: advice giving/uptake, PO, and the management of objects marked as 'delicate'. Also two other areas of note: how clients gain entry into the talk, and the stability of information delivery as the home base, the exception being transcript 2. I might also think about how topics are maintained and changed.

Following this supervision, I then looked further at transcript 6 and identified key points of interest. I will focus on advice giving, agreement/disagreement and experience.

BACK TO THE LITERATURE AGAIN (JANUARY 1994)

Read Sacks's (1992) *Lectures on Conversation*, Vol. 2, p. 32, on completion-transition points. Applying his point to how clients and counsellors operate and get turns as speaker.

Decided to focus on transcripts 2, 4 and 5 to look in more detail at how 'next speaker' is selected or selects self.

SUPERVISION: A NEW TOPIC? (16 JANUARY 1994)

Started thinking about how client and counsellor demonstrate/align selves as 'experts'. We discussed other possible data, e.g. situations where clients ask pharmacists for advice: might be interesting to see how this is constructed/achieved.

We discussed my analysis of transcript 5, looking at how patient gains entry. Key points identified: (i) the stable communication formats; (ii) counsellor's use of perspective-display sequences (PDS) (Maynard, 1991); (iii) the lack of any institutional turn-taking system; (iv) how 'expertise' is accomplished.

WRITING TWO SHORT DATA ANALYSES (FEBRUARY 1994)

First, produced draft paper which looked at: how counsellors' questions and answers are constructed; how clients' questions and answers are constructed. I found: in most interactions counsellors (Cs) are asking questions or delivering information and patients (Ps) are providing answers or response tokens. But transcript 2 is different: P sets up some questions. How is this done?

Second, reanalysed transcript 5 in the light of my review of CA literature on professionality. Paper called 'Doing expertise: the construction of professionality . . .'. Whilst a lot of energy went into this, it felt like I'd reached a blind alley (*perhaps revisit now?*) Feedback by phone: need to review this and revisit paper. Lots of areas identified to look at for future work: formulation of experience; client expertise; is there a dispreference for client initiated questions?

SETBACKS: A NEW JOB (APRIL–MAY 1994)

Did very little: started new job.

A NEW TOPIC (JUNE 1994)

Reread Pomerantz (1984) on pursuing a response and Davidson (1984), and started looking at 'offers'. Revisited extracts 3, 4, 1, 2, 5 in light of PO. Sent DS some draft initial thoughts on findings *re* interactional achievement of acceptance and declination of the offer of screening tests. I felt this was a bit of a breakthrough. Feedback on data – supportive – this was a topic worth focusing on.

PRESENTING WORK (JULY 1994)

Prepared for workshop with DS's other PhD students. Analysed extract from transcript 4 using Davidson's ideas *re* offers. Focused attention on how offers for other tests (i.e. sexually-transmitted diseases, STDs) are made/accepted/declined.

BUILDING ON THE NEW TOPIC (22 JULY 1994)

Looked at other transcripts where screening for other STD tests is offered, focusing on organization and receipt of offers. Feedback from DS: two future extracts analysed and further literature followed up.

FAVOURABLE FEEDBACK (30 AUGUST 1994)
Sent analysis of extract 2 to DS: he says this is the most intense analysis done so far!! (Some comments to incorporate.)

DEVELOPING THE WORK (OCTOBER 1994)
I agreed to write a paper on talking clients into STD tests and to revisit Bergmann (1992) and Maynard's (1992) work on how doctors align their clients to information and/or requests. We also discussed the possibility of a visit to the University of California to work with John Heritage.

WRITING A PAPER FOR PUBLICATION (NOVEMBER–DECEMBER 1994)
First draft of paper on 'talking clients into STD tests'.

FEEDBACK (6 JANUARY 1995)
Discussion with DS of paper. We also discussed the likely outline of the thesis structure.

JOURNAL ARTICLE SUBMITTED (FEBRUARY 1995)
Submitted paper to *Text*: 'Talking clients into STD test'.

A FOREIGN TRIP (APRIL–MAY 1995)
Spent at UCLA: intensive CA work but found that analysis of ordinary conversation lacking on my part. Returned from LA much more aware of what I don't know!

UPGRADING TO PHD STATUS (MAY 1995)
Preparation for upgrading committee. Used paper submitted to *Text* as the basis for the upgrading together with revised outline of PhD thesis.

BUILDING UP THE DATABASE (23 MAY 1995)
Feedback from referee on paper submitted to *Text* [paper rejected]. Discussed with DS together with [successful] outcome of upgrading meeting.
  Action: listen to other audiotape data from HIV centres to find other examples of offers and transcribe them. Develop observations on these transcripts.

DATA SESSION (14 JUNE 1995)
Data session at Goldsmiths: Christian Heath's students plus me.

WORKING THROUGH THE DATA (JUNE–SEPTEMBER 1995)
Review of data and consideration of where and when 'offers' for STD tests made and by whom. Prepared summary of overall structure of counselling interviews.

MAPPING OFFERS IN WHOLE INTERVIEWS (SEPTEMBER–DECEMBER 1995)
Spent time looking in detail where offers were in overall structure of interviews. Mapped what happened in overall interviews, looked at positioning of offers for STDs and offers to see health advisers.

ADDING FURTHER DATA FROM OTHER HIV COUNSELLING CENTRES
(FEBRUARY–MARCH 1996)
Transcribed new material from HIV counselling centres. Also listened to and documented the structure of tapes from another centre where 'offer' to be part of a trial as part of GUM (genito-urinary medicine) consultation. May be useful data to return to.

SOLID PROGRESS (MARCH–MAY 1996)
Continued transcribing extracts. Also wrote chapter on natural history of the research process (to date), chapter on HIV counselling, chapter on offers, sent to DS for comments.

DISASTER (MAY 1996)
Hard disk crashed: lost two chapters and some data files that were not backed up!! Also lost draft chapter prepared on offers.

CONFERENCE (1–5 JULY 1996)
Went to 4th International Social Science Methodology Conference at Essex University. Set out framework for overall PhD and timetable.

WORKSHOP (19–21 SEPTEMBER 1996)
Went to CA weekend data workshop organized by Sarah Collins. This was a good experience for me. I came away feeling very confident about my data and the direction of my research.

DESPAIR (OCTOBER 1996)
Time spent trying to recover data and get transcript back to where had been six months previously – disheartened!!

TIME OUT (OCTOBER 1996 TO JANUARY 1997)
I felt I had achieved next to nothing since my hard disk crashed in May. I took time out and went to Australia to visit my sick brother.

STARTING UP AGAIN (JANUARY–MAY 1997)
Transcribed new data (transcripts 6, 7, 8) and identified other transcripts for transcription and identified extracts within these. Became interested in how doctors' clients responded to the offer to see the health adviser. Key themes: offers of screening tests for other STDs; offers to see the health adviser; and offers by doctors and health advisers.

MINING THE DATA (JULY–OCTOBER 1997)
Sorting out of data, formatting and identifying extracts for future work.

REFOCUSING (16 OCTOBER 1997)
Determined to refocus. Meeting with DS: I set out history of what I had done to date. Discussion around why lost direction: work commitments, confidence, time, UCLA, paper submitted to *Text*, my need to have chapters written!
    From data already looked at, key questions emerge:

25

- Is the format for offers of other STD tests situated? Ideas on paper on what's wrong with ideas about styles of communication – infinitely more skilful, situated contextual.
- Is there anything more culturally delicate about seeing health adviser *vis-à-vis* offers for STDs?
- How do the offer formats for STDs and for going to see the health adviser (HA) vary? Is it to do with individual doctor style?? Is one type of offer more convoluted than another???
- How do HAs' offers for STDs differ from doctors' offers for STDs? Where in the structure of the talk do these offers get made??? Compare same person doing offers to see HAs and STD tests.

Refocus on paper about talking clients into tests, taking referee comments into consideration. Paper to David by 28 November at latest.

Some implications of Vicki's story

Unlike Vicki, Seta and Georgia have successfully completed their PhDs. Yet, as their stories make clear, their path to success was strewn with various dead-ends and the constant need to rethink basic assumptions. As I write, after five years, Vicki is still working on her dissertation. However, having made the big decision to take six months' unpaid leave from her job, she is now making excellent progress, following on the breakthrough that she had made back in June 1994.

Vicki's story of work in progress underlines the highs and lows of working on a piece of research. These are indicated in my summary below, together with rethinks.

HIGH

At the start, Vicki apparently had everything going for her. Her PhD was to be based on her successful MA dissertation. She had a clear theoretical approach and her data were immediately available. Moreover, she could use a helpful model for, in 1993, Anssi Peräkylä had just completed an outstanding thesis under my supervision, using similar data and a similar approach.

RETHINK

However, intelligent researchers like Vicki are rarely content with treading a well-worn path. So, in the autumn of 1993, she explored various ways of refocusing her project: discussing the theoretical background of her research (September 1993), thinking about moving to a new topic (September–October 1993) and even finding new data (November 1993). By the winter of 1993–4, Vicki had decided, for the moment, that her original ideas suited her best. So she began working systematically through the database and discussing workable topics in supervisions (December 1993). However, further experimentation, and even completion of two short papers, left her worried about having reached a dead-end (February 1994).

LOW

In the spring of 1994, a success in getting a better job had a knock-on effect on her research. Predictably, for a while, that came to a halt (April–May 1994).

HIGH

By the summer, Vicki was back at her research. A breakthrough occurred with new reading suggesting a workable topic. When her new-found enthusiasm was supported by her supervisor, Vicki was steaming ahead once more (June 1994). Building on this breakthrough, the summer was a period of steady progress: more analysis, a successful presentation and favourable feedback (July–August 1994). By the autumn, her data analysis was sufficiently advanced to begin writing a paper for a journal. The paper was submitted in February 1995.

RETHINK

At my suggestion, Vicki followed Peräkylä's path of spending two months studying with John Heritage and his students at the Sociology Department, University of California, Los Angeles. However, through nobody's fault, this turned out to be a mixed blessing and her confidence was slightly dented (April–May 1995).

LOW

Her return from UCLA coincided with the news that her paper had been rejected by the journal (May 1995).

HIGH

However, this disappointment was relieved by the very helpful referees' comments and by her success at a viva which upgraded her to PhD standing (May 1995). On this basis, the following ten months turned out to be a period of steady progress, using the referees' comments to rework her data analyses (June 1995 to April 1996).

LOW

Disaster and despair followed when Vicki's hard disk crashed (without back-ups) in May 1996. She felt that she achieved nothing in the following summer apart from attending two conferences. Trying to snap herself out of a vicious circle of despair, Vicki took an extended holiday that winter (November–December 1996).

RETHINK

All was not lost. By the beginning of 1997, Vicki was steadily working on her data once more and rebuilding her confidence.

SUMMARY

Obviously, there are many different stories that research students can tell about their experience and I do not pretend that what you have read was typical or representative. Nonetheless, there are several clear messages in these stories that are worth listening to.

I set these out below as a *twelve-point guide*.[1] Of course, like any recipe, you will need to apply it to your own circumstances. Nevertheless, I believe the points apply to *all levels* of student research from BA and MA dissertations through to the PhD.

1 *Begin in familiar territory* If you can, work with data that are close to hand and readily accessible. For instance, if, as in Vicki's case, your supervisor already has data which you can (re)analyse, grab the opportunity. There are no 'Brownie points' to be obtained for gathering your data in difficult circumstances. Make it easy on yourself at this stage so that you can concentrate your energies on the infinitely more important task of data analysis.

2 *Find a settled theoretical orientation* As I stress throughout this book, research is never just about techniques. All three stories refer to finding a theoretical approach which made sense to the students and then could provide a settled basis for inference and data analysis.

3 *Narrow down your topic* Work at finding a topic that is appropriate to your theory and data and is workable (this issue is discussed at length in Chapter 5). Later, if you wish, like Seta and Vicki, you can broaden out the scope of your research to new data and topics.

4 *Don't try to reinvent the wheel* In Chapter 4, I discuss what 'originality' might mean in research. For the moment, it is worth recalling that both Seta and Vicki used an earlier study as a model for their research. So, at the outset, look at previous successful dissertations in your university library or departmental files and, where possible, focus on work directed by your supervisor.

5 *Keep writing* Commit your ideas to paper. Don't worry how short or draft your papers are. Indeed, in some ways, it makes more sense, initially at least, to submit 500-word pieces so that you can be guided in the right direction before you have expended too much time and effort.

6 *Begin data analysis early* Don't be deflected away from early data analysis by literature reviews and the exigencies of data gathering. If you haven't got any data yourself at an early stage, try analysing someone else's data – published data, your supervisor's data, etc. (see Chapter 10).

7 *Use your supervisor* To test out your ideas and give you confidence.

8 *Use other resources and opportunities* Graduate students should take every opportunity to attend relevant conferences and, better still, to give conference papers, and to take appropriate training courses. Find out if

there are study groups of research students working on similar topics. If not, try to establish such a group.

9 *Do not expect a steady learning curve*   Be prepared for the sequence of highs and lows that will inevitably happen. Treat setbacks as opportunities (e.g. unsuccessful attempts at publication may still produce helpful referees' comments).

10 *Keep a research diary*   Georgia, Seta and Vicki kept a file of their current ideas, hopes and worries. This file is an invaluable resource which, as I suggest in Chapter 19, can be used, in edited form, in your methodology chapter.

11 *Earmark blocks of working time*   If you are researching part-time, it is crucial to find blocks of time in which you can focus solely on your research. Use this time for intensive data analysis and writing.

12 *Do not reproach yourself*   If you experience a setback, it may be best to take some time out to relax before you return to your research.

NOTE

1 Items 11 and 12 were suggested by Vicki Taylor after she read an earlier draft of this chapter.

Further reading

The best place to look for similar research histories is in the writings of students at your own university. BA students should seek to obtain past successful undergraduate dissertations from their department. Graduate students should study MA and PhD theses in the library, focusing particularly on the work of people who had your supervisor. If the methodology chapter does not include an autobiographical account, try to contact the author and discuss what lessons they drew from their experience.

Judith Bell's *Doing Your Research Project* (2nd edn, Open University Press, 1993) is a good introduction to research at the undergraduate level. Estelle Phillips and Derek Pugh's *How To Get a PhD* (2nd edn, Open University Press, 1994) is the best British account of the practical issues involved in the process of writing a PhD. For an American guide, see Kjell Rudestam and Rae Newton's *Surviving Your Dissertation* (Sage, 1992).

Exercise 2.1

Keep a research diary for a given period (one month for an undergraduate dissertation, three months for an MA project, at least six months for a PhD).
Record:

- changes in your ideas about topic, data, theory and method
- new ideas from the literature or from lectures and talk
- meetings with your supervisor and their consequences
- life events and their consequences for your work.

At the end of your chosen period, reread your research diary and assess:

- what you have achieved in that period
- what would be required for you to do better in future
- your achievement targets for the next equivalent period.

3

The Research Experience II

In this part of the book, I have been attempting to set out the context in which qualitative research dissertations are written. We began with a brief overview of qualitative research. Then, in Chapter 2, we considered the lessons that could be drawn from two completed research dissertations and one unfinished study beginning its sixth year.

Yet, for many readers of this book, their own completed graduate or undergraduate dissertation is a distant, desired object. So, in this chapter, we draw upon the accounts of research students at an early stage of their research. Through these accounts, we discuss the analytical, methodological and practical problems that confront the beginning researcher.

In some senses, the beginning researcher has far less to prove than established scholars. If you imagine a sliding scale of levels of achievement, then journal articles, as the stock-in-trade of established scholars, are (or should be) at the pinnacle of scholarly accomplishment. Somewhat surprisingly, books are a little further down the scale since they do not depend on the same degree of independent review. Further down the scale are completed research dissertations which, I suggest, are properly viewed as displays of successful apprenticeship.

However, my sense of a sliding scale in research is intended simply to mark a stage of a research career; it is not a moral category. Although it is more than 30 years since I was at that stage, I do not look down upon the work of first-year research students. Indeed, frankly, I sometimes come across more exciting ideas in a first-year graduate seminar than in many journal articles!

What follows is by no means a representative survey of qualitative research at its early stages. Instead, the material has been drawn from research students in my own department and in various social science and humanities departments of Finnish universities.[1]

While the range of research covered is limited, I hope you will eventually agree that it is not narrow. In other words, I hope and expect that readers will find at least some echo of their own ideas and interests represented.

In collating these presentations for this chapter, I had to decide upon an organizing principle. In particular, I had to choose whether to organize the material by topic, theory or methodology. I reasoned that grouping by topic would be lively but might appear to exclude readers working on different topics. By contrast, a theory grouping might be too abstract and, perhaps, confusing for an audience coming from a disparate range of disciplines. By taking a methodological perspective, I hope to be more inclusive by encompassing many of the methods used (and contemplated) by qualitative researchers.

My discussion is thus organized by method, with sections on interview studies, ethnographies, textual analysis, work with videotapes and audiotapes, and multiple methods. However, such a focus on method is not narrowly technical. As I make clear, methods only acquire meaning and vitality by their embeddedness in particular theoretical perspectives.

As in Chapter 2, I will proceed case by case, offering some comments with each example and then summarizing the points that emerge from each methodology. The chapter concludes with some suggestions about managing the early stages of research.

After each topic heading, I have noted the social science discipline in which the student is working as well as the student's name.

INTERVIEWS

Living and coping in a community of elderly people (information studies/sociology: Tippi)

Tippi writes about her joint research: 'We wanted to ask how the inhabitants feel about living in the community where they have lived for many years.' Her study is based upon thematic interviews with a random sample of eight elderly people from the community. As she puts it, the aim of this study 'is to [clarify] . . . the basic meaning of living [in this community]'. This is how she describes her interviews: 'The elderly people were asked about their daily schedules, their attitudes to relatives, services, neighbourhood and environment, their interests and their opinions about society today compared with their earlier life experiences.'

Preliminary findings suggest two things. First, members of the community told the same kinds of life stories. Second, such people described themselves as more independent than she had thought. They described 'coping' by attempting to keep control of four issues: financial, social, health-related and security.

An analytic issue potentially arises in such studies where interviews are used to elicit respondents' perceptions. How far is it appropriate to think that people attach a single meaning to their experiences? In this case, may not there be multiple meanings of living in the community, represented by what people say to the researcher, to each other, to carers and so on (Gubrium, 1997)?

This raises the important methodological issue about whether interview responses are to be treated as giving direct access to 'experience' or as actively constructed 'narratives' (Silverman, 1993; Holstein and Gubrium, 1995). Both positions are entirely legitimate but the position taken will need to be justified and explained.

Students' views of evaluation and feedback (behavioural sciences: Laura)

Laura is examining students' responses to the assessment of their distance education essays. Her research question is: 'Does it deliver the feedback that is needed and when it is needed?' Her data are derived from thematic interviews with eleven students chosen from four different localities. Her preliminary findings suggest that students want more detailed, critical feedback on their essays so that they can know what are the gaps in their knowledge and what they can do about them.

Laura describes the theoretical basis of her research as a 'hermeneutic' method based on how researcher and subjects interpret the world and attempt to merge their horizons of meaning. This is ambitious and its value will need to be demonstrated in the data analysis. Indeed, it might be simpler to settle on presenting her research as a descriptive study based upon a clear social problem. Either way, the issues about the status of interview data, also raised in Tippi's project, will need to be engaged.

Football and masculinity (sociology: Steven)

Steven's approach is based upon theories of masculinity within the general area of gender studies. More specifically, his work is concerned with football supporters and masculinity. He is particularly interested in understanding the experience of football supporters as opposed to the way in which their behaviour is represented (for instance in the media).

Care needs to be taken in how such appeals to 'experience' are described. This is one way of 'slicing the cake' and other approaches (e.g. studies of media representations of sport), using other forms of data, are not directly competitive.

The data he is using derive from interviews with football supporters. As Steven acknowledges, he still needs to sort out tricky methodological issues relating to his sampling procedure, his involvement with his interviewees and how he analyses his data. A possible resource is Jocelyn Cornwell's study of health, gender and poverty, *Hard Earned Lives* – an interview study which shares some of his ambitions.

It is always sensible, in this situation, to familiarize yourself more deeply with the methodological literature on analysing interview data. Even if you choose to take a position opposed to such texts, you will need to be able to justify it. Without doing this, you are in danger of trying to reinvent the wheel.

Text processing in foreign-language classrooms (English: Pia)

In Finland, foreign languages are primarily taught through textbooks. Yet textbook-based learning is often defined as monotonous or boring by students.

Pia's topic is whether there are different ways of talking about foreign-language teaching and whether there is a conflict between them. Her broader concern is with what hinders change in classroom practices.

Her data consist of twelve interviews (half with teachers and half with students). She also has five 'think aloud' sessions in which students were asked to do an exercise from a text and think aloud at the same time. This is an interesting idea because it attempts to relate what people say to a particular task they are doing – although it has to cope with the likelihood that people's practical skills are far more complicated than they could tell you in so many words (Garfinkel, 1967).

Pia describes her analytical approach as discourse analysis (DA). This implies that she is more interested in identifying different ways of *talking* about foreign-language reading than in addressing the actual experiences of learning a foreign language through a textbook. Given that the latter can be seen as a social problem, there may be a mismatch between DA, which assumes that issues of social definition are paramount, and a direct address of social problems. This might suggest either dropping DA or reconceptualizing the problem.

If we are interested in what happens in the classroom, there is a further issue about the appropriateness of interview data. Shouldn't we observe what people do there instead of asking them what they think about it? Is how we talk about schooling directly related to what happens in schooling?

The family grief and recovery process as narratives (psychiatry: Katarin)

Katarin is analysing interviews with couples after the loss of their baby. She is interested in how family members construct stories about their grief and recovery processes after such a loss. She has identified three discourses at work here:

- a religious discourse ('everything is clear . . . I think my faith is strengthened')
- a medical discourse ('our baby did not have a chance to live, this is better, the lungs were undeveloped')
- a protest discourse ('who can decide who is allowed to live and who isn't?').

Katarin calls her work 'narrative analysis'. By treating her respondents' accounts as skilfully structured stories, she gets a lively, theoretically informed grip on her data.

Only two cautions are appropriate here. First, the mere identification of different discourses in respondents' talk can lead to a simple, reductive list. At some stage, it is analytically productive to move beyond such a list in order to attempt to map the skilful way in which such discourses are laminated on one another (see Silverman, 1993: 50, 76–8).

Second, the assembly of narratives in interviews (or conversations) is always a two-way process. Therefore, we must treat the interviewer's questions not as (possibly distorted) gateways to the authentic account but as part of the process through which a narrative is collectively assembled (see Holstein and Gubrium, 1995).

Narratives by bereaved relatives (sociology: Monica)

Using interview data drawn from an earlier study, Monica, like Katarin, is concerned with how bereaved relatives organize their initial stories of their bereavement. Monica's approach is drawn from ethnomethodology's concern with how people demonstrate the rationality and moral accountability of their talk. In their stories, people show that they hear (and pre-emptively manage) possible charges against them. By doing this, the analysis can fully show how people are not 'judgemental dopes' but rather display a lively concern for the maintenance and repair of the moral order.

Her method derives from Sacks's membership categorization analysis, using Baruch's work on the 'moral tales' of mothers of handicapped children as an example. As we saw in the previous chapter, basing your work on an earlier study deriving from a clear-cut theoretical approach can be a short cut to a successful research dissertation (see also Chapter 5).

In her presentation, Monica showed how she had started to analyse five data extracts using this method. At a later point, in line with her theoretical approach, the analysis can be deepened by working more intensively with small pieces of data to delineate precisely how particular descriptions serve to support particular activities like 'doing a complaint', 'excusing oneself' and so on. In this way, like Katarin, she can avoid the temptation simply to list different categories.

Interviews: summary

Common themes have emerged from our six interview studies which I summarize below. For the sake of simplicity, I present this summary in the form of a list of questions that you need to think about if you are planning to do an interview study.

It should be apparent that here, as elsewhere, I am concerned with data *analysis* rather than the mechanics of data gathering. I strongly believe that to provide recipes for data gathering is to risk either gross oversimplification or utter triteness. Moreover, in qualitative research, what happens 'in the field' as you attempt to gather your data is itself a source of data rather than just a technical problem in need of a solution (see Chapter 15).

WHAT STATUS DO YOU ATTACH TO YOUR DATA?
Many interview studies are used to elicit respondents' perceptions. How far is it appropriate to think that people attach a single meaning to their

experiences? May not there be multiple meanings of a situation (e.g. living in a community home) or of an activity (e.g. being a male football fan) represented by what people say to the researcher, to each other, to carers and so on (Gubrium, 1997)?

This raises the important methodological issue about whether interview responses are to be treated as giving direct access to 'experience' or as actively constructed 'narratives' involving activities which themselves demand analysis (Silverman, 1993; Holstein and Gubrium, 1995). Both positions are entirely legitimate but the position you take will need to be justified and explained.

IS YOUR ANALYTIC POSITION APPROPRIATE TO YOUR PRACTICAL CONCERNS?

Some ambitious analytic positions (e.g. hermeneutics, discourse analysis) may actually cloud the issue if your aim is simply to respond to a given social problem (e.g. living and coping in a community of elderly people, students' views of evaluation and feedback). If so, it might be simpler to acknowledge that there are more complex ways of addressing your data but to settle on presenting your research as a *descriptive* study based upon a clear social problem.

DO INTERVIEW DATA REALLY HELP IN ADDRESSING YOUR RESEARCH TOPIC?

If you are interested in, say, what happens in school classrooms, should you be using interviews as your major source of data? Think about exactly why you have settled on an interview study. Certainly, it can be relatively quick to gather interview data but not as quick as, say, texts and documents. How far are you being influenced by the prominence of interviews in the media (see Atkinson and Silverman, 1997)?

In the case of the classroom, couldn't you observe what people do there instead of asking them what they think about it? Or gather documents that routinely arise in schools, e.g. pupils' reports, mission statements and so on?

Of course, you may still want to do an interview study. But whatever your method you will need to justify it and show you have thought through the practical and analytical issues involved in your choice.

ARE YOU MAKING TOO LARGE CLAIMS ABOUT YOUR RESEARCH?

It always helps to make limited claims about your own research. Grandiose claims about originality, scope or applicability to social problems are all hostages to fortune. Be careful in how you specify the claims of your approach. Show that you understand that it constitutes one way of 'slicing the cake' and that other approaches, using other forms of data, may not be directly competitive.

PROPER ANALYSIS GOES BEYOND A LIST

Identifying the main elements in your data according to some theoretical scheme should only be the first stage of your data analysis. By examining how these elements are linked together, you can bring out the active work of both interviewer and interviewee and, like them, say something lively and original.

We now turn to ethnographic studies that involve some element of observation. As we shall see, these kinds of studies also raise complex methodological and analytic issues.

ETHNOGRAPHIES

Ethnographies are based on observational work in particular settings. The initial thrust in favour of ethnography was anthropological. Anthropologists argue that, if one is really to understand a group of people, one must engage in an extended period of observation. Anthropological fieldwork routinely involves immersion in a culture over a period of years, based on learning the language and participating in social events with the people of that culture.

By contrast, non-anthropologists are more likely to study particular milieux or 'subcultures' in their own society. We will see examples of this latter approach in the studies discussed, where activities in classrooms, in hospitals and on the Internet become objects of research observation.

The analysis of communicative functions of peer interaction during small group learning (education: Caroline)

Working in small groups has become a common feature of modern education. The exact nature of such 'learning' presents a clear and apparently under-researched topic tied to a recognizable social problem. As Caroline remarks: 'The ways in which knowledge is constructed in children's verbal interactions during small group work learning without direct teacher control has not yet been fully researched.'

Caroline has gathered data from children aged 10–12 in small classroom groups working on mathematics, science and language. Her focus is on 'the socio-cognitive and interpersonal dynamics of peer interaction' using categories 'based on the communicative functions identified in the interactions'.

This is a theoretically defined topic which nonetheless might have a clear practical input. It uses a clearly defined method derived from certain forms of discourse analysis. However, Caroline's study also raises a more general issue about how a researcher goes about identifying features in her data.

Caroline's use of the passive voice in her reference to 'the communicative functions *identified* in the interactions' draws attention to a neglected issue in social research, namely, how does the analyst go about 'identifying features' in her data? One common answer is to claim to follow proper procedural rules. For instance, coders of data are usually trained in procedures with the aim of ensuring a uniform approach.

This is a tried and trusted method designed to improve the reliability of a research method. However, it is sensible to be conscious that 'coding' is not the preserve of research scientists. In some sense, these students, like all of us, 'code' what they hear and see in the world around them. Moreover, this 'coding' has been shown to be mutual and interactive (Sacks, 1992; Silverman, 1998a).

Of course, as I said earlier, the research 'cake' can be legitimately sliced in many ways. So I am *not* suggesting that the vast mass of researchers who treat 'coding' as purely an analyst's problem abandon their work. Instead, my minimalist suggestion is that they mention and respond to this well-established critique (for an example, see Clavarino et al., 1995).

Analysing how radiologists work (information processing science: Julia)

Radiology, like many health professions, has recently experienced a sea change of technologies with the conventional X-ray image being complemented by computer-based, digitalized images. As Julia points out, any new technology creates new constraints as well as new possibilities. Her focus is on such technologically mediated interaction in workplace settings.

Using videotapes, observation and interviews, Julia has gathered data about radiological image interpretation conferences. By examining actual workplace interaction she hopes to contribute to the growing body of knowledge about human–computer interaction and to inform future technological design (see Suchman, 1987; Heath, 1997).

I hope you will agree with me that this is an exciting combination of a theoretically defined approach with clear practical relevance. However, Julia writes that she is concerned about what is *missing* from both her interviews and her videos. As she puts it:

> Thus far in my research it has become clear that there are aspects of work which I can't 'reach' through interviews (people can't readily articulate aspects that are so familiar to them as to be unremarkable) or through observation and interactional analysis of video recordings (those aspects of work that are not evident in what people can actually be seen to do).

In a sophisticated way, Julia raises a problem that often troubles research students: the necessarily 'partial' character of any data source. I believe this problem is potentially huge yet, in a practical sense, easily resolved. One simply avoids trying to find the 'whole picture'. Instead, one analyses different kinds of data separately, aware that all data are partial.

So make do with what you have and understand that there are multiple phenomena available in any research setting. If you must go beyond any particular dataset, save that until you have completed smaller-scale analyses. Worrying about the 'whole picture' at the outset is, in my view, a recipe for stalling your research (see Silverman and Gubrium, 1994).

Newsgroups on the Internet
(sociology: Danny)

Danny's topic is the Internet. He is concerned with how people assemble themselves as a community via the net, without recourse to speech inflections or body language. Broader issues relate to how the net is regulated, how it developed and what is exchanged on it. He proposes to focus on newsgroups on the net since their messages are publicly available and offer an interesting way to look at how a 'community' is assembled and develops.

Danny's approach derives from his interest in the Internet as a possible new locus of power and, to this end, he plans to draw upon the German critical theorist Jurgen Habermas's conception of distorted communication. In this way, he will compare how people actually communicate with Habermas's normative theory.

Danny's study shows the implications of making theoretical choices. Using Habermas's concept of 'distorted communication' will give a particular thrust to his study very different from other kinds of theory.

Even if you decide to eschew such grand theories, that itself is a theoretical choice! In this sense, there is no escape (nor should there be) from theory. At the same time, however, there is nothing wrong with a descriptive study providing that the researcher is conscious about the choice that is being made.

Ethnographies: summary

Once more, I have been concerned with how you analyse your data. I deal below with three issues that have arisen above.

WHAT IS INVOLVED IN CODING DATA?
As we have seen, coders of data are usually trained in procedures with the aim of ensuring a uniform approach. Later in this book, we examine how computer-aided qualitative data analysis can help in such coding (see Chapter 12).

However, as I pointed out, it is sensible to be conscious that 'coding' is not the preserve of research scientists. All of us 'code' what we hear and see in the world around us.

One response is to make this everyday 'coding' (or 'interpretive practice') the object of inquiry. Alternatively, we can proceed in a more conventional manner but mention and respond to this well-established critique.

ARE MY DATA 'PARTIAL'?
Of course they are. But this is not a problem – unless you make the impossible claim to give 'the whole picture'. So celebrate the partiality of your data and delight in the particular phenomena that they allow you to inspect (hopefully in detail).

IS MY THEORY APPROPRIATE?
Your theory must be appropriate to the research questions in which you are

interested. Indeed, rather than being a constraint, a theory should generate a series of directions for your research.

TEXTS

To introduce a separate section on 'texts' can look a little artificial. After all, aren't people on the Internet constructing texts? Again, if we treat an interview as a narrative, this can mean looking for the same textual features as researchers working with printed material. Indeed, the mere act of transcription of an interview turns it into a written text.

In this section, I use 'text' as a heuristic device to identify data consisting of words and images which have become recorded without the intervention of a researcher (e.g. through an interview). I examine five studies of texts.

Analysing classroom religious textbooks (teacher education: Pertti)

Since 1985 Finnish schools have had a religious instruction syllabus mainly based on three textbooks deriving from the Finnish Lutheran Church. Pertti's approach treats such textbooks as a form of literary genre (see Silverman, 1993: 72–5) which filters certain values into the school. He is examining such features as contents lists in order to ask 'how is otherness constructed in these texts through particular methods of classification?' His analysis derives from Michel Foucault's (1977; 1979) discussion of the construction of subjects and disciplines.

This study benefits from a manageable body of data: three textbooks are more than enough to carry out the analysis Pertti proposes. The analysis derives from a clearly defined theoretical approach although it may be uneconomical to work with both Foucaultian ideas and writers on literary genre. In particular, from a Foucaultian position, one would want to study education in its own right not in terms of ideas developed to study literature.

The form of Japanese 'modernity' (sociology: Yoji)

Yoji is interested in how far Japanese modernity depends upon concepts and practices deriving from the West (e.g. the assumption that history involves 'progress') and how far it is a feature of Western colonialization. His data will be drawn from representations of urban space in Tokyo. Although a major focus will be on the family, Yoji is also interested in other institutions including prisons, the police, the hospital, the school and the factory.

Yoji's approach derives from Foucault's (1977) account of the micropolitics of space. From this perspective, he is concerned with how space is racialized, colonized and gendered. It also leads to a concern with how space constructs 'modern' subjects (e.g. 'us' and 'them') and the 'inside' and 'outside' (for instance, the inner city, the ghetto etc.).

Like Pertti, Yoji is working with a clear analytic approach. However, he might learn from Pertti's limited database by focusing on one archive or body of data. He is currently working with historical data from around the Meiji Restoration and it may be fruitful just to focus on one such period and/or to limit the material to visual images or certain texts.

The medicalization of the middle-aged female body in the twentieth century
(sociology: Greta)

Greta is interested in the way in which middle-aged women have become a topic for medicine and the 'psy' sciences. Like Pertti and Yoji, Greta's analysis is based upon a Foucaultian discourse analytic approach, concerned with the construction of subjects within various forms of power/knowledge. Using this approach, she is able to chart how the medical gaze has moved from a biomedical model to medico-psy models and, most recently, a medico-psychosocial model.

Her data derive from the *British Medical Journal*, medical textbooks and a history of menopause clinics in the 1970s. Simple keyword analysis has proved fruitful in the early stages of her research, illustrating for instance how the clinical type of 'the chronic pelvic woman' emerged into discourse.

As Greta's research develops, like Katarin's and Monica's interview studies (discussed earlier), she will want to map how different discourses are laminated on each other. She will also have to decide whether to look for yet more sources of data (e.g. articles and letters on advice pages in women's magazines) or to narrow down the amount of data she has already collected.

The representation of 'crime' in local newspapers
(sociology: Chloe)

Analysis of newspapers in the UK has usually focused on the mass circulation press and has used theoretical models deriving from either Marxism or literary studies. Chloe's work is distinctive in that it uses data taken from small, local newspapers and draws on the small corpus of newspaper studies using Sacks's membership categorization analysis (see Silverman, 1998a; Chs 5 and 7). The research incorporates a nice comparative perspective as the two newspapers Chloe is studying derive from different geographical locations: suburban London and a Northern Ireland city. The value of this comparison can be explored by examining the local categories that the newspapers use in their descriptions of crime (e.g. national and local boundaries).

Like Pertti, Chloe has a manageable body of data. By limiting her data simply to two newspapers' headlines on 'crime' stories she is in a good position to say 'a lot about a little'. Like Greta, her clear analytic approach will pay off when used as more than a simple listing device in order to reveal the precise sets of relationships locally constructed in her data.

'Enterprise Discourse' in Higher Education (sociology: Neil)

Neil's research is concerned with strategic development documents from a higher-education college arising from recent changes in the tertiary sector. He is focusing on what he calls 'enterprise discourse' and how it constitutes the professional's conception of identity.

Like Chloe's, Neil's original approach derives from ethnomethodology and was based on Sacks's membership categorization analysis. However, Neil acknowledges the attraction of the Foucaultian approach and aims to recast his concerns in terms of Foucault's conception of the 'architecture of the text'.

Neil's problem is that Foucault provides no clear methodology (but see Kendall and Wickham, 1998). He is attempting to find a usable method from the 'critical linguistics' of Norman Fairclough and from semiotics' concern with syntagmatic and paradigmatic relations (see Silverman, 1993: 71–2). Using these approaches, the aim is to analyse whole texts rather than a few extracts. The value of these approaches will be clearer when Neil presents an extensive piece of data analysis.

However, I feel there is less to worry about in relation to Neil's concerns that working on a single case might mean that he has too few data. As Mitchell (1983) shows, the validity of qualitative analysis depends more on the quality of the analysis than on the size of the sample. Moreover, the comparative method can be used on a single case by isolating and comparing different elements.

Texts: summary

LIMITING YOUR DATA

Like many other qualitative approaches, textual analysis depends upon very detailed data analysis. To make such analysis effective, it is imperative to have a limited body of data with which to work. So, while it may be useful initially to explore different kinds of data (e.g. newspaper reports, scientific textbooks, magazine advice pages), this should usually only be done to establish the dataset with which you can most effectively work. Having chosen your dataset, you should limit your material further by only taking a few texts or parts of texts (e.g. headlines).

HAVE A CLEAR ANALYTIC APPROACH

All the textual studies discussed have recognized the value of working with a clearly defined approach. Even Neil, who was unsure which approach to use, was convinced that such a choice is crucial. Having chosen your approach (e.g. Foucaultian discourse analysis, Saussurian semiotics, Sacks's analysis of membership categorizations), treat it as a 'toolbox' providing a set of concepts and methods to select your data and to illuminate your analysis.

PROPER ANALYSIS GOES BEYOND A LIST

I make no apology for repeating a point that I made earlier in my discussion of interview studies. It seems to me that the distinctive contribution qualitative research can make is by utilizing its theoretical resources in the deep analysis of small bodies of publicly shareable data. This means that, unlike much quantitative research, we are not satisfied with a simple coding of data. Instead, we have to show how the (theoretically defined) elements we have identified are assembled or mutually laminated.

AUDIOTAPES

The three types of qualitative data discussed so far all end up in the form of some kind of text. For instance, in interviews the researchers usually work with written transcripts and in ethnographies one often records and analyses written fieldnotes.

In the same way, audiotapes of naturally occurring interaction are usually transcribed prior to (and as part of) the analysis. The two main social science traditions which inform the analysis of transcripts of tapes are conversation analysis (CA) and discourse analysis (DA). For an introduction to CA, see ten Have (1998); for DA, see Potter and Wetherell (1987) and Potter (1997). Both examples below involve the use of CA (a further example is found in Vicki's research, discussed in Chapter 2).

Team meetings at a hospice
(sociology: Anthony)

While studying for his MA, Anthony started to do voluntary work at a hospice in a London suburb. Staff at the hospice were later happy to grant him access to tape-record some of their work. He chose team meetings for two reasons. First, focusing on such data meant that he did not need to trouble patients. Second, team meetings in which patients were discussed were scheduled events so Anthony did not have to waste time waiting for 'relevant' data to appear. Moreover, another researcher had already tape-recorded some team meetings at the hospice and was happy to lend him her good quality tapes.

Anthony had used conversation analytic methods for his MA dissertation and applied the Jeffersonian CA transcription method to his new data. He then inspected his transcripts informed by CA's focus on the sequential organization of talk.

After an initial series of discrete observations, he selected a number of sequences in which disagreements emerged and were resolved by team members. The management of agreements and disagreements has been extensively analysed within CA through the concept of 'preference organiz-ation' (Heritage, 1984: 265–9). However, Anthony now realizes that his data allowed a new twist to be given to such analyses by looking at how 'third parties' manage disagreements by others. This looks likely to be both ana-lytically interesting and practically relevant to medical staff concerned with effective decision-making.

Asymmetry in interactions between native and non-native speakers of English (English: Marla)

Marla is working with taped naturally occurring conversations in English between native speakers of English and Finnish (both informal conversations and professional/client encounters). As she notes: 'Research in pragmatics and sociolinguistics has shown that various forms of communicative trouble may arise where the linguistic and sociocultural resources of the participants are not shared.'

However, she is taking a different approach. Rather than treat asymmetries as a 'trouble', her initial idea is to examine how the participants 'use emerg-ing asymmetries as a resource through which they can renegotiate the current context of discourse and their interpersonal relationship'.

Like much good research, this is based on a nicely counter-intuitive idea which derives from a clear theoretical perspective (CA suggests that partici-pants can treat apparent troubles as local resources). As in Anthony's case, Marla's data, method and analytical approach are elegantly intertwined.

Audiotapes: summary

NARROW DOWN TO A SINGLE CONCEPT/ISSUE

Choosing a clear analytic approach is a help but is not everything. The danger is that you seek to apply too many findings or concepts deriving from that approach. This can make your analysis both confused and thin, or a naive listing of observations consonant with each of these concepts. By narrowing down to a single issue (e.g. preference organization or troubles as a local resource), you may begin to make novel observations.

GIVE AN ISSUE A NEW TWIST

As the data analysis proceeds, you should aim to give your chosen concept or issue a new twist. In the studies above, we have seen this done by pursuing a counter-intuitive idea and by noting an additional feature little addressed in the literature.

MAKE DATA COLLECTION AS EASY AS POSSIBLE

There are no 'Brownie points' given by most disciplines for having gathered your own data – perhaps with the exception of anthropology's expectation that most researchers will have spent their statutory year with their 'tribe'. Indeed, by choosing 'difficult' situations to gather data (either because nothing 'relevant' may happen or even because background noise may mean you have a poor quality tape), you may condemn yourself to have less time to engage in the much more important activity of data analysis.

Marla and Anthony found practical ways of efficiently gathering data. Both chose to study scheduled encounters and Anthony was able to supplement his own data with tapes collected by somebody else. As I pointed out in the previous chapter, secondary analysis of other people's data is to be commended rather than condemned.

VIDEOTAPES

When people interact face to face, they do not use merely verbal cues – except if they are on the telephone. Researchers who work with videos have access to many non-verbal cues. However, as we shall see, complicated data can often mean complicated analysis!

Talk, text and visual communication in desktop video-conferencing environments (English: Erkki)

Erkki is studying a one-month teaching experiment in which a university course was given on the Internet in two places in Finland and Sweden. Ideas and papers were regularly exchanged and weekly presentations and feedback sessions were held through video conferencing (Internet seminars). Recordings of the video-mediated sessions between the two centres were obtained and transcribed (see Heath, 1997).

Erkki is combining CA with ideas from Erving Goffman (1974) about 'participation frameworks' adopted in particular settings. This setting is, of course, pretty unusual in that participants' sharing of time and space is technologically mediated. In some sessions, the camera positions were fixed. In others, the camera zoomed in and out on the participants. This is allowing Erkki to get a hold on how different use of video-conferencing technology affects interaction.

Erkki's work combines a manageable body of data, a clear theoretical approach ('participation frameworks') and a likely practical input for systems design. As she recognizes, however, it is very complex to work with video data since both transcription and analysis are more complex than is the case with audio data. Fortunately, there is a growing body of CA-inspired work on technologically mediated interaction which Erkki can use as a model (see Heath, 1997).

The early interaction between a mother and a baby aged under one (Finnish: Suzanne)

This is a study of interaction between Suzanne's own baby, Sara, and others based on 9.5 hours of videos of 22 episodes up till Sara's first birthday.

Suzanne's initial interest was at what age a baby begins to imitate other people. Consequently, she is attempting to describe what she says to her baby at different ages (and how she says it) and what linguistic elements begin to emerge in the baby's vocalizations.

Like Erkki, she is using transcription methods and analytic ideas from CA. Based on this approach, she is treating mother–baby talk as interactional, e.g. how does the mother interpret baby's utterances and behaviour in concrete situations and how does she act in response to them?

At the time of her presentation, Suzanne submitted a set of written questions which I set out below with my answers:

- *Is one baby (my own) enough data?* For qualitative work, one case study is sufficient. Obviously, there are issues to be thought through where you are yourself a principal actor. However, from a CA point of view, the complexity of what all of us do is so great that we are unable to grasp it or indeed to change it significantly at the time.
- *Is one videocamera enough, particularly as you don't always see mother and baby together?* This is not a major objection. Once you recognize that there can be no 'perfect' recording of interaction, it is always a case of making do with what you have.
- *How far can you reconstruct all aspects of the interaction between a baby and her family from ten hours of videotape?* Never attempt to reconstruct *everything* about an interaction! Not only is this an impossible task but it is likely to deflect you from establishing a clear focus on one manageable topic.
- *Does an analysis of interactional situations give any hints as to how the baby reciprocally interprets her mother's actions?* Who knows what baby (and mother) are thinking? CA instructs us to look at what each party does without speculating about what they are thinking.
- *Should imitations associated with gestures and expressions be analysed separately from vocal imitations?* No! Use your rich video data to examine the interweaving of talk, gesture and expression.
- *Should more approaches be used (e.g. hermeneutics)?* Don't even think about it! Once you have found an approach which suits you, stick with it. Using multiple approaches is uneconomical and likely to delay completion of your research.
- *How do we distinguish 'imitation' from other activities such as 'repetition'?* Look at how baby's utterances are treated by mother, e.g. praise. But be prepared to change topic. 'Imitation' may give you an early hold on the topic but detailed description may lead in different directions.

The construction of ethnic identity among Spanish immigrants in London (sociology: Viviana)

Viviana's work focuses on styles of cultural consumption in relation to inter-generational differences within families of first- and second-generation immigrants. She has moved from an interview-based study to one based largely on observation and videotaping of Spanish families watching television together.

Viviana's research involves two overlapping areas – media studies and nationality. It is important for her to think through whether her main focus is on media reception or, as I think, on national identity, using the media as a case study. Again, although video data are potentially exciting material, they are notoriously difficult to analyse. Even though the analysis of interview data has all kinds of difficulties attached to it (see earlier), it may be more suited to her focus on ethnic identity. With a video, you have to infer identities. Through interviews, you can ask people to speak about their identity.

How 'female experience' is presented and problematized on TV
(sociology: Nora)

Nora's research is concerned with 'confessional' television as represented by Oprah Winfrey and other 'chat' shows. She has a particular interest in how 'psychological health' is invoked in such programmes.

She argues that most existing research focuses on audience participation in terms of issues relating to democracy and resistance. As she pointed out, the problem with such studies is that they simply posit general structures of power, class and gender. Instead, Nora, following Foucault, wants to problematize subjectivity. In particular, she is interested in the productivity of power in relation to what it means to be a woman; the kind of ethical agent who might adopt this subject position; and the forms of knowledge that have helped to construct it.

By its focus on media products from a Foucaultian perspective, her research promises to break new ground. Her major difficulty is the lack of any detailed direction for empirical work on media products within Foucault's work. Given this absence, I suggest that she speedily review methodologies deriving from other traditions to see if there are any useful points to be derived. In particular, CA offers a detailed way of transcribing video material and is beginning to address issues of validity and reliability in relation to single case studies (Peräklyä, 1997).

Videotapes: summary

All the points made earlier about audio data apply here, so I limit myself to a few additional observations arising from our four video studies.

BEWARE OF COMPLEXITY

Although video data are very attractive, they are very complex to work with since both transcription and analysis are more difficult than is the case with audio data. So think very carefully about whether you need video data for

47

your research. For instance, unlike CA, neither Foucault nor theories of identity provide a clear template for video analysis.

KEEP IT SIMPLE

You are not making a feature film! One videocamera is fine for most purposes. When you have your data, maintain a clear focus. Never attempt to reconstruct all aspects of the interaction from the videotape.

STICK WITH ONE APPROACH

By all means test out different ways of analysing your data but always settle on one clear analytic approach. Draw on other approaches only for particular technical skills (e.g. in transcribing video data).

MULTIPLE METHODS

Researchers are often tempted to use multiple methods. For instance, ethnographers often seek to combine observation with the interviewing of 'key informants'. In this section, I consider four examples of ethnographic work involving methods additional to observation.

How texts are reconstructed (sociology: Anne)

Anne's research is concerned with how a text changes as it moves from a book to television or radio. She is also concerned with the effects of mediation on performance.

Her approach derives from an extensive literature on theories of mediation dealing with literary products, film, sound/music and art. This seems to form a good basis for her research, although perhaps more work needs to be done on distinguishing these theories from our everyday assumption that something is 'lost' when books are turned into mass media products.

Anne intends to study media practices during the process of production as well as to interview translators, scriptwriters and actors to try to understand the principles that inform mediators. This looks like an interesting project working with accessible data, but I wonder if her data analysis might be simplified by focusing on media practice and products and leaving out any reference to the 'intentions' of those involved in the process and/or by just following through the transformation of one text.

Botswana women in public life (from 1800) (sociology: Mercy)

This study is a development of Mercy's earlier research. It centres around questions of women, power and politics in the context of Botswana society and culture. Her research derives from a feminist focus on the factors limiting women's political influence in Botswana. This means concentrating on forms of patriarchy as expressed in the *kgotla* system and in women's fragile citizenship rights. The research questions that flow from this concern women's changing experiences, the limits to women's participation in political life and the role of outside influences.

To answer these questions, Mercy proposes to use three methods: interviews, focus groups and the analysis of archive material perhaps using ideas from Foucault. However, she may be limited by the need to obtain government approval for her research.

This is an ambitious project which may be made more manageable by considering using only *one* dataset and not pursuing her reading of Foucault unless she decides to make the textual data her primary focus. However, as in all field research, it makes sense to treat her dealings with official authorities as data rather than as a technical difficulty prior to data gathering (see Chapter 15).

American 'concert dance' in the post-war era (sociology: Rita)

Rita's background is in dance studies and, more recently, sociology. Rita has found that, after World War II, the US government was building a new relationship with the dance community through sending out cultural 'ambassadors'. The period also coincided with the development of an American dance 'style' eschewing expressionism in favour of formalism.

Rita wants to explain both the politics of US support for dance and the emergence of a style which avoided seeking to express the 'self' or 'inner emotions'. She will focus on two groups of dance companies, as well as examining performances and texts by dance theorists.

Rita describes her approach as deriving from the work of Pierre Bourdieu, drawing upon his account of the body as embodying the social and a theory of fields in which agents struggle for domination. Bourdieu's work should help her achieve her ambitious aim to bring together history and social theory.

It remains to be seen whether it will be possible effectively to combine data deriving from different methods. Not only does this increase the scope of the research but it raises complicated issues about how to 'map' one set of data upon another (see my critique of 'triangulation' in Chapter 13).

How women experience depression (sociology: Philippa)

Philippa's research is concerned with how women, as users of psychiatric services, experience depression, self and identity. Her interest in this topic arose partly from family and work experience and partly because of her curiosity about the statistics which seem to show that women are twice as likely as men to be diagnosed as 'depressives'.

Her approach derives from Foucaultian 'genealogical' analysis and hence leads to a focus on how 'depression' is discursively constituted. This approach differs from feminist concerns with patriarchy and misogyny and from an interactionist focus on labelling by psychiatrists. The research questions that arise for her from this approach are: how do women speak of themselves as subjects who are 'depressed'? How do women position and speak about themselves compared with 'normal' gendered subjects? And how far do we find traces of a 'pharmacological culture' in how depression is constituted and treated?

Her data are drawn from women whom she meets through her work as a counsellor. Unusually, given her approach, Philippa has opted initially at least for a questionnaire (partly this reflects her lack of confidence in interviewing women she also counsels). A pilot of this questionnaire showed a high rate of non-response. She is currently revising her questionnaire as well as planning to do some archive analysis.

Philippa is aware that there might be more fruitful research designs. In particular, the use of focus groups or of open-ended interviews based on a single question (such as 'Would you like to tell me your story?') might overcome the problem of using leading or incomprehensible questions. Nonetheless, her project is ambitious and she might consider working entirely with available archives in the usual Foucaultian manner.

Multiple methods: summary

KEEP IT SIMPLE I

Like videotapes, multiple methods are tempting because they seem to give you a fuller picture. However, you need to be aware that multiple sources of data mean that you will have to learn many more data analysis skills. You will need to avoid the temptation to move to another dataset when you are having difficulties in analysing one set of material.

KEEP IT SIMPLE II

Often the desire to use multiple methods arises because you want to get at many different aspects of a phenomenon. However, this may mean that you have not yet sufficiently narrowed down your topic. Sometimes a better approach is to treat the analysis of different kinds of data as a 'dry run' for your main study. As such, it is a useful test of the kind of data which you can most easily gather and analyse.

KEEP IT SIMPLE III

'Mapping' one set of data upon another is a more or less complicated task depending on your analytic framework. In particular, if you treat social reality as constructed in different ways in different contexts, then you cannot appeal to a single 'phenomenon' which all your data apparently represent.

Research design should involve careful thought rather than seeking the most immediately attractive option. However, none of the points above exclude the possibility of using multiple means of gathering data. Ultimately, everything will depend on the quality of your data analysis rather than upon the quality of your data.

SUMMARY

I now want to pull together the points that I have been making in my discussion of the studies in this chapter. I have made the following suggestions:

- Define your research problem analytically.
- Limit your data.
- Demonstrate that your data analysis goes beyond a list.
- Limit the claims you make about your study.
- Think about the relevance of your research for other scholars and for 'society'.

Since each of these issues is discussed in later chapters, I will limit myself here to a few observations about each of them.

Defining your problem

1 Research 'problems' do not arise out of a clear blue sky! Sometimes their source is a scholarly debate, sometimes a pressing social problem. In any event, you will need to think through the *analytic basis* of your way of defining your research problem. Having chosen an approach, treat it as a 'toolbox' providing a set of concepts and methods to select your data and to illuminate your analysis.
2 Your approach must be appropriate to the research questions in which you are interested. Indeed, rather than being a constraint, a theory should generate a series of directions for your research (see Chapter 6). It will influence what status you attach to your data – for instance, as a true or false representation of reality – and how you code them.

Limiting your data

1 Decide which data to use by asking yourself which data are most appropriate to your research problem. For instance, are you more interested in what people are thinking or feeling or in what they are doing?
2 To make your analysis effective, it is imperative to have a limited body of data with which to work. So, while it may be useful initially to explore different kinds of data, this should usually only be done to establish the dataset with which you can most effectively work (see Chapter 8).
3 Make data collection as easy as possible. There are no 'Brownie points' given by most disciplines for having gathered your own data. Indeed, by

choosing 'difficult' situations to gather data (either because nothing 'relevant' may happen or even because background noise may mean you have a poor quality tape), you may condemn yourself to have less time to engage in the much more important activity of data analysis.

4 Beware of complexity. For instance, as we have seen, although video data are very attractive, they are very complex to work with. So keep data-gathering simple. Go for material that is easy to collect. Do not worry if it only gives you one 'angle' on your problem. That is a gain as well as a loss!

Data analysis goes beyond a list

1 Choosing a clear analytic approach is a help but is not everything. The danger is that you seek to apply too many findings or concepts deriving from that approach. This can make your analysis both confused and thin or a naive listing of observations consonant with each of these concepts. By narrowing down to a single issue, you may begin to make novel observations.

2 Identifying the main elements in your data according to some theoretical scheme should only be the first stage of your data analysis. Go on to examine how these elements are linked together (see Chapters 10 and 11).

3 As the data analysis proceeds, you should aim to give your chosen concept or issue a new twist, perhaps by pursuing a counter-intuitive idea or by noting an additional feature little addressed in the literature.

Limiting the claims you make about your research

It always helps to make limited claims about your own research. Grandiose claims about originality, scope or applicability to social problems are all hostages to fortune. Be careful in how you specify the claims of your approach. Show that you understand that it constitutes one way of 'slicing the cake' and that other approaches, using other forms of data, may not be directly competitive.

Issues of relevance

1 When you have finished, reflect upon the contribution that your research makes to contemporary scholarly debates. How does it add to knowledge or change our sense of the role of particular methods or concepts (see Chapter 21)?

2 Is your analytic position appropriate to any practical concerns you have? For instance, many contemporary social theories look at the world quite differently from respondents, policy-makers or practitioners. If you use such an approach, you will need to think carefully about what you can offer such groups – although it may well turn out that you can offer them more interesting findings than rather more conventional research (see Chapters 15 and 24).

NOTE

1 These research ideas derive from presentations during graduate workshops I co-ordinated at Goldsmiths College and at Oulu University, Finland. In the Finnish material, I have been able to draw upon research abstracts written by the students prior to the workshop. I was dependent on my contemporary notes for the Goldsmiths material and apologize for any inaccuracies present. In any event, it should be borne in mind that this is an account of the early stages of research studies which, no doubt, have developed and changed since then. Because of this, student's names have been anonymized.

Further reading

An excellent practical guide to the business of writing a dissertation is Pat Cryer's *The Research Student's Guide to Success* (Open University Press, 1996). Judith Bell's *Doing Your Research Project* (2nd edn, Open University Press, 1993) is a much more basic treatment, mainly aimed at under-graduate dissertations.

Exercise 3.1

This exercise is meant to help you think through the issues raised in this chapter about the value and implications of different ways of gathering and analysing qualitative data. Please go through the following steps, ideally with another student:

1 Define your research topic in no more than two sentences.
2 Explain which method you propose to use to gather data. Why that method?
3 Why would other methods not be possible or appropriate?
4 How big a data sample do you intend to collect? Could you manage with fewer data? Might you need more?
5 What theoretical approach do you favour? How will it help or hinder you in the analysis of your data?
6 What other approaches might be appropriate/inappropriate? Why?
7 Is there anything about your theory/method/data that could be simplified to make a more effective study?

4

What Counts as Originality?

All students speculate about the standards through which they will be assessed. Many students beginning a research study crave to be 'original'. Whether the research is for a PhD, an MA or only a humble BA dissertation, 'originality' is, for many, both a goal and a perceived critical standard which will be used by your examiners to beat you with!

Such fears are associated with a lack of knowledge about what is expected at a new, 'higher' level of your education. In this respect, we are talking about a common experience when we reach the next step on any ladder.

Many social transitions are associated with rites of passage and educational careers are no exception. In English secondary schools, after the age of 16, one enters the sixth form where one is expected to specialize narrowly and to become more self-reliant and less spoonfed. At my own school, boys just out of short trousers suddenly found themselves addressed by their sixth-form teacher as 'gentlemen'. We looked round the room but, weirdly, the appellation was directed at us.

The process is repeated in some form all over the world when you begin a BA at a university. Now, it seems, you are truly on your own, having to meet strange new criteria of achievement without any obvious means of support. Your time tends to be much more your own and you have to decide how much time to allocate to the library, the computer centre – or, at British universities, the students' union bar.

How much worse, then, when you register to do an MA or a PhD. Suddenly, everything you could count on in the past now seems to amount to nothing. You are no longer the outstanding undergraduate but just one of many students all of whom, presumably, achieved good first degrees. In the past, university examinations were mysteries that you had cracked. Now, although some further written examinations may await, you know that this is not how you are going to be mainly judged.

To some extent, this transition from BA to PhD is eased by the provision of taught courses for first-year research students, many of whom will have already taken an MA. However, a nagging doubt is still likely to torment many beginning PhD students. Are you 'up to it'? Above all, do you have the capacity to be 'original'? Or is 'originality', like so many things these days, something you can learn?

ORIGINALITY

> *Original*: not derived, copied, imitated or translated from anything else; novel; creative; independent in invention. (*Chambers English Dictionary*, 1990)

Consulting a dictionary about 'originality' brings mixed blessings. You are not planning to plagiarize anybody else and so should have no problem in meeting the 'negative' definition of 'originality' given above: your dissertation is unlikely to be 'derived, copied, imitated or translated from anything else'.

But how about the 'positive' components of 'originality'? Can you be 'novel; creative; independent in invention'? Moreover, since 'imaginativeness' is linked to 'originality' by Roget's *Thesaurus*, have you the talent to be 'imaginative'?

However you answer these questions, you are going to be in trouble! Obviously, if you don't feel that your intellect is especially 'novel', 'creative', 'inventive' and 'imaginative', then you are going to worry yourself sick about whether you are up to doing a worthwhile piece of research. Conversely, if you are full of confidence about these matters, it is very likely that you are under-estimating what is required to be granted these epithets.

If you doubt me, scan the book review pages in a journal in your field. My guess is that you will not find such words thrown around freely. And, remember, many of the books reviewed will be authored by established scholars, well past their own PhDs.

If the work of established scholars is not regularly judged to be 'novel', 'creative', 'inventive' or 'imaginative', what chance do you have? The answer is surprising: you have no problem.

Such epithets are rarely used by the examiners of successful PhD dissertations. Most dissertations are no more than solid and workmanlike. Indeed, it would cheapen the currency of academic description to use the vocabulary of 'originality' too frequently. Even Nobel Prize laureates never fail to cast doubt on their own supposed 'genius'. Instead, they regularly refer to the support of their research teams and to Edison's aphorism: 'Genius is one per cent inspiration and ninety-nine per cent perspiration' (see Mulkay, 1984).

As Phillips and Pugh point out, in the context of a PhD, 'an original contribution to knowledge' is a very shaded term: 'It does not mean an enormous breakthrough which has the subject rocking on its foundations' (1994: 34). In Kuhn's (1970) terms, PhD research is unlikely to involve a 'paradigm shift' in your discipline. Instead, Phillips and Pugh suggest, it demonstrates that you have a good grasp of how research is normally done in your field (i.e. that you can do what Kuhn calls 'normal science').

What does this mean in practice? Among other things, it can mean:

> making a synthesis that hasn't been made before; using already known material but with a new interpretation, bringing new evidence to bear on an old issue . . . [and] adding to knowledge in a way that hasn't been done before. (1994: 61–2)

So Phillips and Pugh suggest that a PhD is less to do with 'originality' and more about displaying that you are 'a fully professional researcher' (1994: 19). In turn, this means showing:

- that you have something to say to which your peers will want to listen
- that you are 'aware of what is being discovered, argued about, written and published by your academic community across the world' (1994: 19).

The upshot of this is that a PhD is best viewed as an apprenticeship prior to the admission to a community of scholars. This implies that:

> you are not doing research in order to do research; you are doing research in order to demonstrate that you have learned *how* to do research to fully professional standards. (1994: 20)

BEING A 'PROFESSIONAL'

'Originality' is only one of four criteria upon which examiners of the University of London PhD must report. For someone to get a London PhD, the examiners must report:

- that the thesis is genuinely the work of the candidate
- that the thesis forms a distinct contribution to the knowledge of the subject, and affords evidence of originality by the *discovery of new facts* and/or *the exercise of independent critical power* (my emphasis)
- that the thesis is satisfactory as regards literary presentation
- that the thesis is suitable for publication . . . as submitted or in abridged or modified form.

Despite the passing reference to 'originality' in the second item, all these criteria are really about professionality. We only need to concern ourselves about the second criterion: the discovery of new facts and the exercise of independent critical thought.

Considered on its own, 'the discovery of new facts' is rarely an important or even a challenging criterion in most of the social sciences. In the natural sciences, perhaps, a PhD researcher may discover a new substance or process and be applauded. But, in my experience, it is much rarer for qualitative social science PhDs to argue that they have found new 'facts'. Indeed, if they did so, they would most likely be greeted with the riposte: 'So what?'

For example, say such a dissertation claims that it has discovered that a particular group has beliefs or displays behaviours that were previously unknown. Any examiner worth their salt would then want to ask: 'Why, on earth, should it matter that this is the case?' In other words, what analytical or practical significance are we being asked to attach to this 'finding'?

Such a line of questioning is *not* a case of the examiner being difficult. As

I argue in Chapter 6, any scientific finding is always to be assessed in relation to the theoretical perspective from which it derives and to which it may contribute.

This means that, while 'facts' are never unimportant, they derive their relevance from the theoretical perspectives from which they stem and to which they contribute. The clear implication is that 'the exercise of independent critical thought' is the major criterion through which your dissertation will be assessed.

How can you satisfy this criterion? If professionality consists in the display of independent critical thought, what is the secret of being independent, critical and professional?

INDEPENDENT CRITICAL THOUGHT

In fact, as is the usual case in research, there is no secret or magic process to be revealed. In Chapter 2, we saw how Georgia, Seta and Vicki went about their research as solid craftpersons. Although occasionally they may have jumped out of their bath shouting 'eureka', most of the time they just plodded along, building a workmanlike analysis in the face of setbacks and opportunities.

Using their experience and the work of other students I have supervised, I outline below three procedures which contribute to the successful display of 'independent critical thought':

- developing a concept and/or a methodology
- thinking critically about your approach
- building on an existing study.

Developing a concept and/or a methodology

In 1997, Paul Acourt completed a theoretical dissertation on the emergence and apparent disappearance of discussion of 'progress' in the social science literature. Armed with a well-supported argument about the analytical and practical relevance of such a concept, he was able to convince his examiners of his 'independent critical thought'.

Many social science dissertations have a more empirical content. Georgia and Seta employed the concepts and methodology that the sociologist Harvey Sacks used to study the descriptive process. Georgia worked with the records of a further education college and Seta analysed referral letters and interviews gathered from an alcohol treatment centre.

Fifteen years earlier, Geoffrey Baruch (1981) had used the same approach (membership categorization analysis) on transcripts of interviews with parents of handicapped children. Like Georgia and Seta, he showed the ability to work with and to advance Sacks's specialist approach.

In the normal way, Georgia, Seta and Geoffrey were influenced by the interests and skills of their supervisor. In my case, I had a long-standing interest in making Sacks's work more widely known (see Silverman, 1998a).

Two of my other successful PhD students have used the concepts and methodology of the subdiscipline Sacks founded. As we saw in Chapter 3, conversation analysis (CA) is the study of talk-in-interaction. CA was used, in part, by Barry Sandywell in his research in the 1970s on mothers' expansions of their children's utterances. Twenty years later, Anssi Peräkylä (1995) developed CA's account of 'institutional' talk by his analysis of a video archive of AIDS counselling.

Of course, social science has a broad and rich stream of concepts and methodologies and my students' work has expressed this breadth while reflecting my interests in processes of language and representation. So Kobena Mercer (1990) used some ideas from the French tradition of semiotics in his research on the speeches of an English politician, Enoch Powell. The related concepts of Foucaultian discourse analysis were used by Mary Fraser (1995) in her study of representations of children in a British nursing journal.

In all these cases, because the approach was theoretically informed, the dissertation could justifiably argue that it had contributed to conceptual development.

Thinking critically about your approach

As we saw in Chapter 2, reflecting their prior experience as (respectively) psychotherapist and quantitative researcher, both Georgia and Seta originally proposed to use a quite different approach. Such changes of mind are not inevitable but are more likely when your supervisor comes from a different intellectual background to your own. However, as I noted in Chapter 2, only plodding students blindly follow every whim of their supervisor. Neither Georgia nor Seta accepted their new approach totally uncritically.

Ten years earlier, Gill Chapman (1987) had devised an unusual way of demonstrating her independent critical thought. Having discussed a range of possible ways of analysing her audiotapes of nurses' meetings, she decided to experiment with a wide range of concepts and methodologies. Each of the empirical chapters of her dissertation is thus both an analysis of her data and a critical evaluation of the approach used.

Building on an existing study

Don't try to reinvent the wheel! Seek to find a previous study that, in some respect, mirrors your own interests and topic. Then model your own research on that study and develop some aspect of it.

Of course, with limited resources, you are unlikely to be able to offer a complete 'test' of the findings of that study. But by careful analysis of your limited data, you can reflect on its approach and conclusions in an informed way.

Sometimes a more realistic model is a previous PhD thesis. It is worth recalling that both Seta and Vicki used an earlier PhD that I had supervised as a model for their research. So, at the outset, look at earlier dissertations in your university library and, where possible, focus on work directed by your supervisor.

CONCLUDING REMARKS

The message of this chapter is that a successful dissertation does not require genius. Once one defines the task of the research student in terms of the display of professional competence, then one can abandon those sessions in front of the mirror wondering whether you really look like Einstein, Keynes or Marie Curie!

In any event, you are likely to discover these things after a while through the response of your supervisor to your work. As Phillips and Pugh (1994) point out, worrying about the originality of your thought tends to be a concern only during the first few months. After then, this problem tends to disappear.

SUMMARY

Students at all levels desire to be original. However, BA and MA students can comfort themselves that even PhDs are rarely awarded for originality. In the context of a research degree, 'originality' is largely about your ability to display 'independent critical thought'. In turn, such thought can be shown by:

1   developing a concept and/or a methodology
2   thinking critically about your approach
3   building on an existing study.

Further reading

Estelle Phillips and Derek Pugh's *How To Get a PhD* (2nd edn, Open University Press, 1994), Chapters 3–6 gives a realistic, supportive account of what is required to achieve a PhD. Another helpful account of what counts as 'originality' in student research is Pat Cryer's *The Research Student's Guide to Success* (Open University Press, 1996), Chapters 15–17.

Exercise 4.1

Pat Cryer has suggested that we can understand originality in research through an analogy with a travel expedition: 'the research student is the explorer and the expedition is the research programme' (1996: 145). Cryer uses the expedition analogy to suggest different senses of 'original research'.

Review each of the following kinds of originality in terms of what you think your research might contribute and decide which kind is most likely to be applicable to your work:

- originality in tools, techniques and procedures
- originality in exploring the unknown
- originality in exploring the unanticipated
- originality in use of data
- originality in outcomes
- originality in byproducts (1996: 146–8).

You might return to this exercise at regular intervals to review any changes in how you view your research.

5

Selecting a Topic

Many undergraduate social science programmes reward passive knowledge rather than the ability to use ideas for yourself. They often leave students better able to leap the hurdles to pass their assessments than to use their knowledge for research or practice.

In qualitative methodology courses, this phenomenon is seen when courses encourage rote learning of critiques of quantitative research and offer minimal practice of alternative methods. By contrast, in quantitative methods courses, one tends to learn by rote recipe knowledge which *is* of practical use in drafting a research proposal (e.g. defining variables and measures).

In this context, selecting a research topic to be studied through qualitative methods is a very risky activity. This is because it involves committing yourself to a particular course of action rather than reiterating spoonfed 'critiques'.

Faced with this risk, students often try to play safe by opting for one of three apparently 'low-risk' strategies:

* simplistic inductivism
* the 'kitchen sink' gambit
* grand theory.

I briefly discuss each below before offering some more satisfactory solutions.

SIMPLISTIC INDUCTIVISM

In many social sciences, the qualitative tradition was initially characterized by its opposition to the strict research designs demanded in most quantitative work. So anthropologists would select their tribe, take up residence, learn the language and do no more than keep a field diary. Similarly, socio-logical ethnographers would identify an activity, institution or subculture and just 'hang out'. In both cases, the idea was to grasp 'reality' in its daily accomplishment.

The hope was that somehow meaning would 'emerge' by itself from such 'in-depth' exposure to the field. It was believed that any prior definitions of topics or concepts would only stand in the way of a sensitive understanding of the slice of the cultural world to which one was being exposed.

In the 1960s, this belief was apparently supported by Glaser and Strauss's (1967) famous idea of theory 'grounded' in data rather than presumed at the outset of a research study. Ironically, but understandably, the idea of quali-tative research as unstructured 'exposure' to the world was also supported by quantitative researchers. So we learn, in one quantitative text, that:

> Field research is essentially a matter of immersing oneself in a naturally occurring
> . . . set of events in order to gain firsthand knowledge of the situation. (Singleton
> et al., 1988: 11)

In common with crude inductivists, Singleton et al. refer to 'the situation' as if 'reality' were a single, static object awaiting observation. Like such quali-tative researchers, they emphasize 'immersion' which they implicitly con-trast with later, more focused research. This is underlined in their subsequent identification of qualitative or field research with 'exploration' and 'descrip-tion' (1988: 296) and their approval of the use of field research 'when one knows relatively little about the subject under investigation' (1988: 298–9).

This apparent unanimity at both ends of the research spectrum is noted by the authors of one qualitative methodology text:

> The conventional image of field research is one that keeps prestructuring and tight
> designs to a minimum. (Miles and Huberman, 1984: 27)

Miles and Huberman note two objections to this position and the cosy consensus that supports it: the omnipresence of theory and the need for a research design. I will briefly consider each in turn.

First, 'any researcher, no matter how unstructured or inductive, comes to fieldwork with *some* orienting ideas, foci and tools' (1984: 27). As Gubrium and Holstein note, the apparently atheoretical position of some ethnogra-phers itself derives from a theory:

> The directive to 'minimize presuppositions' in order to witness subjects' worlds on
> their own terms is a key to *naturalistic* inquiry. (1997: 34, my emphasis)

So the idea of just 'hanging out' with the aim of faithfully representing sub-jects' worlds is a convenient myth derived from a theory that Gubrium and Holstein term 'naturalism'. Of course, without some conceptual orientation, one would not recognize the 'field' one was studying. So the problem is that many closet naturalists fail to come clean about the theory dependence of their research.

A second objection to simply going out into the field and inducing observations is that it can be an excuse for sloppy, unfocused research. Mason (1996: 6) rejects the suggestion that qualitative research can just 'describe' or 'explore' the social world. As Miles and Huberman point out, such unfocused research can be a recipe for disaster:

> the looser the initial design, the less selective the collection of data; *everything* looks important at the outset to someone waiting for the key constructs or regularities to emerge from the site, and that wait can be a long one. (1984: 28)

Moreover, such a purely inductive approach can be blind to the need to build cumulative bodies of knowledge. If this is not an intentionally anti-scientific ploy, it can be just naive. In the 1920s and 1930s, research students in Chicago, following Robert Park's injunction to get out of their armchairs into the virgin territory of urban streetlife (see Bulmer, 1984), could justify their inductivist aims. By the 1960s, however, even Glaser and Strauss (1967) were requiring that field researchers think about the 'formal theories' that might be developed out of apparently isolated substantive, inductive studies.

At the turn of the century, qualitative research would indeed be in a sorry state if it had not developed such theories and related cumulative bodies of knowledge. As I commented recently:

> we no longer need to regard qualitative research as provisional or never based on initial hypotheses. This is because qualitative studies have already assembled a usable, cumulative body of knowledge. (Silverman, 1997a: 1)

Sometimes, the previous literature or (for experienced researchers) one's own work will suggest a hypothesis crying out to be tested or a finding ripe for retesting. Where this happens, particularly where the earlier study derived from a theoretical approach to which you are sympathetic, an attempt to strike out afresh would be in danger of reinventing the wheel.

Of course, as Chapter 2 shows, this does not mean that you should necessarily be stuck with your original ideas. The beauty of qualitative research is that its rich data can offer the opportunity to change focus as the ongoing analysis suggests. However, such changes of direction, like the original research proposal, do not come out of the blue but reflect the subtle interplay between theory, concepts and data.

THE 'KITCHEN SINK' GAMBIT

Like any piece of advice, you can take too far the advice to avoid simplistic inductivism. In drafting your first research proposal, it is tempting to select a very broad topic. By including every aspect of a problem that you can think of, you hope to show the breadth of your knowledge and to impress potential supervisors.

Unfortunately, this 'kitchen sink' approach is a recipe for disaster. Unless you have the resources for a big team of researchers, depth rather than breadth is what characterizes a good research proposal. If you define your topic very widely, you will usually be unable to say anything at great depth about it.

As I tell my students, your aim should be to say 'a lot about a little (problem)'. This means avoiding the temptation to say 'a little about a lot'. Indeed, the latter path can be something of a 'cop-out'. Precisely because the topic is so wide-ranging, one can flit from one aspect to another without being forced to refine and test each piece of analysis.

GRAND THEORY

While the kitchen-sinker flits about trying this and that, the grand theorist is kept busy building theoretical empires. Stuck firmly in their armchairs, such theorists need never trifle with mere 'facts'. Instead, they may sometimes spin out cobwebs of verbiage which, as C. Wright Mills (1959) said, can be reduced to a few sentences.

Nonetheless, a situation in which you can obtain a research degree without ever leaving your familiar university library is not to be despised. Indeed, I should be the last to criticize grand theory since my own PhD was obtained by this very method!

However, it is usually wise to assume that every 'solution' contains seeds of further problems. In the case of grand theory, these problems include:

- Can you ever get out of the library in order to write your thesis? One book will surely have a list of further 'crucial' references and so on, *ad infinitum*. Anybody who thinks a library PhD is a 'quick fix' would be well advised to ponder whether they have the willpower to stop reading. They would also be wise to consult Borges's short story 'The Library of Babel' which tells a chastening tale of scholars who believe that, if they only keep on looking, all knowledge will finally be revealed by yet another book.
- Theoretical fashions change – nowhere more so than in the social sciences. If you commit yourself to a theoretical topic, you must always be looking over your shoulder at the prospect of some change in direction in the theoretical wind from, say, Paris to an obscure location with a school of thought of which you are totally unfamiliar.
- If you do grand theory, you may spend so much time constructing elegant accounts of the world that you never touch base with the ground upon which the world rests. Kafka's (1961) wonderful short story 'Investigations of a Dog' creates a marvellous image of 'airdogs' (*Lufthunde*) who float on cushions above the ground, surveying the world from on high,

yet cut off from any contact with it (so cut off that Kafka's doggy investigator wonders how they manage to reproduce themselves!).

However, readers of this book will be more interested in solutions than in critiques. In response to this, I set out below some practical strategies that may be of use to potential 'simplistic inductivists', 'kitchen-sinkers' and 'grand theorists'.

STRATEGIES FOR SIMPLISTIC INDUCTIVISTS

If your previous education has equipped you with few research ideas of your own, comfort yourself that your predicament is not unusual and can be resolved.

I outline below three strategies that you can use if you find yourself in this boat. Each seeks to encourage you to use the knowledge you have already gained as a resource in generating a researchable problem. The three strategies I discuss are:

- using concepts as sensitizing resources
- using other people's generalizations
- introducing a third variable.

Using sensitivities

Treating the knowledge you have learned as a resource involves thinking about how it can sensitize you to various researchable issues. In an earlier book (Silverman, 1993: 6–8), I sought to distinguish three types of sensitivity:

- historical
- cultural
- political
- contextual.

Most of this is self-explanatory. Historical sensitivity means that, wherever possible, one should examine the relevant historical evidence when setting up a topic to research. Cultural sensitivity reveals how the kind of 'experiences' reported in our four critiqued research studies are shaped by particular forms of cultural representation. Political sensitivity shows the vested interests behind current media 'scares' and reveals that this way of determining our research topics is just as fallible as designing research in accordance with administrative or managerial interests.

Contextual sensitivity is the least self-explanatory and most contentious category in the present list. A longer explanation is as follows:

By 'contextual' sensitivity, I mean two things:

(a) the recognition that apparently uniform institutions like 'the family', 'a tribe' or 'science' take on a variety of meanings in different contexts;

(b) the understanding that participants in social life actively produce a context for what they do and that social researchers should not simply import their own assumptions about what context is relevant in any situation. (1993: 8)

Such contextual sensitivity would suggest that matters like 'recovery from depression', 'quality care' and 'urban healing' are not uniform phenomena but take on particular meanings in different local contexts and local cultures (Gubrium, 1988), depending, among other things, on who is the audience for the description.[1]

One final point. The four kinds of sensitivity we have been considering offer different, sometimes contradictory, ways of generating research topics. I am not suggesting that all should be used at the beginning of any research study. However, if we are not sensitive to *any* of these issues, then we run the danger of lapsing into a commonsensical way of defining our research topics. This is a topic to which I shall return, particularly in Chapter 6.

Using earlier findings or theories

Phillips and Pugh (1994: 49–52) suggest that one aid for the sluggish research imagination is to begin with previously proposed generalizations and then try to find their limits by postulating new conditions.

Since most undergraduate social science teaching places a great deal of emphasis on the 'classic' literature, you can sometimes mobilize your knowledge of 'classical' work in order to generate a research problem. In an earlier book (Silverman, 1985: 10–11), I gave two sociological examples of postulating a new condition for a classical generalization.

First, Alvin Gouldner (1954) observed that Max Weber's 'ideal type' of bureaucracy was largely based on studies of government bureaucracies. This meant that Weber stressed the role of democratically defined formal rules in obtaining consent. By studying rule-following in the private sector, Gouldner was able to identify varying levels and bases of consent by staff to rules.

Second, Lipset et al. (1962) noted that Robert Michels's 'iron law of Oligarchy' had encouraged a focus on the factors that make organizations un-democratic. By studying a highly democratic organization, Lipset et al. identified both anti-democratic and democratic pressures in how organizations operate. By doing so, they were able to question the inevitability of this iron law.

More recently, I became interested in the conditions under which clients were likely to demonstrate uptake of the advice that they were given in interviews with health professionals. In a study of interviews between British health visitors and first-time mothers, Heritage and Sefi (1992) had found that mothers were more likely to acknowledge the relevance of advice which was related to their expressed concerns.

In my own study of HIV-test counselling (Silverman, 1997b), I began with

Heritage and Sefi's findings as my initial research focus. However, I observed that time constraints in many counselling centres meant that it was very difficult for counsellors to adopt such an apparently 'client-centred' approach. My research question now changed to considering how both parties acted to prevent open disagreements while giving or receiving potentially irrelevant advice (1997b: 154–81).

Introducing a third variable

As described by Rudestam and Newton (1992, 12–16), introducing a third variable involves adding a focusing factor to your area of research interest. These authors give the example of a student interested in how young people view the elderly. You can make this topic less general, more researchable and more interesting by introducing a third variable. For instance, you can ask: does living with a grandparent influence this? Alternatively, you can focus on the effect on young people of media representations of the elderly. Further, using 'contextual sensitivity', as described above, you can limit your focus even more by asking how, when and where young people generate descriptions of elderly people.

If you have a tendency to be a 'simplistic inductivist', you should now attempt Exercise 5.1 at the end of this chapter.

STRATEGIES FOR KITCHEN-SINKERS

> Do less, more thoroughly. (Wolcott, 1990: 62)

Wolcott's advice is sound. Narrowing down is often the most crucial task when drafting a research proposal. Kitchen-sinkers have so many ideas buzzing around in their heads that getting down to a focused piece of research is entirely beyond them.

Every issue seems so fascinating. Each aspect seems interconnected and each piece of reading that you do only adds further ideas (and suggests further readings). So, while you can grasp the value of making a lot out of a little, it is easier said than done. The question remains: how do you go about narrowing your ideas down? I set out below three practical techniques which help to answer this question:

* drawing a flow chart
* finding a puzzle
* looking through a zoom lens.

The flow chart

Dealing with data means moving from passive reading to active analysis. If you have failed to use the early stages of your research to narrow down your topic, data analysis is going to be very difficult:

having a large number of research questions makes it harder to see emergent links across different parts of the data base and to achieve successful integration of findings. (Miles and Huberman, 1984: 36)

To help you narrow down, it can make sense to do an early flow chart setting out your key concepts and how they might relate. Following Miles and Huberman:

Conceptual frameworks are best done graphically, rather than in text. Having to get the entire framework on a single page is salutary. (1984: 33)

The single-page flow chart is a useful technique in writing books as well as in doing research. For instance, as I write these words, I regularly move to a second document which houses the outline of this book. This outline was continually revised as I did my preliminary reading. It is still being revised as I write each chapter.

Several attempts will usually be needed to get your flow chart into a state that will be useful to you. Miles and Huberman recommend experimenting with different ways of specifying your research focus. But their basic advice is to 'begin with a foggy research question and then try to defog it' (1984: 35).

Finding a puzzle

One way to break out of the vicious circle of unending facts and theories is to put your books on one side and to ask yourself: what am I really trying to find out? More specifically, what *puzzle* am I trying to solve?

Think of research as one of many kinds of puzzle-solving among a set of activities like doing jigsaws, completing crosswords or solving crimes. Each activity will be associated with its own set of more or less unique activities (but see Alasuutari, 1995, on the parallel between the qualitative researcher and Sherlock Holmes). Jennifer Mason has argued that 'all qualitative research should be formulated around an intellectual puzzle' (1996: 6). She distinguishes three kinds of question that may generate the type of intellectual puzzle which qualitative researchers would recognize, namely:

- How or why did X develop? (a developmental puzzle)
- How does X work? (a mechanical puzzle)
- What causes X or what influence does X have on Y? (a causal puzzle) (1996: 14)

Let us consider how, following Mason, you might find a puzzle. Say you have a general interest in 'child abuse'. You might narrow down your topic by choosing among the following questions:

- How or why was 'child abuse' first recognized? (a developmental puzzle)
- How (and by whom) is 'child abuse' identified? (a mechanical puzzle)

- What are the characteristics of child abusers and abused children? What effect does child abuse have on each group? (a causal puzzle)

Once you make a list of this kind, you should see that it is impossible to solve satisfactorily all these puzzles. So which puzzle do you choose? The following are some further questions that are worth asking:

- Which puzzle most interests me?
- Which puzzle might most interest my supervisor or funding body?
- Which puzzle most relates to issues on which I already have some theoretical or empirical background?
- Which puzzle would generate questions that could be answered using my own resources and with readily available data?

The zoom lens

Wolcott (1990) gives the example of one PhD student who never finished his study of classroom behaviour. The true 'kitchen-sinker', this poor student was always reading more or gathering yet more data.

Wolcott uses the analogy of a zoom lens to suggest a practical solution. Say you want to take some photographs of a holiday resort. You could find some suitably high place, say a nearby hill, and try to take a picture of the whole resort. Then, as Wolcott points out, 'if you want to take in more of the picture, you must sacrifice closeness of detail' (1990: 63).

Alternatively, you can zoom in on one small image. What you lose in breadth, you may well gain in telling detail – say a particular dish that you enjoyed, or the interaction between two local people.

Now apply the zoom lens analogy to defining your own research task. Wolcott suggests 'taking some manageable "unit of one" as a focus' (1990: 69). So if, like his student, you are interested in classroom behaviour, focus on one student, one day, one lesson or one critical event.

The beauty of this narrowing of focus is that it will produce a manageable and achievable research task. Moreover, you are not locked forever in this close-up picture. Just like the photographer, you can 'zoom in progressively closer and closer until your descriptive task is manageable, then zoom back out again to regain perspective' (1990: 69).

Following Wolcott, later on you can always attempt to broaden your generalizations through more data at different levels of 'reality'. But your initial 'zooming in' will have got you going – out of the library and into dealing with data.

If you have a tendency to be a 'kitchen-sinker', you should now attempt Exercise 5.2.

A caution: avoiding reductionism

One of the advantages of introducing a third variable is that it guards against the tendency to try to explain complex social processes in terms of a single cause. Such reductionism is regularly demanded both in legal cross-examinations ('answer yes or no'!) and in media interviews (where the demand for simplification sometimes makes research scientists seem like incoherent babblers).

So my diagnosis of 'kitchen-sinking' and my recommendations for specifying a research problem should not be confused with attempts to reduce the complexities of the social world to a single variable. Just as doctors talk about meeting patients who make their hearts sink, there is nothing worse than when a detailed seminar on one's research is greeted by some bright spark with a version of: 'That's all very interesting. But surely what you've described is all to do with power/gender/postmodernity etc.'

What a nice, simple world it would be if everything reduced to one factor! For the moment, however, we should leave the pursuit of this kind of simplicity to bigots and to those theoretical physicists who are valiantly seeking a single theory of matter.

Unfortunately, this does not put off those social scientists who claim that one factor or institution ('power', 'gender') is the cause of everything and do 'research' in order to 'prove' this. For instance, in a study of doctor–patient communication, Waitzkin had the laudable aim of relating 'the everyday micro-level interaction of individuals' to 'macro-level structures of domination' (1979: 601). However, as Rayner and Stimson (1979) point out, Waitzkin used a mechanistic version of Marxism based on notions of the material base and the superstructure, which reduces the doctor–patient relationship simply to an ideological state apparatus of the capitalist state.

Knowing what he was going to find, Waitzkin appeared to treat his data largely as illustrative of a preconceived theory. For instance, he asserts that doctors send ideological messages about the 'work ethic' to their patients. Yet he rests his case on a small part of a medical interview in which, hearing that his patient is tired, the doctor asks whether he is 'able . . . to work a regular day'. When the patient confirms this, the doctor says: 'Wonderful' (1979: 604–5).

As I commented in an earlier book:

> At the very least, Waitzkin is making very limited data do a great deal of analytic work. Without any evidence to the contrary, the reader might prefer to read the doctor's question about the patient's employment as simply establishing the status of the latter's comment about feeling tired. (Silverman, 1985: 186)

So narrowing down a research problem should not be confused with this kind of reductionism. I can only echo the arguments of the authors of a recent qualitative methodology textbook:

> Such reductive arguments are always distressing, given the variety and complex organization of social worlds. They reflect mentalities that cannot cope with the uncertainties and ambiguities of social research. (Coffey and Atkinson, 1996: 15)

STRATEGIES FOR GRAND THEORISTS

Reducing 'reality' to ungrounded sets of categories is an obvious potential failing of grand theorists. However, the minority of readers who feel they have the flair and temperament for theorizing will not, I suspect, be dissuaded by anything I might write. Indeed, sometimes, as I have already remarked, library-based work can be a quick way to write an acceptable thesis.

In this situation, all I can usefully do is wish you luck and offer you a couple of suggestions to speed you on your way. First, try to ignore fashions. Second, think about how some data may actually help you to theorize better. I set out these suggestions below.

Ignore fashions

Having found the corner of the intellectual garden which suits you, stick with it. Don't worry about those smart alecs who have always read a 'crucial' book by some new author: nine times out of ten, it will just distract you. Guided by your supervisor, work out the set of readings that will be your central material and stay with them. When you have written most of your thesis, you may then have the luxury of reading more widely and using that reading to reflect on the implications and limitations of your position – perhaps for your final chapter. Till then, don't be distracted.

Find some data

Even the most active minds can become a little stilted when confined to their armchairs. So think about examining some empirical materials of some kind. Even though these may not be central to your thesis, they may work as an aid to the sluggish imagination.

Take the case of two students in my own department currently writing 'theoretical' PhDs. Nick is interested in what he calls 'the refusal of work' which he links to theoretical ideas about 'the ontology of desire'. Despite this highly complex theory, Nick still feels it worthwhile to gather material on the history of Autonomia – an Italian movement to refuse work – and the organization of unemployment benefit in the UK.

Jake is interested in a critique of existing theories of the community. In this context, he is attempting what he describes as largely a philosophical exercise. Nonetheless, to aid his thinking, he is observing and interviewing homeless people, beggars and the mainstream community. He is attempting what he calls 'a situated phenomenology of the moral encounter', and the data are intended to be only illustrative.

CONCLUDING REMARKS

As with most dispositions, whether you tend to be a simplistic inductivist, a kitchen-sinker or a grand theorist is likely to arise from a combination of temperament and experience. As such, you are unlikely to be deflected by anything I write. So this chapter will have succeeded not by converting you but if it helps you to speed along your ordained path.

On the other hand, it may be over-reductionist to view these three tendencies as personal dispositions. Jay Gubrium (personal correspondence) has suggested to me that simplistic inductivism, kitchen-sinkism and grand theory are occupational hazards of all social science inquiry. In this sense, they are tendencies present in all of us and we need to be constantly wary of them if our enterprise is going to be theoretically informed *and* empirically grounded.

SUMMARY

Selecting a research topic can be made easier if you resist three temptations.

First, *simplistic inductivism* assumes that we need make no assumptions in studying the world. Instead, hypotheses will somehow emerge if we just 'hang out' with the aim of faithfully representing subjects' worlds. Simplistic inductivism is at best a convenient myth which ignores the theory-saturated nature of any observation and can be an excuse for sloppy, unfocused research. It is best countered by:

- using concepts as sensitizing resources
- using other people's generalizations
- introducing a third variable.

Second, *the kitchen sink gambit* seeks to include every aspect of a problem that you can think of in order to show the breadth of your knowledge and to impress potential supervisors. However, if you define your topic very widely, you will usually be unable to say anything at great depth about it. Depth rather than breadth is what characterizes a good research proposal. Kitchen-sinking can be countered by:

- drawing a flow chart
- finding a puzzle
- looking through a zoom lens.

Third, *grand theorists* build theoretical empires. Stuck firmly in their armchairs, such theorists need never trifle with mere 'facts'. The consequence may not be enlightenment but merely cobwebs of verbiage. This tendency can be countered by:

- ignoring the latest fashions
- finding some data.

NOTE

1 See Chapter 26 for further discussion of studies of these topics in relation to assessing the 'quality' of qualitative research.

Further reading

To help you think some more about defining your research, I recommend three basic texts: Amanda Coffey and Paul Atkinson, *Making Sense of Qualitative Data* (Sage, 1996), Chapter 1; Jennifer Mason, *Qualitative Researching* (Sage, 1996), Chapters 1–2; and David Silverman, *Interpreting Qualitative Data: Methods for Analysing Talk, Text and Interaction* (Sage, 1993), Chapter 1.

Useful but more specialist texts are: Pertti Alasuutari, *Researching Culture* (Sage, 1995), Chapter 13; Martyn Hammersley and Paul Atkinson, *Ethnography: Principles in Practice* (Tavistock, 1983), Chapter 2; and Anselm Strauss and Juliet Corbin, *Basics of Qualitative Research* (Sage, 1990), Chapters 1–4.

Exercise 5.1: strategies for simplistic inductivists

1 Attempt to relate your research ideas to *one* or *all* of the types of 'sensitivity' discussed in the chapter:

- historical
- cultural
- political
- contextual.

How might this lead you to reformulate your research interest?
2 Review any theoretical or research study with which you are familiar. Try to postulate new conditions which might allow you to develop a new but related research topic.
3 Try adding a few extra variables into your area of research interest. Now work out which of these variables would add most depth to your project and/or be most simply researched (e.g. are the data available, and can they be relatively easily gathered?)

Exercise 5.2: strategies for kitchen-sinkers

1 Draw a flow chart of no more than one page, setting out your key concepts and how they relate.
2 Review your area of research interest in terms of the following questions and formulate your research problem in terms of *one* kind of puzzle:

  • How or why did *X* develop? (a developmental puzzle)
  • How does *X* work? (a mechanical puzzle)
  • What causes *X* or what influence does *X* have on *Y*? (a causal puzzle) (Mason, 1996: 14)

3 Use the zoom lens technique to focus in on some manageable 'unit of one' which might serve as an initial dataset to resolve your puzzle.

6

Theory in Qualitative Research

Some people become qualitative researchers for rather negative reasons. Perhaps they are not very good at statistics (or think they are not) and so are not tempted by quantitative research. Or perhaps they have not shone at library work and so are not tempted to write a purely theoretical dissertation.

However, the latter disposition begs the question of the relevance of theory to research. In part, this varies between social science disciplines. For, at least until recently, the different social sciences seemed to vary in the importance that they attached to theory. To take just two examples, psychologists and anthropologists, for all their differences, seemed to downplay theory.

In psychology, the benchmark was the laboratory study. For psychologists, the motto seemed to be: 'demonstrate the facts through a controlled experiment and the theories will take care of themselves'. Anthropologists were just as interested in 'the facts'. However, their most important facts were revealed in observational case studies of groups or tribes usually found in faraway lands. Nonetheless, until recently, most English-speaking anthropologists followed psychologists in elevating 'facts' above 'theories'.

By contrast, generations of sociology students have been made very aware of the primary importance attached to theory in their discipline. For instance, although undergraduate sociology courses tend to be split into three main areas (the 'holy trinity' of social theory, social structure and research methods), it is the course in social theory which is usually given the most prestige. Moreover, theory has recently become much more important in psychology and anthropology, as battles have commenced between traditionalists and qualitative 'discourse analysts' (in psychology) and 'postmodern' and gender theorists (in anthropology).

The social sciences' concern with theory is reflected in how PhD dissertations are assessed. As we saw in Chapter 4, 'the discovery of new facts' is rarely an important or even a challenging criterion in the assessment of most qualitative research. Any scientific finding is usually to be assessed in relation to the theoretical perspective from which it derives and to which it may contribute. This means that, while 'facts' are never unimportant, they are always subsidiary to theories. Successful dissertations display 'independent critical thought' (in the words of the University of London PhD regulations) by engaging with theory.

However, this begs an important question. What is 'theory'? In the following section I show why, for qualitative researchers, theory is altogether more interesting than the dry pages of theory textbooks.

WHAT IS THEORY?

Martin O'Brien (1993) has used the example of a kaleidoscope to answer this question. As he explains:

> a kaleidoscope . . . [is] the child's toy consisting of a tube, a number of lenses and fragments of translucent, coloured glass or plastic. When you turn the tube and look down the lens of the kaleidoscope the shapes and colours, visible at the bottom, change. As the tube is turned, different lenses come into play and the combinations of colour and shape shift from one pattern to another. In a similar way, we can see social theory as a sort of kaleidoscope – by shifting theoretical perspective the world under investigation also changes shape. (1993: 10–11)

How theory works as a kaleidoscope can be vividly seen in a concrete example taken from Eric Livingston (1987). Livingston asks us to imagine that we have been told to carry out some social research on city streets. Where should we begin? Some alternatives are set out in Table 6.1.

As Livingston points out, each of these different ways of looking involves basic theoretical as well as methodological decisions. Very crudely, if we are attached to social theories which see the world in terms of correlations between social facts (think of demography or macroeconomics), we are most likely to consider gathering official statistics (option 1 in Table 6.1). By contrast, if we think that social meanings or perceptions are important (as in certain varieties of sociology and psychology), we may be tempted by the interview study (option 2). Or if we are anthropologists or those kinds of sociologists who want to observe and/or record what people actually do *in situ*, we might elect for options 3 or 4. But note the very different views of people's behaviour we get from looking from on high (3), where people look like ants forming geometrical shapes like wedges, and from street level (4), where behaviour seems much more complex.

The point is that none of these data are more real or more true than the others. For instance, people are not really more like ants or complex actors. It all depends on our research question. And research questions are inevitably

TABLE 6.1 **Viewing a street: data possibilities**

1   Official statistics (traffic flow, accidents)
2   Interviews (how people cope with rush hours)
3   Observation from a tower (viewing geometric shapes)
4   Observation/video at street level (how people queue/organize their movements)

Source: adapted from Livingston, 1987: 21–7

theoretically informed. So we *do* need social theories to help us to address even quite basic issues in social research.

However, O'Brien's analogy of a kaleidoscope and Livingston's example of viewing a city street only take us so far. What precisely is a 'theory'? And how does it differ from a 'hypothesis'?

Questions like this mean that I can no longer postpone the potentially tiresome business of defining my terms. Once I have completed these definitions, I will, once again, provide a set of concrete examples to clarify what I mean.

THEORIES, MODELS AND HYPOTHESES

In this section, we shall be discussing models, concepts, theories, hypotheses, methodologies and methods. In Table 6.2, I set out how each term will be used.

As we see from the table, *models* provide an overall framework for how we look at reality. In short, they tell us what reality is like and the basic elements it contains ('ontology') and what is the nature and status of knowledge ('epistemology'). In this sense, models roughly correspond to what are more grandly referred to as 'paradigms' (see Guba and Lincoln, 1994).

In social research, examples of such models are functionalism (which looks at the functions of social institutions), behaviourism (which defines all behaviour in terms of 'stimulus' and 'response'), symbolic interactionism (which focuses on how we attach symbolic meanings to interpersonal relations) and ethnomethodology (which encourages us to look at people's everyday ways of producing orderly social interaction).

Within the narrower sphere of qualitative research, Gubrium and Holstein (1997) use the term 'idiom' to encompass both the analytical preferences indicated by 'model' and tastes for particular vocabularies, investigatory

TABLE 6.2 **Basic terms in research**

Term	Meaning	Relevance
Model	An overall framework for looking at reality (e.g. behaviouralism, feminism)	Usefulness
Concept	An idea deriving from a given model (e.g. 'stimulus–response', 'oppression')	Usefulness
Theory	A set of concepts used to define and/or explain some phenomenon	Usefulness
Hypothesis	A testable proposition	Validity
Methodology	A general approach to studying research topics	Usefulness
Method	A specific research technique	Good fit with model, theory, hypothesis and methodology

Source: revised version of Silverman, 1993: 1

77

styles and ways of writing. They distinguish (and criticize) four different 'idioms':

- *Naturalism* A reluctance to impose meaning and a preference to 'get out and observe the field'.
- *Ethnomethodology* Shares naturalism's attention to detail but locates it in talk-in-interaction.
- *Emotionalism* Desires 'intimate' contact with research subjects and favours the personal biography.
- *Postmodernism* Seeks to deconstruct the concepts of the 'subject' and the 'field'.

Concepts are clearly specified ideas deriving from a particular model. Examples of concepts are 'social function' (deriving from functionalism), 'stimulus/response' (behaviouralism), 'definition of the situation' (interactionism) and 'the documentary method of interpretation' (ethnomethodology). Concepts offer ways of looking at the world which are essential in defining a research problem.

Theories arrange sets of concepts to define and explain some phenomenon. As Strauss and Corbin put it: 'Theory consists of plausible relationships produced among concepts and sets of concepts' (1994: 278).

Without a theory, such phenomena as 'death', 'tribes' and families' cannot be understood. In this sense, without a theory there is nothing to research.

So theory provides a footing for considering the world, separate from, yet about, that world. In this way, theory provides both:

- a framework for critically understanding phenomena
- a basis for considering how what is unknown might be organized (Gubrium, personal correspondence).

By provoking ideas about the presently unknown, theories provide the impetus for research. As living entities, they are also developed and modified by good research. However, as used here, models, concepts and theories are self-confirming in the sense that they instruct us to look at phenomena in particular ways. This means that they can never be disproved but only found to be more or less useful.

This last feature distinguishes theories from *hypotheses*. Unlike theories, hypotheses are tested in research. Examples of hypotheses, discussed in Silverman (1993), are:

- How we receive advice is linked to how advice is given.
- Responses to an illegal drug depend upon what one learns from others.
- Voting in union elections is related to non-work links between union members.

In many qualitative research studies, there is no specific hypothesis at the outset. Instead, hypotheses are produced (or induced) during the early stages of research. In any event, unlike theories, hypotheses can, and should be, tested. Therefore, we assess a hypothesis by its validity or truth.

A *methodology* defines how one will go about studying any phenomenon. In social research, methodologies may be defined very broadly (e.g. qualitative or quantitative) or more narrowly (e.g. grounded theory or conversation analysis). Like theories, methodologies cannot be true or false, only more or less useful.

Finally, *methods* are specific research techniques. These include quantitative techniques, like statistical correlations, as well as techniques like observation, interviewing and audio recording. Once again, in themselves, techniques are not true or false. They are more or less useful, depending on their fit with the theories and methodologies being used and the hypothesis being tested and/or the research topic that is selected. So, for instance, behaviouralists may favour quantitative methods and interactionists often prefer to gather their data by observation. But, depending upon the hypothesis being tested, behaviouralists may sometimes use qualitative methods – for instance in the exploratory stage of research. Equally, interactionists may sometimes use simple quantitative methods, particularly when they want to find an overall pattern in their data.

The relation between models, concepts, theories, hypotheses, methodology and methods can be set out schematically as in Figure 6.1. Reading the

FIGURE 6.1   *Levels of analysis*

figure downwards, each concept reflects a lower level of generality and abstraction. The arrow from 'findings' to 'hypotheses' indicates a feedback mechanism through which hypotheses are modified in the light of findings.

Let me now try to put flesh on the skeleton set out in Figure 6.1 through the use of some concrete examples. Imagine that we have a general interest in the gloomy topic of 'death' in society. How are we to research this topic?

Before we can even define a research problem, let alone develop a hypothesis, we need to think through some very basic issues. Assume that we are the kind of social scientist that prefers to see the world in terms of how social structures determine behaviour, following the sociologist Emile Durkheim's (1951) injunction to treat social facts as real 'things'.

Such a model of social life will suggest concepts that we can use in our research on death. Using such a model, we will tend to see death in terms of statistics relating to rates of death (or 'mortality'). And we will want to explain such statistics in terms of other social facts such as age or social class.

Armed with our concepts, we might then construct a theory about one or other aspect of our topic. For instance, working with our assumption that death is a social fact, determined by other social facts, we might develop a theory that the rate of early death among children, or 'infant mortality', is related to some social fact about their parents, say their social class. From this theory, it is a quick step to the hypothesis that the higher the social class of its parents, the lower the likelihood of a child dying within the first year of its life. This hypothesis is sometimes expressed as saying that there is an 'inverse' relationship between social class and infant mortality.

As already implied, a model concerned with social facts will tend to favour a quantitative methodology, using methods such as the analysis of official statistics or the use of large-scale social surveys based on apparently reliable fixed-choice questionnaires. In interpreting the findings of such research, one will need to ensure that due account is taken of factors that may be concealed in simple correlations. For instance, social class may be associated with quality of housing and the latter factor (here called an 'intervening' variable) may be the real cause of variations in the rates of infant mortality. This overall approach to death is set out schematically in Figure 6.2.

Figure 6.3 sets out a very different way of conceiving death. For certain sociologists, social institutions are created and/or stabilized by the actions of participants. A central idea of this model is that how we label phenomena defines their character. This, in turn, is associated with the concept of 'definitions of the situation' which tells us to look for social phenomena in how meaning gets defined by people in different contexts. The overall message of this approach is that 'death' should be put in inverted commas and hence leads to a theory in which 'death' is treated as a social construct.

Of course, this is very different from the 'social fact' model and, therefore, nicely illustrates the importance of theories in defining research problems. Its immediate drawback, however, may be that it appears to be counter-intuitive. After all, you may feel, death is surely an obvious fact. Either we are dead or not dead and, if so, where does this leave social constructionism?

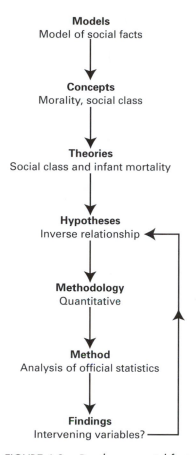

FIGURE 6.2   *Death as a social fact*

Let me cite two cases which put the counter-argument. First, in 1963, after President Kennedy was shot, he was taken to a Dallas hospital with, according to contemporary accounts, half of his head shot away. My hunch is that if you or I were to arrive in a casualty department in this state, we would be given a cursory examination and then recorded as 'dead on arrival' (DOA). Precisely because they were dealing with a President, the staff had to do more than this. So they worked on Kennedy for almost an hour, demonstrating thereby that they had done their best for such an important patient (cf. Sudnow, 1968a).

Now think of contemporary debates about whether or when severely injured people should have life-support systems turned off. Once again, acts of definition constitute whether somebody is alive or dead. And note that such definitions have real effects.

Of course, such a way of looking at how death is socially constructed (sometimes called 'social constructionism') is just one way of theorizing this phenomenon, not intrinsically better or worse than the 'social fact' approach.

81

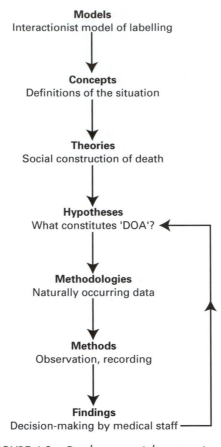

FIGURE 6.3   *Death as a social construction*

But, once we adopt one or another model, it starts to have a big influence upon how our research proceeds. For instance, as we have seen, if 'dead on arrival' can be a label applied in different ways to different people, we might develop a hypothesis about how the label 'dead on arrival' is applied to different hospital patients.

Because of our model, we would then probably try to collect research data that arose in such 'naturally occurring' (or non-research-generated) contexts as actual hospitals, using methods like observation and/or audio or video recording. Note, however, that this would not rule out the collection of quantitative data (say from hospital records). Rather, it would mean that our main body of data would probably be qualitative. Following earlier research (e.g. Jeffery, 1979; Dingwall and Murray, 1983), our findings might show how age and presumed moral status are relevant to such medical decision-making as well as social class. In turn, as shown in Figure 6.3, these findings would help us to refine our initial hypothesis.

GENERALIZATIONS AND THEORY BUILDING

Theorizing about data does not stop with the refinement of hypotheses. In this section, I will show how we can develop generalizations out of successfully tested hypotheses and, thereby, contribute to *building* theories.

First, we need to recognize that case studies, limited to a particular set of interactions, still allow one to examine how particular sayings and doings are embedded in particular patterns of social organization.

A classic case of an anthropologist using a case study to make broader generalizations is found in Mary Douglas's (1975) work on a Central African tribe, the Lele. Douglas noticed that an anteater, that Western zoologists call a 'pangolin', was very important to the Lele's ritual life. For the Lele, the pangolin was both a cult animal and an anomaly. It was perceived to have both animal and human characteristics: for instance, it tended only to have one offspring at a time, unlike most other animals. It also did not readily fit into the Lele's classification of land and water creatures, spending some of its time on land and some time in the water. Curiously, among animals that were hunted, the pangolin seemed to the Lele to be unique in not trying to escape but almost offering itself up to its hunter.

Fortunately, Douglas resisted what might be called a 'tourist' response, moving beyond curiosity to systematic analysis. She noted that many groups who perceive anomalous entities in their environment reject them out of hand. To take an anomalous entity seriously might cast doubt on the 'natural' status of your group's system of classification.

The classic example of the rejection of anomaly is found in the Old Testament. Douglas points out that the reason why the pig is unclean, according to the Old Testament, is that it is anomalous. It has a cloven hoof which, following the Old Testament, makes it clean; but it does not chew the cud, which makes it dirty. So it turns out that the pig is particularly unclean precisely because it is anomalous. Similarly, the Old Testament teachings on inter-marriage work in relation to anomaly. Although you are not expected to marry somebody of another tribe, to marry the offspring of a marriage between a member of your tribe and an outsider is even more frowned upon. In both examples, anomaly is shunned.

However, the Lele are an exception: they celebrate the anomalous pangolin. What this suggests to Douglas is that there may be no *universal* propensity to frown upon anomaly. If there is variability from community to community, then this must say something about their social organization.

Sure enough, there is something special about the Lele's social life. Their experience of relations with other tribes has been very successful. They exchange goods with them and have little experience of war.

What is involved in relating well with other tribes? It means successfully crossing a frontier or boundary. But what do anomalous entities do? They cut across boundaries. Here is the answer to the puzzle about why the Lele are different.

Douglas is suggesting that the Lele's response to anomaly derives from experiences grounded in their social organization. They perceive the pangolin favourably because it cuts across boundaries just as they themselves do. Conversely, the Ancient Israelites regard anomalies unfavourably because their own experience of crossing boundaries was profoundly unfavourable. Indeed, the Old Testament reads as a series of disastrous exchanges between the Israelites and other tribes.

By means of this historical comparison, Douglas has moved from a single-case explanation to a far more general theory of the relation between social exchange and response to anomaly. Glaser and Strauss (1968) have described this movement towards greater generality as a move from *substantive* to *formal* theory. In their own research on hospital wards caring for terminally ill patients, they show how, by using the comparative method, we can develop accounts of people's own awareness of their impending death (i.e. a substantive theory) and move to accounts of a whole range of 'awareness contexts' (formal theory).

Douglas's account of the relation between responses to anomaly and experiences of boundary crossing can also be applied elsewhere. Perhaps bad experiences of exchanges with other groups explains why some Israeli Jews and Palestinian Muslims are so concerned to mark their own identity on the 'holy places' in Jerusalem and reject (as a hateful anomaly) multiple use of the same holy sites.

In any event, Douglas's study of the Lele exemplifies the need to locate how individual elements are embedded in forms of social organization. In her case, this is done in an explicitly Durkheimian manner which sees behaviour as the expression of a 'society' which works as a 'hidden hand' constraining and forming human action. Alternatively, using a constructionist framework, one can look at the fine detail of people's activities without treating social organization as a purely external force (e.g. Moerman, 1974). In the latter case, people cease to be 'cultural dopes' (Garfinkel, 1967) and skilfully reproduce the moral order.

HOW TO THEORIZE ABOUT DATA

Unlike Moerman or Douglas, most readers will not bring to their research any very well-defined set of theoretical ideas. If you are in this position, your problem will be how you can use data to think in theoretical terms. The following list is intended merely as a set of suggestions. Although it cannot be exhaustive, it should serve as an initial guide to theorizing about data. It can also be read in conjunction with my discussion of the three kinds of research sensitivity in Chapter 5.

In carrying out your research, it is suggested that you think about the following five issues:

1 *Chronology*   Can you gather data over time in order to look at processes of change? If not, it is worth searching out historical evidence which may at least suggest how your research problem came into being.

2 *Context* How are your data contextualized in particular organizational settings, social processes or sets of experiences? For instance, as Moerman shows, answering an interviewer's question may be different from engaging in the activity which is the topic of the interview. Therefore, think about how there may be many versions of your phenomenon.

3 *Comparison* Like Mary Douglas, who generated her theory by comparing how different groups treated anomalies, always try to compare your data with other relevant data. Even if you cannot find a comparative case, try to find ways of dividing your data into different sets and compare them. Remember that the comparative method is the basic scientific method.

4 *Implications* When you are reporting your research, think about how what you have discovered may relate to broader issues than your original research topic. In this way, a very narrow topic (e.g. how the Lele perceive the pangolin) may be related to much broader social processes (e.g. how societies respond to anomalous entities).

5 *Lateral thinking* Be like the Lele. Don't erect strong boundaries between concepts but explore the relations between apparently diverse models, theories and methodologies. Celebrate anomaly!

CONCLUSION

The philosopher of science Thomas Kuhn (1970) has described some social sciences as lacking a single, agreed set of concepts. In Kuhn's terms, this makes social research 'pre-paradigmatic' or at least in a state of competing paradigms. As I have already implied, the problem is that this has generated a whole series of social science courses which pose different social science approaches in terms of either/or questions.

Such courses are much appreciated by some students. They learn about the paradigmatic oppositions in question, choose A rather than B, and report back, parrot fashion, all the advantages of A and the drawbacks of B. It is hardly surprising that such courses produce very little evidence that such students have ever thought about anything; even their choice of A is likely to be based on their teacher's implicit or explicit preferences. This may, in part, explain why so many undergraduate social science courses actually provide a learned incapacity to go out and do research.

Learning about rival 'armed camps' in no way allows you to confront research data. In the field, material is much more messy than the different camps would suggest. Perhaps there is something to be learned from both sides, or, more constructively, perhaps we start to ask interesting questions when we reject the polarities that such a course markets?

Even when we decide to use qualitative and/or quantitative methods, we involve ourselves in theoretical as well as methodological decisions. These decisions relate not only to how we conceptualize the world but also to our theory of how our research subjects think about things.

But theory only becomes worthwhile when it is used to explain something.

Howard Becker (1998: 1) reports that the great founder of the Chicago School, Everett Hughes, responded grumpily when students asked what he thought about theory. 'Theory of what?,' he would reply. For Hughes, as for me, theory without some observation to work upon is like a tractor without a field.

Theory, then, should be neither a status symbol nor an optional extra in a research study. Without theory, research is impossibly narrow. Without research, theory is mere armchair contemplation.

SUMMARY

Research questions are inevitably theoretically informed. So we *do* need social theories to help us to address even quite basic issues in social research. But theories need to be distinguished from models and concepts:

- *Models* provide an overall framework for how we look at reality.
- *Concepts* are clearly specified ideas deriving from a particular model.
- *Theories* arrange sets of concepts to define and explain some phenomenon.
- *Hypotheses* are testable propositions.
- *Methodologies* define how one will go about studying any phenomenon.
- *Methods* are specific research techniques.

You can improve your ability to theorize about data by thinking about:

1 *Chronology*   Gathering data over time in order to look at processes of change.
2 *Context*   Considering how your data are contextualized in particular organizational settings, social processes or sets of experiences.
3 *Comparison*   Trying to find ways of dividing your data into different sets and comparing each.
4 *Implications*   Thinking about how what you have discovered may relate to broader issues than your original research topic.
5 *Lateral thinking*   Exploring the relations between apparently diverse models, theories and methodologies.

Further reading

Becker's book *Tricks of the Trade* (University of Chicago Press, 1998) contains two chapters which are highly relevant to learning how to theorize about your data (Chapter 2 on 'Imagery' and Chapter 4 on 'Concepts'). Jaber Gubrium and James Holstein's book *The New Language of Qualitative Method* (Oxford University Press, 1997) is an invaluable, thought-provoking guide to the vocabularies, investigatory styles and ways of writing of different theoretical 'idioms'.

Exercise 6.1

Howard Becker reports that his colleague Bernard Beck responded to students seeking to theorize about their data by instructing them: 'Tell me what you've found out, but without using any of the identifying characteristics of the actual case' (1998: 126).

Becker gives the example of his own research on Chicago teachers which seemed to show that these teachers sought to improve their situation by moving to different schools rather than trying to get promoted in their present school. Using his data, but forbidden to talk about 'teachers' or 'schools', how might Becker have generated an account of his research that would have satisfied Beck?

7

Choosing a Methodology

> Knowing what you want to find out leads inexorably to the question of *how* you
> will get that information. (Miles and Huberman, 1984: 42)

In Chapter 6, I defined 'methodology' as 'a general approach to studying
research topics'. In this sense, your choice of method should reflect an
'overall research strategy' (Mason, 1996: 19) as your methodology shapes
which methods are used and how each method is used.

In quantitative research, it is expected that you begin by establishing a set
of variables and methods (often using already existing, proven measures).
However, when you are at the start of a piece of qualitative research, how far
are you forced to choose between different methods?

This question is raised by Miles and Huberman (1984) who suggest
that qualitative researchers have a range of options in how far they use
what the authors call 'prior instrumentation' (i.e. pre-defined methods and
measures):

- *No prior instrumentation* Fieldwork must be open to unsuspected
  phenomena which may be concealed by prior instrumentation'; all you
  really need are 'some orienting questions, some headings for observations [and] a rough and ready document analysis form' (Miles and
  Huberman, 1984: 42).
- *Considerable prior instrumentation* If the research is not focused, you will
  gather superfluous data; using measures from earlier studies allows for
  comparability.
- *An open question* Exploratory studies need to be far less structured than
  confirmatory studies; if your sample size is very small then cross-case
  comparison will be more limited and, therefore, the need for standardized research instruments will be less.

Miles and Huberman show that, although prior structuring of a research
design is more common in quantitative studies, such structuring is worth
considering in more qualitative work. Thus there have to be good reasons
for any decision to begin a study with 'no prior instrumentation'. Qualitative research can be highly structured and what Miles and Huberman call

TABLE 7.1   Different uses for four methods

| Method | Methodology | |
	Quantitative research	Qualitative research
Observation	Preliminary work, e.g. prior to framing questionnaire	Fundamental to understanding another culture
Textual analysis	Content analysis, i.e. counting in terms of researchers' categories	Understanding participants' categories
Interviews	'Survey research': mainly fixed-choice questions to random samples	'Open-ended' questions to small samples
Transcripts	Used infrequently to check the accuracy of interview records	Used to understand how participants organize their talk

Source: Silverman, 1993: 9

'no prior instrumentation' should not be regarded as the default option for non-quantitative research.

Moreover, most research methods can be used in either qualitative or quantitative studies. This is shown in Table 7.1. The table underlines my earlier point that methods are techniques which take on a specific meaning according to the methodology in which they are used. All this means that we need to resist treating research methods as mere *techniques*.

To take just one example, although there are quantifiable, standardized observation schedules, observation is not generally seen as a very important method of data collection in quantitative research. This is because it is difficult to conduct observational studies on large samples. Quantitative researchers also argue that observation is not a very 'reliable' data-collection method because different observers may record different observations. If used at all, observation is held to be only appropriate at a preliminary or 'exploratory' stage of research.

Conversely, observational studies have been fundamental to much qualitative research. Beginning with the pioneering case studies of non-Western societies by early anthropologists (Malinowski, 1922; Radcliffe-Brown, 1948) and continuing with the work by sociologists in Chicago prior to the Second World War (Thomas and Znaniecki, 1927), the observational method has often been the chosen method to understand another culture.

The methods used by qualitative researchers exemplify a common belief that they can provide a 'deeper' understanding of social phenomena than would be obtained from purely quantitative data. Such purportedly 'deep' understanding arises in qualitative researchers' claims to have entered and mapped such territories as 'inner experiences', 'language', 'cultural meanings' or 'forms of social interaction'. Some of these claims, associated with different qualitative methods, are set out in Table 7.2.

Two further points need to be made about Table 7.2. First, each claim shown there is not neutral but depends upon an implied model of how social reality works. In terms of Gubrium and Holstein's (1997) four 'idioms', discussed in

TABLE 7.2 **Methods of Qualitative Research**

Method	Features	Claim
Observation	Extended periods of contact	Understanding of 'subcultures'
Texts and documents	Attention to organization and use of such material	Understanding of language and other sign systems
Interviews	Relatively unstructured and 'open-ended'	Understanding 'experience'
Audio and video recording	Precise transcripts of naturally occurring interactions	Understanding how interaction is organized

Chapter 6, naturalists give priority to understanding 'subcultures', emotionalists favour understanding 'experience', ethnomethodologists prefer to understand 'interaction' and postmoderns prioritize sign systems.

Such idioms or models are a necessary but not sufficient warrant for a claim that any given research method has been properly used. So a purely theoretical warrant does not guarantee that a method will be appropriately used in a particular data analysis.

Second, there is a broader, societal context in which methods are located and deployed. As a crude example, texts depended upon the invention of the printing press or, in the case of television or audio recordings, upon modern communication technologies.

Moreover, such activities as observation and interviewing are not unique to social researchers. For instance, as Foucault (1977) has noted, the observation of the prisoner has been at the heart of modern prison reform, while the method of questioning used in the interview reproduces many of the features of the Catholic confessional or the psychoanalytic consultation. Its pervasiveness is reflected by the centrality of the interview study in so much contemporary social research. Think, for instance, of how much interviews are a central (and popular) feature of mass media products, from 'talk shows' to 'celebrity interviews'. Perhaps we all live in what might be called an 'interview society' in which interviews seem central to making sense of our lives (see Atkinson and Silverman, 1997).

This broader societal context may explain qualitative researchers' temptation to use methods such as the interview (see Chapter 26). Of course, such a link between culture and method should be an opportunity to question ourselves about our methodological preferences. However, such self-questioning (sometimes, mistakenly I think, referred to as reflexivity) does not itself provide a warrant for the choices we make. As I argue below, such a warrant depends on the robustness and credibility of our research design.

Qualitative research is, by definition, stronger on long descriptive narratives than on statistical tables. The problem of credibility that arises here is how such a researcher goes about categorizing the events or activities described. This is sometimes known as the problem of *reliability*.

Reliability is one of two key criteria through which we can assess any research study. The other key criterion is *validity*.

The issue of validity is usually posed in terms of what constitutes a credible claim to truth. It is in these terms that Denzin and Lincoln discuss the approach of what they call 'conventional positivist social science' to 'disciplined inquiry':

> *internal validity*, the degree to which findings correctly map the phenomenon in question; *external validity*, the degree to which findings can be generalized to other settings similar to the one in which the study occurred; *reliability*, the extent to which findings can be replicated, or reproduced, by another inquirer; and *objectivity*, the extent to which findings are free from bias. (1994: 100)

I will return to the issues of validity and reliability in Part Three of this book when I discuss ways to analyse your data. However, even in the early stages of designing a methodology, it is worth considering these issues. In particular, you should ask yourself how far the methods you are contemplating will provide valid, reliable and objective data.

However, abstract discussion of such matters is not always enlightening. In order to concretize things, I will now show how I considered these issues in the early stages of designing a recent study that I carried out. This involved research on the HIV-test counselling that emerged following the AIDS epidemic identified in the early 1980s.

A CASE STUDY: HIV COUNSELLING

The context

The counselling study discussed here emerged out of my work as a medical sociologist. Between 1979 and 1985, I worked on data from British outpatient consultations which involved parents and children. At the same time, I also conducted a small study of adult oncology clinics, comparing National Health Service (NHS) and private consultations conducted by the same doctor. This research was reported in a number of papers (Silverman, 1981; 1983; 1984; Silverman and Bloor, 1989) and brought together in a book (Silverman, 1987). In that book, I focused on how apparently 'patient-centred' medicine can work in many different directions.

In 1987, I was given permission to sit in at a weekly clinic held at the genito-urinary department of an English inner-city hospital (Silverman, 1989). The clinic's purpose was to monitor the progress of HIV-positive patients who were taking the drug AZT (Retrovir). AZT, which seems able to slow down the rate at which the virus reproduces itself, was then at an experimental stage of its development.

Like any observational study, the aim was to gather first-hand information about social processes in a 'naturally occurring' context. No attempt was made to interview the individuals concerned because the focus was upon what they actually did in the clinic rather than upon what they thought about what they did. The researcher was present in the consulting room at a side angle to both doctors and patient.

Patients' consent for the researcher's presence was obtained by the senior doctor. Given the presumed sensitivity of the occasion, tape-recording was not attempted. Instead, detailed handwritten notes were kept, using a separate sheet for each consultation. The sample was small (fifteen male patients seen in thirty-seven consultations over seven clinic sessions) and no claims were made about its representativeness. Because observational methods were rare in this area, the study was essentially exploratory. However, as we shall see, an attempt was made to link the findings to other social research about doctor–patient relations.

As Sontag (1979) has noted, illness is often taken as a moral or psychological metaphor. The major finding of this early study was the moral baggage attached to being HIV-positive. For instance, many patients used a buzzer to remind them to take their medication during the night. As one commented: 'It's a dead giveaway. Everybody knows what you've got.'

However, despite the social climate in which HIV infection is viewed, there was considerable variation in how people presented themselves to the medical team. Four styles of 'self-presentation' (Goffman, 1959) were identified which I called 'cool', 'anxious', 'objective' and 'theatrical' (see Silverman, 1989). But there was no simple correspondence between each patient and a particular 'style' of self-presentation. Rather, each way of presenting oneself was available to each patient within any one consultation, where it might have a particular social function. So the focus was on social processes rather than on psychological states.

Along the way, I also discovered how an ethos of 'positive thinking' was central to many patients' accounts and how doctors systematically concentrated on the 'bodies' rather than the 'minds' of their patients. This led on to some practical questions about the division of labour between doctors and counsellors.

About the time I was writing up this research, Kaye Wellings, who then was working for the publicly funded Health Education Authority (HEA), approached me about the possibility of extending my research to HIV counselling. Until that time, the HEA had been funding research on the effectiveness of 'safer sex' messages carried in the mass media. In the light of the explosion in the number of HIV tests in the UK in the late 1980s, Kaye thought it might be useful to take a longer look at the effectiveness of the health promotion messages being delivered in counselling people around the HIV antibody test.

I was interested in such a study for two reasons. First, it was the logical development of my study of medical interviews with AIDS patients. Second, it offered the opportunity to pursue my interest in looking at how communication between professionals and their clients worked out in practice – as opposed to the injunctions of textbooks and training manuals. Consequently, I submitted a research proposal and received funding from the HEA for 30 months beginning in late 1988.

The quantitative bias

John McLeod has recently reminded us that 'almost all counselling and psychotherapy research has been carried out from the discipline of psychology' (1994: 190). One consequence has been a focus on quantitative studies concerned with the attributes of individuals. This has meant that linguistic and sociological issues, such as language use and social context, have been downplayed (see Heaton, 1979).

Such a psychological focus has also had an impact on research design, leading to the dominance of experimental and/or statistical methods favoured in psychology. Of course, no research method is intrinsically better than any other; everything will depend upon one's research objectives. So it is only a question of restoring a balance between different ways of conceiving counselling research.

In designing my research proposal, I therefore needed to balance two competing objectives:

- my desire to examine how HIV counselling worked in actual counsellor–client interviews
- having to adjust to a context in which most counselling research had been informed either by a quantitative methodology or by normative assumptions about what constitutes 'good' counselling.

Designing a methodology: three familiar options

Quantitative or normative approaches suggest three obvious ways of researching counselling, all of which appear to take seriously the demands of validity and reliability. These three methodologies are set out in Table 7.3.

In order to underline the methodological options that arise in the early stages of research design, I review each strategy below. In doing so, we will see that each raises both methodological and analytic questions. I shall suggest that, in terms of either or both these questions, none of these three strategies is entirely satisfactory.

TABLE 7.3   **Three methodologies for counselling research**

1   Measuring clients' response to counselling by means of research interviews which elicit their knowledge and reported behaviour. This would involve a longitudinal study, following a cohort of patients. The study could have either an experimental or non-experimental design
2   Measuring clients' response to counselling by means of objective behavioural indicators. This also would involve a longitudinal study, following a cohort of patients
3   Measuring the degree of fit between actual counselling practice and certain agreed normative standards of 'good counselling'

Source: Silverman, 1997b: 16

THE RESEARCH INTERVIEW

As already noted, this might have either an experimental or a non-experimental design.

In the experimental design, we might randomly assign clients to two groups. In group 1, clients are counselled, while in group 2, the control group, no counselling is provided. Both groups are then interviewed about their knowledge of AIDS and how they intend to protect themselves against the disease. This interview is followed up, some months later, with a further interview examining their present behaviour compared with their reported behaviour prior to the experiment.

In the non-experimental design, existing counselling procedures are evaluated by a cohort of patients. Again, we might follow up a cohort some time later.

The advantage of such research designs is that they permit large-scale studies which generate apparently 'hard' data, seemingly based on unequivocal measures. However, a number of difficulties present themselves. Of course, I accept that these problems are recognized by researchers who use such research instruments. In turn, they have ingenious methods for dealing with them. Let me list a few:

1 How seriously are we to take patients' accounts of their behaviour? Isn't it likely that clients will tend to provide answers which they think the counsellors and researchers will want to hear (see McLeod, 1994: 124–6)?
2 Doesn't the experimental study ignore the *organizational* context in which health care is delivered (e.g. relations between physicians and other staff, tacit theories of 'good counselling', resources available, staff turnover etc.)? Such contexts may shape the nature and effectiveness of counselling in non-laboratory situations.
3 Even if we can overcome the practical and ethical problems of not providing, say, pre-test counselling to a control group, may not the experience of being allocated to a control group affect the reliability of our measures and the validity of our findings (see McLeod, 1994: 124)?
4 Don't both studies treat subjects as 'an aggregation of disparate individuals' who have no social interaction with one another (Bryman, 1988: 39)? As such, they give us little hold on how counselling is organized as a local, step-by-step social process and, consequently, we may suspect that we are little wiser about how counselling works in practice.

The non-experimental study may have either a quantitative or a qualitative design. In the latter case, we might expect to carry out a relatively small number of open-ended interviews in order: 'to enter, in an empathic way, the lived experience of the person or group being studied' (McLeod, 1994: 89). This pursuit of 'lived experience' means that many qualitative researchers favour the open-ended interview (see Chapter 3). Both the 'in-depth' accounts apparently provided by the 'open-ended' interview and the apparently unequivocal measures of information retention, attitude and behaviour that we obtain via laboratory or questionnaire methods have a tenuous basis in what people may be saying and doing in their everyday lives. Moreover, if our interest is in the relation of counselling to health-related behaviour, do such studies tell us how people actually talk with professionals and with each other as opposed to via responses to researchers' questions?

An example makes the point very well. At a recent meeting of social scientists working on AIDS, much concern was expressed about the difficulty of recruiting a sample of the population prepared to answer researchers' questions about their sexual behaviour. As a result, it was suggested that a subsequent meeting should be convened at which we could swap tips about how to recruit such a sample.

Now, of course, this issue of recruiting a sample is basic to survey research. And for potentially 'delicate' matters, like the elicitation of accounts of sexual behaviour, survey researchers are quite properly concerned about finding willing respondents.

At the same time, it is generally acknowledged that the best chance of limiting the spread of HIV may be by encouraging people to discuss their sexual practices with their partners. This implies something about the limits of interview-based research in this area. Such research necessarily focuses on finding people prepared to talk about their sexuality in an interview. However, it can say nothing about how talk about sexuality is organized in 'naturally occurring' environments such as talk between partners or, indeed, talk about sexuality in the context of real-time counselling interviews.

BEHAVIOURAL INDICATORS

This method seeks to elicit behavioural measures which reliably report the effectiveness of counselling. Its advantage is that, unlike the research interview, it does not depend upon potentially unreliable client perceptions and self-reports of behaviour and behavioural change. Moreover, by eliminating a concern with the information that clients may acquire from counselling, it takes on board the research that shows that acquired knowledge does not have any direct link with behavioural change.

In relation to HIV-test counselling, it was suggested to me by a senior physician at an AIDS unit in Sweden that an appropriate behavioural indicator is seroconversion (developing antibodies to the virus). Presumably, then, we would need to study a cohort of patients who test seronegative and are counselled. We would then retest them after a further period, say twelve months, to establish what proportions from different counselling centres and with different counsellors have seroconverted. In this way, it would be claimed, we could measure the effectiveness of counselling in relation to promoting safer behaviour.

As already noted, the advantage of this approach is that it generates quantitative measures of behaviour which are apparently objective. However, like the research interview, its reliability also has serious shortcomings:

1 How do we know that the counselling alone is the variable that has produced the reported behaviour? Although we may be able to 'control' for some gross intervening variables (like gender, age, sexual preference, drug use etc.), it is likely that some non-measured variables may be associated with the reported behaviour (e.g. access to other sources of information, availability of condoms or clean injecting equipment etc.).

2 How do we know that an initial seronegative test means that the client is not infected with HIV? The problem is created by the fact that there is a 'window period' of up to six months during which the body does not produce antibodies despite the presence of the virus. Consequently, if any of the cohort has been exposed to risk of infection during that period, any negative result would have a dubious status.

3 A major problem for many counsellors in using behavioural measures is that such measures do not fit with how the purposes of counselling are usually defined. As we shall see below, 'effective' counselling is often defined in terms of criteria which are either only indirectly linked to behavioural change or related to behavioural changes other than particular physical outcomes. Hence lack of seroconversion could not be treated as a reliable measure of effective counselling.

MEETING NORMATIVE STANDARDS

To many counsellors, the only sensible means of evaluating their work is to start from their own objectives. These objectives will reflect their normative theories of 'good practice'.

Like sociology, counselling has been a site for many competing theoretical orientations (see McLeod, 1994: 142–64). In the counselling centres I studied, two main normative approaches were found. The first used a primarily 'medical' model. This meant that, after a brief 'history-taking', the counsellor spent most of her time delivering information to the client with the avowed aim of ensuring that the HIV test only took place with the client's informed consent. The second approach involved much more extended periods of questioning, and unsolicited information giving and advice was rarely seen.

However, in practice, it has proved difficult to establish reliable measures to evaluate counselling. As McLeod (1994: 150–64) has noted, several problems have confronted attempts at evaluation by means of normative standards, namely:

1 Observers find it difficult to differentiate different measures (e.g. 'congruence', 'empathy' and 'acceptance') and instead rate counsellors ac-cording to 'their image of a "good therapist"' (1994: 150).

2 *Ad hoc* decisions are often made about which part of a counselling interview should be assessed. The scope extends from a whole counselling interview (or even several interviews with the same client) down to a microsegment of one interview. The latter, narrow approach may gain in precision but at the cost of understanding the context of the surrounding

talk. The broader approach may find it hard to make detailed assessments of whole interviews.

3   Even if such measures are reliable and precise, the result 'assesses only the presence or absence of a mode, and not the skilfulness with which it is delivered' (1994: 151).

Such problems in attempts to use internal, 'normative' standards of evaluation look even worse when viewed in the context of studies which seek to relate such measures to particular outcomes. As McLeod (1994) notes, one such study (Hill, 1989) found that only 1 per cent of variance in client responses was related to observed measures of counsellor behaviour!

The methodology chosen

It is now time to lay my cards on the table and to offer the alternative approach on which my research was based – conversation analysis (henceforth CA). CA, as we saw in the studies discussed in Chapters 2 and 3, is centrally concerned with the organization of talk, although its concern with social organization leads it to describe its subject-matter as 'talk-in-interaction'.

Equally, counsellors, by definition, treat talk as a non-trivial matter. However, even if we concede the centrality of talk to social life, why should counselling researchers give priority to recording and transcribing talk? Given the usefulness of other kinds of data derived, say, from observations of behavioural change or interviews with clients, what is the special value of transcripts of tape-recordings of conversation?

One way to start to discuss this question is to think about how research based upon data which arise in subjects' day-to-day activities can seek to preserve the 'phenomenon' of interactions like counselling interviews. Although such 'naturally occurring' data are never uncontaminated (for instance, they may need to be recorded and transcribed), they usually give us a very good clue about what participants usually do outside a research setting.

Conversely, in research interviews, as Heritage puts it: 'the verbal formulations of subjects are treated as an appropriate substitute for the observation of actual behaviour' (1984: 236). The temptation here is to treat respondents' formulations as reflections of some pre-existing social or psychological world.

However, even when counselling researchers contemplate tape-recording actual interactions, they sometimes become easily deflected away from the counselling session itself. For instance, although McLeod calls for a study of 'the interior of therapy', he also cites favourably attempts at 'interpersonal process recall' where participants are played back the tape 'to restimulate the actual experience the person had during the session' (1994: 147). Thus, in common with many qualitative researchers, what matters for McLeod is what people think and feel rather than what they do.

However, if we follow this temptation in counselling research, then we deny something that all counsellors recognize: namely, that talk is itself an activity. Although this is recognized in many normative versions of counselling, to base our research on such versions would be to narrow our focus to those activities which we already know about.

An alternative is to investigate how counselling interviews actually proceed without being shackled by normative standards of 'good' communication. In this way, we might discover previously unnoticed skills of both counsellors and clients as well as the communicational 'functions' of apparently 'dysfunctional' counsellor behaviour.

Summary and implications

In this section, I have used the case of a study of HIV counselling to illustrate several of the options that are available in designing a qualitative methodology. I did not want to imply that a CA study of counselling interviews is the 'one right method'. Instead, I wanted to demonstrate that choosing a particular method always has more implications than you might think. I have shown here how those implications encompass preferred analytical models, questions of reliability and validity and, in this particular case, relevance for professional practice. To follow up this point, you should attempt Exercise 7.1 now.

MULTIPLE METHODS?

So far I have been assuming that you will always want to choose just one method. However, the methods presented in Table 7.2 are often combined. For instance, many qualitative case studies combine observation with interviewing. This may be because you have several research questions or 'because you want to use different methods or sources to corroborate each other so that you are using some form of methodological "triangulation"' (Mason, 1996: 25).

For instance, Miles and Huberman (1984: 42) give the example of research on how police suspects are arrested and booked. You might think here of combining several methods, e.g.:

• interviews (with suspects, police and lawyers)
• observation (of arrests and bookings)
• collecting documents (produced by this process)
• recording (of arrests and bookings) (1984: 42).

If you are a pure empiricist, uninterested in the theoretical bases of research design, multiple methods may look like a good idea. By having a cumulative view of data drawn from different contexts, we may, as in trigonometry, be able to triangulate the 'true' state of affairs by examining where the different data intersect. In this way, some qualitative researchers believe that triangulation may improve the reliability of a single method. But do multiple methods always make analytical sense?

As I remarked in Chapter 3, 'mapping' one set of data upon another is a more or less complicated task depending on your analytic framework. In particular, if you treat social reality as constructed in different ways in different contexts, then you cannot appeal to a single 'phenomenon' which all your data apparently represent (see Silverman, 1993: 156–8).

Mason (1996: 27) gives the example of the mistaken attempt to combine (say) interview data on individuals' perceptions with discourse analysis (DA) of particular texts. The mistake arises because DA treats all accounts as socially constructed and, therefore, cannot treat interview accounts as providing a definitive version of reality.

Such triangulation of data seeks to overcome the context-boundedness of our materials at the cost of analysing their sense in context. For purposes of social research, it may simply not be useful to conceive of an overarching reality to which data, gathered in different contexts, approximate.

At the very least, we need to note Fielding and Fielding's (1986) suggestion that the use of triangulation should operate according to the following ground rules:

- Always begin from a theoretical perspective (e.g. interactionism).
- Choose methods and data which will give you an account of structure and meaning from within that perspective (e.g. by showing the structural contexts of the interactions studied).

Many theoretical perspectives in sociology and elsewhere suggest we cannot simply aggregate data in order to arrive at an overall 'truth'. This implies that we should receive with caution the clarion calls for multiple methods in areas like nursing, family medicine and elsewhere. As Hammersley and Atkinson point out: 'one should not adopt a naively "optimistic" view that the aggregation of data from different sources will unproblematically add up to produce a more complete picture' (1983: 199).

As already noted in Chapter 3, multiple methods are often adopted in the mistaken hope that they will reveal 'the whole picture'. But this 'whole picture' is an illusion which speedily leads to scrappy research based on under-analysed data and an imprecise or theoretically indigestible research problem. For instance, multiple methods may tempt novice researchers to move to another dataset when they are having difficulties in analysing one set of material. It is usually far better to celebrate the partiality of your data and delight in the particular phenomena that it allows you to inspect (hopefully in detail).

CONCLUDING REMARKS

The debate about multiple methods illustrates the theoretically laden environment in which we make methodological choices. It underlines the fact that many apparently technical choices are saturated with theoretical import.

Of course, to some extent this complicates the picture when you are attempting to design a research study. However, a concern at this stage with theoretical issues also helps in at least two ways. First, it may allow you to simplify your research design as you realize that it is often misleading to attempt to research 'the whole picture'. Second, thereby, it may add theoretical consistency and even some elegance to the research design. As I remarked in Part One, often the best research says 'a lot about a little'.

SUMMARY

1   Your choice of method should reflect an 'overall research strategy' (Mason, 1996: 19) as your methodology shapes which methods are used and how each method is used.
2   Although most research methods can be used in either qualitative or quantitative studies, research methods are more than mere *techniques*. Different theoretical idioms or models provide different justifications for using particular research methods.
3   Methods do not just belong to social researchers. Before choosing a method, you should reflect upon the broader, societal context in which this method is located and deployed.
4   You should ask yourself how far the methods you are contemplating will provide valid, reliable and objective data.
5   Think carefully before adopting multiple methods. Many models suggest that we cannot simply aggregate data in order to arrive at an overall 'truth'. Choose simplicity and rigour rather than the often illusory search for the 'full picture'.

Further reading

David Silverman (ed.), *Qualitative Research: Theory, Method and Practice* (Sage, 1997) provides state of the art accounts by leading scholars of the uses of interviews, observations, texts and audio- and videotapes. Other useful books on methodology are: Amanda Coffey and Paul Atkinson, *Making Sense of Qualitative Data* (Sage, 1996); Jennifer Mason, *Qualitative Researching* (Sage, 1996); Pertti Alasuutari, *Researching Culture* (Sage, 1995) and David Silverman, *Interpreting Qualitative Data: Methods for Analysing Talk, Text and Interaction* (Sage, 1993).

Exercise 7.1 Choosing a Methodology

Mason (1996: 19) notes that your choice of a methodology is likely to reflect your own biography and the knowledge and training your education has given you. As she comments: 'Whilst practical issues to do with training and skill are . . . relevant in your choice of method . . . they should not govern your choice' (1996: 19). She suggests instead making a list of possible research methods and data source options and thinking through why you are accepting or rejecting each one.

1   Follow Mason's suggestion about making a list of possible research methods and data source options. Explain why you are accepting or rejecting each one.
2   Answer the following questions (adapted from Mason, 1996: 20–1):
    (a) What data sources and methods of data generation are potentially available or appropriate?
    (b) What can these methods and sources feasibly tell me?
    (c) Which phenomena and components or properties of social 'reality' might these data sources and methods potentially help me to address?
    (d) Which of my research questions could they help me to address?

8

Selecting a Case

I concluded the previous chapter with my favourite research maxim: 'make a lot out of a little'. If you take me seriously, you will have every chance of producing a thorough, analytically interesting research study. However, a nagging doubt may well remain.

This doubt surfaces in a regular refrain I hear from student researchers. 'I have so few data, only just one case,' they say, 'how can I possibly generalize about it?'

Generalizability is a standard aim in quantitative research and is normally achieved by statistical sampling procedures. Such sampling has two functions. First, it allows you to feel confident about the representativeness of your sample: 'if the population characteristics are known, the degree of representativeness of a sample can be checked' (Arber, 1993: 70). Second, such representativeness allows you to make broader inferences:

> The purpose of sampling is usually to study a representative subsection of a precisely defined population in order to make inferences about the whole population. (1993: 38)

Such sampling procedures are, however, usually unavailable in qualitative research. In such studies, our data are often derived from one or more cases and it is unlikely that these cases will have been selected on a random basis. Very often a case will be chosen simply because it allows access. Moreover, even if you were able to construct a representative sample of cases, the sample size would be likely to be so large as to preclude the kind of intensive analysis usually preferred in qualitative research (Mason, 1996: 91).

This gives rise to a problem, familiar to users of quantitative methods:

> How do we know ... how representative case study findings are of all members of the population from which the case was selected? (Bryman, 1988: 88)

GENERALIZABILITY IN QUALITATIVE RESEARCH

For a few writers who see qualitative research as purely descriptive, generalizability is not an issue. For example, Stake refers to the *'intrinsic case study'* where 'this case is of interest ... in all its particularity and ordinariness'

(1994: 236). In the intrinsic case study, according to Stake, no attempt is made to generalize beyond the single case or even to build theories.

This is resisted by many qualitative researchers. As Jennifer Mason puts it:

> I do not think qualitative researchers should be satisfied with producing explanations which are idiosyncratic or particular to the limited empirical parameters of their study . . . Qualitative research should [therefore] produce explanations which are *generalizable* in some way, or which have a wider resonance. (1996: 6)

So, unlike Stake, the problem of 'representativeness' is a perennial worry of many qualitative or case study researchers. How do they attempt to address it? Can we generalize from cases to populations without following a purely statistical logic?

In the rest of this chapter, I will discuss four different but positive answers to this question of how we can obtain generalizability:

- combining qualitative research with quantitative measures of populations
- purposive sampling guided by time and resources
- theoretical sampling
- using an analytic model which assumes that generalizability is present in the existence of *any* case.

COMBINING QUALITATIVE RESEARCH WITH QUANTITATIVE MEASURES OF POPULATIONS

Quantitative measures may sometimes be used to infer from one case to a larger population. Hammersley (1992) suggests three methods through which we can attempt to generalize from the analysis of a single case:

- obtaining information about relevant aspects of the population of cases and comparing our case with them
- using survey research on a random sample of cases
- co-ordinating several ethnographic studies.

Hammersley argues that such comparisons with a larger sample may allow us to establish some sense of the representativeness of our single case.

However, two of Hammersley's methods are very ambitious for the student researcher. For instance, you are unlikely to have the funds for even a small piece of survey research, while the co-ordination of several ethnographic studies requires substantial resources of time and personnel as well as good contacts with other researchers. Such contacts allowed Miller and Silverman (1995) to apply the comparative approach in describing talk about troubles in two counselling settings: a British haemophilia centre counselling patients who are HIV-positive, and a family therapy centre in the US. In this study, we focused on similarities in three types of discursive practices in these settings: those concerned with trouble definitions, trouble remedies, and the social contexts of the clients' troubles (see also Gubrium, 1992).

Without such contacts and resources, the student researcher is left with Hammersley's first method: obtaining information about relevant aspects of the population of cases and comparing our case with them. This is more useful because, at its simplest, this method only involves reading about other cognate studies and comparing our case with them. For instance, in my study of HIV counselling (Silverman, 1997b), I compared my counsellor–client interviews with Heritage and Sefi's (1992) data on interviews between health visitors and first-time mothers. Although this had little to do with establishing the representativeness of my sample, it gave a firmer basis to my generalizations about advice sequences in my data (1997b: 124–8).

The comparative method used here allows you to make larger claims about your analysis without leaving your library. As Peräkylä puts it:

> The comparative approach directly tackles the question of generalizability by demonstrating the similarities and differences across a number of settings. (1997: 214)

In this sense, your literature review (see Chapter 18) has as much to do with the issue of generalizability as with displaying your academic credentials.

PURPOSIVE SAMPLING

Before we can contemplate comparing our case with others, we need to have selected our case. Are there any grounds other than convenience or accessibility to guide us in this selection?

Purposive sampling allows us to choose a case because it illustrates some feature or process in which we are interested. However, this does not provide a simple approval to any case we happen to choose. Rather purposive sampling demands that we think critically about the parameters of the population we are interested in and choose our sample case carefully on this basis. As Denzin and Lincoln put it:

> Many qualitative researchers employ . . . purposive, and not random, sampling methods. They seek out groups, settings and individuals where . . . the processes being studied are most likely to occur. (1994: 202)

Stake (1994: 243) gives the example of a study of interactive displays in children's museums. He assumes that you only have resources to study four such museums. How should you proceed?

He suggests setting up a *typology* which would establish a matrix of museum types as in Table 8.1. The typology yields six cases which could be increased further by, say, distinguishing between museums located in small and big cities – bringing up the cases to twelve. Which cases should you select?

TABLE 8.1   A typology of children's museums

| Programme type | Type of museum | | |
	Art	Science	History
Exhibitory	1	2	3
Participative	4	5	6

Source: adapted from Stake, 1994: 243

You will be constrained by two main factors. First, there may not be examples to fit every cell. Second, your resources will not allow you to research every existing unit. So you have to make a practical decision. For instance, if you can cover only two cases, do you choose two participatory museums in different locations or in different subjects? Or do you compare such a museum with a more conventional exhibit-based museum?

Provided you have thought through the options, it is unlikely that your selection will be criticized. Moreover, as we see below, how you set up your typology and make your choice should be grounded in the theoretical apparatus you are using. Sampling in qualitative research is neither statistical nor purely personal: it is, or should be, theoretically grounded. To improve your understanding of this point, you could now attempt Exercise 8.1.

THEORETICAL SAMPLING

Theoretical and purposive sampling are often treated as synonyms. Indeed, the only difference between the two procedures applies when the 'purpose' behind 'purposive' sampling is not theoretically defined.

Bryman argues that qualitative research follows a theoretical, rather than a statistical, logic: 'the issue should be couched in terms of the generalizability of cases to *theoretical* propositions rather than to *populations* or universes' (1988: 90, my emphasis).[1]

The nature of this link between sampling and theory is set out by Jennifer Mason:

> theoretical sampling means selecting groups or categories to study on the basis of their relevance to your research questions, your theoretical position . . . and most importantly the explanation or account which you are developing. Theoretical sampling is concerned with constructing a sample . . . which is meaningful theoretically, because it builds in certain characteristics or criteria which help to develop and test your theory and explanation. (1996: 93–4)

Theoretical sampling has three features which I discuss below:

- choosing cases in terms of your theory
- choosing 'deviant' cases
- changing the size of your sample during the research.

Choosing cases in terms of your theory

Mason writes about 'the wider universe of social explanations in relation to which you have constructed your research questions' (1996: 85). This theoretically defined universe 'will make some sampling choices more sensible and meaningful than others'. Mason describes choosing a kind of sample which can represent a wider population. Here we select a sample of particular 'processes, types, categories or examples which are relevant to or appear within the wider universe' (1996: 92). Mason suggests that examples of these would include single units such as 'an organization, a location, a document . . . [or] a conversation'.

Mason gives the example of a DA study of gender relation as discourses which construct subjects of gender relations. In this approach, as she puts it: 'you are . . . unlikely to perceive the social world in terms of a large set of gender relations from which you can simply draw a representative sample of people by gender' (1996: 85).

So in qualitative research the relevant or 'sampleable' units are often seen as theoretically defined. This means that it is inappropriate to sample populations by such attributes as 'gender', 'ethnicity' or even age because how such attributes are routinely defined is itself the *topic* of your research.

As an example of theoretically defined sampling, Bryman uses Glaser and Strauss's discussion of 'awareness contexts' in relation to dying in hospital:

> The issue of whether the particular hospital studied is 'typical' is not the critical issue; what is important is whether the experiences of dying patients are typical of the broad class of phenomena . . . to which the theory refers. Subsequent research would then focus on the validity of the proposition in other milieux (e.g. doctors' surgeries). (1988: 91)

We can understand better the theoretical logic behind choice of a sample in a further example of a study of police work. Say you are interested in the arrest and booking of suspects (see Miles and Huberman, 1984: 37–8). You are now confronted with a series of choices which relate to:

- the particular setting to be studied
- the elements or processes on which you will focus
- how you might generalize further.

Let us look at each of these in turn.

SETTINGS

In independent, unfunded research, you are likely to choose any setting which, while demonstrating the phenomenon in which you are interested, is accessible and will provide appropriate data reasonably readily and quickly. In the police study, this might well lead you to study the police station rather than a squad car, the scene of the crime, the suspect's residence or hangout. In the police station, at the very least, you will keep warm and dry, you will be safe and you can expect several arrests and bookings on any visit. However, so far you are being guided by quite practical influences.

THE RESEARCH FOCUS

In focusing your research, you necessarily are making a theoretically guided choice. By opting to focus on particular individuals, events or processes, you are electing particular theoretical frameworks. For instance, a focus on differential behaviour between police officers and suspects with different characteristics may draw on some version of the structural determinants of action. Conversely, a focus on how laws are interpreted in practice (cf. Sudnow, 1968b), may derive from a concern with the creative power of common-sense interpretive procedures.

GENERALIZING FURTHER

When your study is wedded to other studies which share your theoretical orientation, a single police station may provide enough data to develop all the generalizations you want about, say, how common-sense reasoning works. However, if you have a more 'structural' bent, it may now be necessary to widen your sample in two ways: first, to add more observations of arrests in this police station; and second, to compare it with other stations, perhaps in a range of areas.

In all these cases, the sample is not random but theoretical: it is

> designed to provide a close-up, detailed or meticulous view of particular units which may constitute . . . cases which are relevant to or appear within the wider universe. (Mason, 1996: 92)

Choosing 'deviant' cases

Mason notes that you must overcome any tendency to select a case which is likely to support your argument. Instead, it makes sense to seek out negative instances as defined by the theory with which you are working.

For instance, in a study of the forces that may make trade unions undemocratic, Lipset et al. (1962) deliberately chose to study a US printing union. Because this union had unusually strong democratic institutions it constituted a vital deviant case compared with most American unions of the period. Lipset's union was also deviant in terms of a highly respected theory which postulated an irresistible tendency towards 'oligarchy' in all formal organizations.

So Lipset et al. chose a deviant case because it offered a crucial test of a theory. As our understanding of social processes improves, we are increasingly able to choose cases on such theoretical grounds.

Changing the size of your sample during the research

So far we have been discussing theoretical sampling as an issue at the *start* of a research study. However, we can also apply such sampling during the course of a piece of research. Indeed, one of the strengths of qualitative research design is that it often allows for far greater (theoretically informed) flexibility than in most quantitative research designs. As Mason puts it:

> Theoretical or purposive sampling is a set of procedures where the researcher manipulates their analysis, theory, and sampling activities *interactively* during the research process, to a much greater extent than in statistical sampling. (1996: 100)

Such flexibility may be appropriate in the following cases:

• As new factors emerge you may want to increase your sample in order to say more about them.
• You may want to focus on a small part of your sample in early stages, using the wider sample for later tests of emerging generalizations.
• Unexpected generalizations in the course of data analysis lead you to seek out new deviant cases.

Alasuutari has described this process through using the analogy of an hourglass:

> a narrow case-analysis is broadened . . . through the search for contrary and parallel cases, into an example of a broader entity. Thus the research process advances, in its final stages, towards a discussion of broader entities. We end up on the bottom of the hourglass. (1995: 156)

Alasuutari (1995: 155) illustrates this hourglass metaphor through his own study of the social consequences of Finnish urbanization in the 1970s. He chose local pubs as a site to observe these effects and eventually focused upon male 'regulars'. This led to a second study even more narrowly focused on a group where drinking was heavier and where many of the men were divorced. As he puts it: 'Ethnographic research of this kind is not so much generalization as extrapolation . . . the results are related to broader entities' (1995: 155).

GENERALIZABILITY AS PRESENT IN A SINGLE CASE

The fourth and final way of thinking about how we generalize in qualitative research is far more radical than our earlier alternatives. According to this approach, since the basic structures of social order are to be found anywhere, it does not matter where we begin our research. Look at *any* case and you will find the same order.

For this linguistically inspired approach, the possibility something exists is enough. As Peräkylä suggests:

> Social practices that are possible, i.e., *possibilities of language use*, are the central objects of all conversation analytical case studies on interaction in particular institutional

settings. The possibility of various practices can be considered generalizable even if the practices are not actualized in similar ways across different settings. (1997: 215)

Peräkylä illustrates his argument by the example of his own study of AIDS counselling in a London teaching hospital (Peräkylä, 1995). This study focused on specific questioning practices used by counsellors and their clients. As he puts it:

> As possibilities, the practices that I analyzed are very likely to be generalizable. There is no reason to think that they could not be made possible by any competent member of (at least any Western) society. In this sense, this study produced generalizable results. The results were not generalizable as descriptions of what other counsellors or other professionals do with their clients; but they were generalizable as descriptions of what any counsellor or other professional, with his or her clients, *can* do, given that he or she has the same array of interactional competencies as the participants of the AIDS counselling sessions have. (1997: 215–16)

As the most cogent proponent of this view once put it: 'tap into whomsoever, wheresoever and we get much the same things' (Sacks, 1984: 22). Sacks had a strategy of working with any data that crossed his path. This clearly conflicts both with the standard approach of quantitative social scientists, who usually work with random samples from particular populations, and with the common defensiveness of their qualitative brethren about the representativeness of the cases that they study.

Sacks's lack of defensiveness on this issue stems from his argument about the obvious pervasiveness of the social forms (or what he calls the 'machinery') with which he is concerned. For example, Sacks notes the ability of a child to learn a culture from very limited contacts and of the sociolinguist Whorf to build a Navajo grammar from talking to just one person (1992, Vol. 1: 485).

The pervasiveness of structures which these examples suggest implies to Sacks that it does not matter what data you select. As he argues:

> Now if one figures that that's the way things are . . . then it really wouldn't matter very much what it is you look at – if you look at it carefully enough. And you may well find that you [have] got an enormous generalizability because things are so arranged that you *could* get them; given that for a [societal] member encountering a very limited environment, he has to be able to do that, and things are so arranged as to permit him to. (1992, Vol. 1: 485)

However, apprentice researchers have to be very cautious about simply parroting Sacks's 'solution' to the problem of the generalizability of research findings. This solution is really only appropriate to the most basic research on social order guided by theoretically sophisticated positions like Sacks's own conversation analytic (CA) approach (or, perhaps, French structuralism). If you are interested in this sort of research, you should now attempt Exercise 8.2.

Within CA, following Sacks:

> the baseline assumption is that the results are or should be generalizable to the whole domain of ordinary conversations, and to a certain extent even across linguistic and cultural boundaries. (Peräkylä, 1995: 214)

However, Peräkylä notes that even this depends on the type of CA research:

> Even though the most primordial conversational practices and structures – such as turn-taking or adjacency pairs – are almost universal, there are others, such as openings of telephone calls (see Schegloff, 1986; Houtkoop-Steenstra, 1991; Lindström, 1994), which show considerable variation in different cultures. This variation can only be tackled through gradual accumulation of studies on ordinary conversation in different cultures and social milieux. (1995: 214)

Peräkylä's observation about the need for comparative work shows that even the most potentially radical approach, like CA, has to take seriously the issue of the empirical generalizability of its findings. Sometimes, an appeal to 'possibilities' will be sufficient. Often, however, other examples will be required.

CONCLUDING REMARKS

In this chapter, I have set out various strategies which you can use to defend your research against the charge that it 'merely' depends upon a single case. My overall message is that there is usually no need to be defensive about the claims of qualitative research. As Howard Becker argues:

> Sampling is a major problem for any kind of research. We can't study every case of whatever we're interested in, nor should we want to. Every scientific enterprise tries to find out something that will apply to *everything* of a certain kind by studying *a few examples*, the results of the study being, as we say 'generalizable' to all members of that class of stuff. We need the sample to persuade people that we know something about the whole class. (1998: 67)

Following Becker, sampling troubles quantitative researchers too. Indeed, as we have seen, the relative flexibility of qualitative research can improve the generalizability of our findings by allowing us to include new cases after initial findings are achieved.

The crucial issue here seems to be thinking through one's theoretical priorities. Providing that you have done that and can demonstrate a research design driven by those priorities, nobody should have cause for complaint.

So the secret seems to be to substitute theoretical cogency for the statistical language of quantitative research. In this sense, as Alasuutari has suggested, perhaps 'generalizability' is the wrong word to describe what we attempt to achieve in qualitative research. As he puts it:

Generalization is ... [a] word ... that should be reserved for surveys only. What can be analyzed instead is how the researcher demonstrates that the analysis relates to things beyond the material at hand ... *extrapolation* better captures the typical procedure in qualitative research. (1995: 156–7)

SUMMARY

In this chapter, I have discussed four positive answers to the question of how we can generalize from qualitative data:

- combining qualitative research with quantitative measures of populations
- purposive sampling guided by time and resources
- theoretical sampling
- using an analytic model which assumes that generalizability is present in the existence of *any* case.

NOTE

1 As Clive Seale (personal correspondence) has pointed out, theoretical sampling may have more to do with generating theories than with empirical generalization. I take up Seale's point at the end of this chapter in relation to Alasuutari's argument that the idea of empirical generalization 'should be reserved for surveys only' (1995: 156).

Further reading

The most thorough book on this topic is Clive Seale's *The Quality of Qualitative Research* (Sage, 1999).

Other useful discussions are: Jennifer Mason, *Qualitative Research-ing* (Sage, 1996), Chapters 5–7; Pertti Alasuutari, *Researching Culture* (Sage, 1995), Chapter 12 'Generalization'; and Howard Becker, *Tricks of the Trade* (University of Chicago Press, 1998) Chapter 3 'Sampling'.

Robert Stake's chapter 'Case studies' is a good account of the conventional qualitative methods position on generalizability (in N. Denzin and Y. Lincoln (eds), *Handbook of Qualitative Research*, Sage, 1994). Anssi Peräkylä's chapter 'Reliability and validity in research based upon transcripts' is an excellent, more specialist treatment (in David Silverman (ed.), *Qualitative Research*, Sage, 1997).

Exercise 8.1

Imagine that you have the resources to study *four* cases of the phenomenon in which you are interested. Following my discussion of Stake (1994; see Table 8.1), draw up a typology to indicate the universe of cases potentially available. This typology should include between six and twelve possible cases.

Now explain why you propose to select your four cases in terms of the logic of purposive sampling.

Exercise 8.2

Using conversation analysis, Harvey Sacks has argued: 'tap into whomsoever, wheresoever and we get much the same things' (1984: 22).

Consider how far your own theoretical model might allow you to use Sacks's argument to justify working with a very small dataset.

9

Writing a Research Proposal

According to Janice Morse (1994), qualitative research is difficult to sell to funding agencies. This is because:

- Qualitative research is unstructured.
- The results of qualitative research are unpredictable.
- The outcome is uncertain (1994: 227).

How, then, can one convince funders to support a piece of qualitative research? Or a potential university supervisor to support your research proposal?

To answer these questions satisfactorily means shifting away from your own concerns and thinking about the questions that the reader(s) of your research proposal will be asking. Many of these questions are set out in Table 9.1.

TABLE 9.1 **Questions a research proposal must answer**

1	Why should anyone be interested in my research?
2	Is the research design credible, achievable and carefully explained?
3	Is the researcher capable of doing the research?

Source: adapted from Marshall and Rossman, 1989: 23

How can you properly (and successfully) answer these questions?

- Be practical
- Be persuasive
- Make broader links
- Aim for crystal clarity
- Plan before you write.

Each of these suggestions are explained below.

BE PRACTICAL

One way to persuade non-specialists, Morse suggests, is to show the specific ways that your research can address a social problem or solve an organizational trouble (e.g. staff turnover).

Such a concern with practical problems cannot be shrugged off even if you are proposing to do a purely academic piece of research with no expectation that it will be read outside the university. Academic funding bodies are increasingly demanding practical pay-offs as well as analytic insights. For instance, Kelly (1998: 112) quotes a policy statement by the body that funds social science PhDs in the UK:

> Any lingering public perception of social science as a source of irrelevant, introverted and incoherent output is set for radical alteration . . . In future, research which makes a difference to the health and wealth of the population, rather than merely supports 'ivory tower' academic excellence, will be the ESRC's priority. (Student Information: Economic and Social Research Council, 1996)

The issue of *audiences* for your research is discussed further in Chapter 24. However, if what you are proposing is 'basic research', i.e. a study deriving from debates and concepts internal to social science, then all is not lost. You can strengthen the persuasiveness of your case by showing non-specialists why they ought to take your ideas seriously. One way to do that is to write a persuasive proposal as explained below.

BE PERSUASIVE

> It is easy to get very wrapped up in the subject and think that, because we are convinced of the particular value of our research, others will be too. The way in which the proposal is presented can enable the reader to appreciate what you are planning to do. (Kelly, 1998: 121)

Kelly is reminding us that, in framing a research proposal, one must think first of the audience who is going to read it (and judge it). This means that it should set out to convince such readers that this is something worth supporting:

> The first principle of grantsmanship is to recognize that a good proposal is an argument . . . for the researcher's project. The proposal must make a case to the granting agency that the research question is interesting [and] that the study is important . . . Thus the proposal must be written persuasively. (Morse: 1994: 226)

Morse is suggesting that you try to 'sell' your proposal. This means that you must recognize that the craft of selling (your proposal, yourself) is not incongruent with working in a university. 'Ivory towers' were never so isolated as the term suggests!

However, this persuasiveness must be balanced with a realistic understanding about what you can achieve within a few years as a single researcher. Like any good salesperson, do not oversell your goods!

MAKE BROADER LINKS

Realism need not mean that you must present your research as entirely a narrow, anaemic exercise. Even if you cannot cover every aspect of the field yourself, you should demonstrate your understanding of the broader implications of your proposed research.

One way to do that is to hint at a wider context:

> place the problem in context to show, for instance, that 'when we understand this, we will be able to work on that'. (Morse, 1994: 227)

Of course, you will be studying very few cases or maybe only a single case. Be positive about the gains as well as the losses of this! Show how a relatively small database will enable you to conduct an in-depth analysis (see Chapters 8 and 13). And argue that your case can indicate far larger phenomena:

> The writer must show how, in examining a specific setting or group of individuals, she is studying a case of a larger phenomenon. (Marshall and Rossman, 1989: 12)

AIM FOR CRYSTAL CLARITY

> The proposal should use language and terminology that is understandable to an intelligent lay person as well as to a subject expert. (Cryer, 1996: 15)

Although it is tempting to seek to display your newly acquired technical jargon, bear in mind that your proposal is likely to be read, in the first instance, by a faculty member who is not a specialist in your area of the discipline. So never be content with a proposal which can look like a stream of (perhaps undigested) theories or concepts. Always aim for clear language that describes your research in a way that non-specialists can comprehend.

As Morse suggests, this means that you should resist the temptation to lapse into pure jargon: 'because some of the reviewers will be from other disciplines, the proposal writer should assume nothing and explain everything' (Morse, 1994: 227).

By explaining everything, you will have demonstrated the ability to think (and write) clearly. Not only is this the way to write a research proposal, it is also the best indicator that your research itself will be organized in a clear and logical way:

> A sloppily prepared proposal will, at best, send a message to the agency that if it funds the proposal, the research may also be sloppy. (1994: 226–7)

For instance, your objectives 'should be clear and it should be easy to decide whether they have been achieved or not' (Kelly, 1998: 117). The ways to achieve this are:

- Be concise (there is no reason why a proposal for a piece of student research should be more than 500 words).
- Use short, simple sentences.
- Use headings as in Table 9.2.

TABLE 9.2   **A Structure for a Qualitative Research Proposal**

1   Title
2   Abstract (further advice on titles and abstracts is found in Chapter 17)
3   Background or introduction: e.g. contemporary debates in social policy and social
    science
4   Statement of purpose or aims: the research question ('The intellectual problem(s) I may help
    solve through this research is (are) . . .')
5   Review of the relevant literature: showing the importance of the project in the context of the
    classic or definitive pieces of research in this area
6   Methods: description of case(s) chosen, procedures for data collection and data analysis in
    terms of (a) their appropriateness to your theoretical orientation and (b) how they satisfy
    criteria of validity and reliability (see Chapters 7 and 13)
7   Ethical Issues (see Chapter 15)
8   Dissemination and policy relevance: explain how you will communicate your findings (see
    Chapters 16 and 24)
9   Timetable: indicating the length of time to be devoted to each stage of the research
10 References: use a standard system like the Harvard system.[1]

[1] Harvard system: in the main body of your text (not in footnotes), give surname of author, followed
by date and page reference. In your references, give author (with initials), date, title, place of
publication, publisher and page references (for articles or chapters).
Source: adapted from Morse, 1994: 228; Kelly, 1998: 115–21; Rudestam and Newton, 1992: 18

PLAN BEFORE YOU WRITE

> The writer must show that the design is the result of a series of decisions that she
> made because of knowledge gained from the . . . literature. (Marshall and Rossman,
> 1989: 13)

Not only must the proposal demonstrate that it is based on an intelligent
understanding of the existing literature, it must show that you have thought
about the time you will need to conduct each stage of the research from
obtaining access to writing up your data analysis. So, as Sara Arber notes,
your research proposal will partly be judged by how you state you are going
to use your time:

> You need to adopt a systematic and logical approach to research, the key to which
> is the planning and management of your time. (1993: 33)

Kelly (1998: 120–1, adapted here) offers an example from an interview study
planned to last 32 weeks:

Week 2   Submit proposal to University Ethical Committee.
Week 6   Draw up sample.
Week 8   Begin interviews.
Week 15   End interviews.
Week 23   Complete data analysis.

Week 26   First draft sent out for comments.
Week 32   Submission of final report.

We are not born with a natural ability to prepare research timetables! To help you plan such a timetable, seek the assistance of a trusted teacher in your department. Failing that, seek out an existing research student. With their help, make a list of all the options available in relation to your research problem, method and case(s) to be studied. Now you are in a better position to write a reasoned research proposal that explains the actual choices you have made.

Table 9.2 provides a model structure for such a proposal. When you have read it, you should attempt Exercise 9.1.

SUMMARY

When preparing a research proposal, try to find answers to *three* questions:

1   Why should anyone be interested in my research?
2   Is the research design credible, achievable and carefully explained?
3   Is the researcher capable of doing the research?

You can answer these questions better by following *five* principles:

- Be practical
- Be persuasive
- Make broader links
- Aim for crystal clarity
- Plan before you write.

Further reading

A research proposal is crafted according to the level of your research. Beginning researchers should turn to: Moira Kelly, 'Writing a research proposal', in C. Seale (ed.), *Researching Society and Culture* (Sage, 1998), pp. 111–22.

At PhD level, a useful reference is: Pat Cryer, *The Research Student's Guide to Success* (Open University Press, 1996), Chapter 2.

Beyond the PhD, you should consult: Janice Morse 'Designing funded qualitative research', in N. Denzin and Y. Lincoln (eds), *Handbook of Qualitative Research* (Sage, 1994), pp. 220–35.

Exercise 9.1

Prepare a draft proposal about your research (no more than 1500 words) covering the following elements:

1 Title
2 Abstract
3 Background or introduction
4 Statement of Purpose or aims
5 Review of the relevant literature
6 Methods: description of case(s) chosen, procedures for data collection and data analysis
7 Ethical issues
8 Practical relevance
9 Timetable
10 Set of preliminary references.

10

Beginning Data Analysis

After their first year of research, people have varying degrees of certainty about the future. As Coffey and Atkinson (1996) put it, the end of year one sees two kinds of researcher. The uncertain one asks: 'I've collected all these data, now what should I do?' The other, more confident, researcher states: 'I've collected all my data, now I'm going to analyse them and write up the project.'

The temptation might be to find merit in both positions. After all, self-questioning and self-confidence both seem to be worthy qualities in a researcher. In fact, *neither* position is satisfactory and both reflect a more or less wasted first year of research:

> Both positions imply a woeful lack of appreciation of what is and can be meant by analysis ... [Such analysis] is a *pervasive* activity throughout the life of a research project. Analysis is not simply one of the later stages of research, to be followed by an equally separate phase of 'writing up results'. (1996: 10–11, my emphasis)

Research designs which devote the first year solely to a literature review and/or data gathering may look excellent on paper. Indeed, they may be just the thing in quantitative studies more concerned with implementing pre-designed 'measures' than with employing a theoretical imagination. But in most qualitative research, unless you are *analysing* data more or less from day one you will always have to play 'catch-up'.

All very well, you might respond, but where on earth am I going to get my data from on day one? Surely, most of my first year is going to be spent on getting access to some research site or set of respondents and then, if successful, gathering my data. How is it going to be possible to start data analysis so quickly?

KICK-STARTING YOUR ANALYSIS

There are three very practical, complementary solutions to this puzzle:

- Analyse data already in the public sphere.
- Beg or borrow other people's data.
- Analyse your own data as you gather them.

I briefly discuss each strategy below.

Analyse data already in the public sphere

Some types of naturally occurring materials are already waiting for you. For instance, when undergraduate students doing a dissertation at my London college approach me with their concerns about gathering and analysing data in, say, a three-month time-slot, I usually give the following advice. Hop on a train to Colindale in North London. Turn right out of the station and you will come to a big building marked British Museum Newspaper Library. Now select a few newspapers which covered a particular story (e.g. Princess Diana's death, the O.J. Simpson trial or the trial of the British nanny, Louise Woodward).

Of course, you still lack a research problem and a method of analysis and you will need to think long and hard about both. But you have your data, so go to it!

Needless to say, the public sphere contains much more than newspapers. There are all the other kinds of written texts from novels to the contents of different websites on the Internet. There are the products of the broadcast media, radio and TV programmes, from phone-ins to soap operas and news broadcasts. Then there are those rare qualitative studies which reproduce large portions of data, making them available for your own reanalysis, perhaps following up different questions from those originally asked.

Even if you intend, in due course, to gather your own data, these materials are immediately available. As such, they provide a marvellous opportunity to refine your methods and to get a feel of the joys (and torments) of 'hands-on' data analysis.

Beg or borrow other people's data

Perhaps your research interests cannot be accommodated by data in the public sphere. If so, it is always worth making enquiries in your department about relevant data that other people may be willing to share with you.

Your supervisor is an obvious person to turn to. Having agreed to supervise you, and thereby acknowledged a common research interest, it is probable that your supervisor will have already gathered data that may be relevant to your project. Don't be shy to ask if you might have access to them. As we saw in Chapter 2, this was exactly the strategy that my student Vicki Taylor followed.

Of course, there may be ethical or other reasons why such access is not always possible. But most supervisors will be delighted, perhaps even flattered, if you are interested in their own data. After all, your research may lead to new ideas which will help them in their own work.

If your supervisor cannot deliver the goods, explore your various peer groups. Fellow research students in your department, perhaps two or three years into their research, may, like your supervisor, welcome passing on some of their own data. Or perhaps you can turn to members of study groups in your area or even to visiting speakers talking on a relevant topic.

Above all, you must remember that, in most disciplines, no 'Brownie points' are usually given for having your own data. It is the quality of your data *analysis* that will matter, not whether you can show how clever you were to access your data. Perhaps only in anthropology may the display of how, in pursuit of your 'tribe', you have travelled thousands of miles, learnt a foreign language and endured endless hardships count for something – but not much I suspect.

You should now attempt Exercise 10.1.

Analyse your own data as you gather them

Say you decide that you will feel happier to have your own data. The first thing to remember is that this does not exclude the first two strategies. In the early stages, analysis of other people's data or public data may still give you the impetus you need for research 'lift-off' when you are ready to analyse your own materials.

The second thing to remember is that data analysis does not come after data gathering. If you only have one interview or recording or set of field-notes, go to it! Where appropriate, start transcribing. In all cases, start reviewing your data in the light of your research questions.

Now is the time to test out methods, findings and concepts. Do you feel comfortable with your preferred method of data analysis (e.g. grounded theory, conversation analysis, discourse analysis, feminist methodology)? Is it suggesting interesting questions? And is it giving you a strong grip on your data that looks like it might generate interesting generalizations?

Do previous research findings seem to apply to your data? If not, why not? If so, how can you use your data to develop these findings?

How do particular concepts from your preferred model of social research apply to your data? Which concepts work best and hence look likely to be most productive?

None of these questions can be properly answered from the armchair or drawing board. No matter how elegant your original research proposal, its application to your first batch of data is always salutary. In most qualitative research, sticking with your original research design can be a sign of inadequate data analysis rather than demonstrating a welcome consistency.

None of this will you know until you begin analysing your data. Of course, this will mean committing yourself to writing up your analysis at a very early stage. As Wolcott argues: 'You cannot begin writing early enough' (1990: 20). Even a 200-word shot at data analysis will give your supervisor something to go on. And even if understandable initial hesitancy means that you are not 'off and running', at least you will have started.

You should now attempt Exercise 10.2.

So far I have been discussing ways to 'kick-start' your data analysis. However, my attempt to offer useful tips for any kind of study has meant that I have had to talk about qualitative research in general. I now want to move to a lower level of generality and to examine how you may begin to analyse different kinds of qualitative data. I will consider four different kinds of data:

- interviews
- fieldnotes
- texts
- transcripts.

For each data source, I will offer an example of how, in a particular study, data analysis took off.

INTERVIEWS

In Chapter 3, I examined the various ways that researchers can read sense into answers that respondents give to open-ended interviews. The most popular approach is to treat respondents' answers as describing some external reality (e.g. facts, events) or internal experience (e.g. feelings, meanings). Following this approach, it is appropriate to build into the research design various devices to ensure the accuracy of your interpretation. So you can check the accuracy of what your respondents tell you by other observations (see Chapters 8 and 13 on the method of 'triangulation'). And you can treat such measures as inter-coder agreement (see Chapter 13) and computer-assisted qualitative data programs (see Chapter 12) as a means of securing a fit between your interpretations and some external reality. Let us call this a 'realist' approach to interview data.

As Clive Seale (personal correspondence) has pointed out, 'realism' is here used in the sense of the literary genre whose aim is to describe the 'gritty' reality of people's lives. In this approach, typical of tabloid journalism, 'confessional' stories are gathered and presented to the reader as new 'facts' about personalities. This form of realism has had much influence on qualitative research (see Atkinson and Silverman, 1997).

An alternative approach treats interview data as accessing various stories or narratives through which people describe their world (see Holstein and Gubrium, 1995). This approach claims that, by abandoning the attempt to treat respondents' accounts as potentially 'true' pictures of 'reality', we open up for analysis the culturally rich methods through which interviewers and interviewees, in concert, generate plausible accounts of the world. Although this second approach may use similar measures to achieve 'quality control' (e.g. group data sessions to ensure agreement about the researchers' reading of a transcript), these measures are used in pursuit of a different, 'narrated' reality in which the 'situated', or locally produced, nature of accounts is to the fore.

I am aware that many readers of this volume will favour the former approach. At the same time, I do not want to neglect the latter, 'narrative' approach – particularly as it is closer to my own theoretical orientation. Fortunately, there are examples available which show how you can kick-start a piece of interview research using both these approaches.

Jody Miller and Barry Glassner (1997) describe a study involving in-depth, open-ended interviews with young women (aged 13 to 18) who claim affiliation with youth gangs in their communities (Miller, 1996). These interviews follow the completion of a survey interview administered by the same researcher.

Here is how they describe the purposes of each form of data:

> While the survey interview gathers information about a wide range of topics, including the individual, her school, friends, family, neighborhood, delinquent involvement, arrest history, sexual history, and victimization, in addition to information about the gang, the in-depth interview is concerned exclusively with the roles and activities of young women in youth gangs, and the meanings they describe as emerging from their gang affiliation. (1997: 105)

Let us focus on the data that Miller obtained from her in-depth interviews. This is one example:

> Describing why she joined her gang, one young woman told Miller, 'well, I didn't get any respect at home. I wanted to get some love and respect from somebody somewhere else.' (1997: 107)

Here is another respondent's explanation of why she joined a gang:

> 'I didn't have **no** family . . . I had nothin' else.' (1997: 107)

Another young woman, when asked to speculate on why young people join gangs, suggested:

> 'Some of 'em are like me, don't have, don't really have a basic home or steady home to go to, you know, and they don't have as much love and respect in the home so they want to get it elsewhere. And, and, like we get, have family members in gangs or that were in gangs, stuff like that.' (1997: 107)

Let us assume that you have gathered these data and now want to begin analysis. Put at its starkest, what are you to do with them? In line with the realist approach, using programs such as ETHNOGRAPH or NUD•IST (see Chapter 12), you may start by coding respondents' answers into the different sets of reasons that they give for participation in gangs. From these data, two reasons seem to predominate: 'push' factors (unsupportive families) and 'pull' factors (supportive gangs).

Moreover, given the availability of survey data on the same respondents, you are now in a position to correlate each factor with various background characteristics that they have. This seems to set up your research in good shape. Not only can you search for the 'subjective' meanings of adolescent gangs, you can relate these meanings to 'objective' social structures.

The realist approach thus has a high degree of plausibility to social scientists who theorize the world in terms of the impact of (objective) social structures upon (subjective) dispositions. Moreover, the kind of research outputs that it seeks to deliver are precisely those demanded by 'users' in the community, seeking immediate practical pay-offs from social science research.

However, say we are not entirely satisfied by the apparent plausibility of realism. How can the narrative approach kick-start data analysis?

Miller and Glassner (1997: 103–4) suggest that one way to begin is to think about how respondents are using culturally available resources in order to construct their stories. They refer to Richardson's suggestion that:

> Participation in a culture includes participation in the narratives of that culture, a general understanding of the stock of meanings and their relationships to each other. (1990: 24)

How, then, can the data above be read in these terms? The idea is to see respondents' answers as *cultural stories*. This means examining the rhetorical force of what interviewees say:

> Interviewees deploy these narratives to make their actions explainable and understandable to those who otherwise may not understand. (Miller and Glassner, 1997: 107)

In the data already presented, Miller and Glassner note that respondents make their actions understandable in two ways. First, they do not attempt to challenge public views of gangs as bad. But, second, they do challenge the notion that the interviewee herself is bad.

However, Miller and Glassner note that not all their respondents glibly recycle conventional cultural stories. As they put it:

> Some of the young women go farther and describe their gang involvement in ways that directly challenge prevailing stereotypes about gangs as groups that are inherently bad or antisocial and about female roles within gangs. (1997: 108)

This is some of the respondents' accounts that they have in mind:

> 'It was really, it was just normal life, the only difference was, is, that we had meetings.'

'[We] play cards, smoke bud, play dominoes, play video games. That's basically all
we do is play. You would be surprised. This is a bunch of big kids. It's a bunch of
big old kids in my set.' (1997: 109)

In accounts like these, Miller and Glassner argue that there is an explicit
challenge to what the interviewees know to be popular beliefs about youth
gangs. Instead of accepting the conventional definition of their behaviour as
'deviant', the girls attempt to convey the normalcy of their activities.

These narratives directly challenge stereotypical cultural stories of the
gang. Following Richardson, Miller and Glassner refer to such accounts as
'collective stories' which 'resist the cultural narratives about groups of people
and tell alternative stories' (Richardson, 1990: 25).

Miller's research on adolescent gang culture follows an earlier study of
American adolescents' perception and use of illegal drugs. In this study,
Glassner and Loughlin (1987) treat interview responses as *both* culturally
defined narratives and possibly factually correct statements. So, for instance,
when someone says she uses marijuana because her friends do, Glassner and
Loughlin take this to suggest *two* findings:

She has made use of a culturally prevalent way of understanding and talking about
these topics [narrative].

We now have evidence that marijuana smoking is part of peer gatherings [realism].
(1987: 35)

Glassner and Loughlin argue that narrative analysis works through examining the nature and sources of the 'frame of explanation' used by the interviewee. However, the character of what the interviewee is saying can also be
treated, through a realist approach, as a factual statement and validated by
observation (e.g. of the series of interactions through which her friends' use
comes to affect her own).

If we treat interviewees' responses as factual statements, then it becomes
crucial to ask: 'Can we believe the kids?' Clearly, the authors take this to be
a serious question, arguing that, indeed, we should trust (their report of)
what the kids are saying. They base this assertion on a set of claims about
how 'rapport' was established with subjects: interviewers were accepted as
peer-group members, showed 'genuine interest' in understanding the interviewee's experiences and guaranteed confidentiality (1987: 35).

Calling their approach a 'methodology for listening', Glassner and
Loughlin are thus centrally concerned with 'seeing the world from the
perspective of our subjects' (1987: 37). In this respect, they share the same
assumptions about the 'authenticity' of 'experience' as do other realists.
However, their sensitive address of the narrative forms from which perspectives arise suggests an alternative path for interview analysis (for a
more developed version of the narrative approach, see Gubrium and
Holstein, 1997).

FIELDNOTES

Tape-recorded interviews, like texts and tapes of naturally occurring inter-action, allow you to return to your data in their original form as often as you wish. The problem with fieldnotes is that you are stuck with the form in which you made them at the time and that your readers will only have access to how you recorded events.

There are two partial solutions to this problem: following strict con-ventions in writing fieldnotes; and adhering to a consistent theoretical orien-tation. The issue of fieldnote conventions will be discussed in Chapter 11. In this chapter, I discuss an observational research study which began from a well-defined theory.

In the early 1980s, I obtained access to a number of clinics treating cancer patients in a British National Health Service (NHS) hospital. Following Phil Strong's (1979) account of the 'ceremonial order of the clinic', I was interested in how doctors and patients presented themselves to each other. For instance, Strong had noted that NHS doctors would adhere to the rule 'politeness is all' and rarely criticize patients to their faces.

While at the hospital, I noticed that one of the doctors regularly seemed to 'go missing' after his morning clinics. My curiosity aroused, I made enquiries. I discovered that most afternoons he was conducting his 'private' practice at consulting rooms in a salubrious area of London's West End.

Nothing ventured, nothing gained, I tried asking this doctor if I could 'sit in' on his private practice. To my great surprise, he consented on condition that I did not tape-record. I happily agreed, even though this meant that my data were reduced to (what I saw as) relatively unreliable fieldnotes.

Obviously, in making fieldnotes, one is not simply recording data but also analysing them. The categories you use will inevitably be theoretically satu-rated – whether or not you realize it! Given my interest in Strong's use of Goffman's (1974) concept of 'framing', I tried to note down the activities through which the participants managed their identities. For instance, I noted how long the doctor and patient spent on social 'small-talk' and how subsequent appointments were arranged.

However, if the researcher is physically present, two different kinds of issues should never be neglected:

- what you can see (as well as hear)
- how you are behaving and being treated.

What you can see

Both NHS clinics were held in functional rooms, with unadorned white walls, no carpets, simple furniture (a small desk, one substantial chair for the doctor and a number of stacking chairs for patients, families and students). As in most NHS hospitals, heating pipes and radiators were very obtrusive.

To enter the consulting rooms of the private clinic is to enter a different world. The main room has the air of an elegant study, perhaps not unlike the kind of room in a private house where a wealthy patient might have been visited by an eighteenth-century doctor. The walls are tastefully painted and adorned with prints and paintings. The floor has a fine carpet. The furniture is reproduction antique and includes a large, leather-topped desk, several comfortable armchairs, a sofa, a low table covered with books and magazines, and a bookcase which holds ivory figures as well as medical texts. Plants are placed on several surfaces and the room is lit by an elegant central light and a table lamp. To add an executive touch, there are three phones on the desk, as well as a pen in a holder.

This room establishes an air of privacy as well as luxury. At the NHS clinics, patients are nearly always examined in curtained-off areas. Here, however, the examination couch is in a separate room which can only be entered through the consulting room. Although more functional than the latter, it is nonetheless carpeted and kept at a high temperature to keep patients warm. Even the doctor himself may knock before entering this examination room while the patient is dressing or undressing.

How you are being treated

The emphasis on privacy in British 'private' medicine creates a special problem for the researcher. While at the NHS clinics I sheltered happily behind a name-tag, at the private clinic my presence was always explained, if ambiguously ('Dr Silverman is sitting in with me today if that's alright?'). Although identified and accepted by the patient, I remained uncomfortable in my role in this setting. Its air of quiet seclusion made me feel like an intruder.

Like the doctor, I found myself dressing formally and would always stand up and shake hands with the patient. I could no longer merge into the background as at the NHS clinics. I regularly experienced a sense of intruding on some private ceremony.

My impression was that the private clinic encouraged a more 'personalized' service and allowed patients to orchestrate their care, control the agenda, and obtain some 'territorial' control of the setting. In my discussion of the data Silverman (1984), like Strong, I cite extracts from consultations to support these points, while referring to deviant cases and to the continuum of forms found in the NHS clinics.

My interest in how observers are treated in medical settings is nicely demonstrated in Anssi Peräkylä's (1989) study of a hospital ward for terminally ill people. Peräkylä shows how staff use a 'psychological' frame to define themselves as objective surveyors of the emotional reactions of such patients. The psychological frame is a powerful means of resolving the identity disturbances found in other frames: where a patient is resisting practical or medical framing, for instance, this can be explained in terms of his psychological state.

However, the psychological frame also turns out to be highly relevant to understanding the staff's response to Peräkylä himself. By seeing him as a researcher principally interested in patients' feelings, the staff had a ready-made explanation of his presence to give to patients and also were able to guess which of their own activities might need explaining to him.

Like Peräkylä, by examining my own involvement in the 'framing' of the interaction, and using my eyes as well as my ears, I had kick-started my analysis. However, were there other ways in which I could systematically compare the two NHS clinics with the private clinic? In Chapter 11, I discuss some simple quantitative measures I used in order to respond to this problem.

TEXTS

Quantitative researchers try to analyse written material in a way which will produce reliable evidence about a large sample. Their favoured method is 'content analysis' in which the researchers establish a set of categories and then count the number of instances that fall into each category. The crucial requirement is that the categories are sufficiently precise to enable different coders to arrive at the same results when the same body of material (e.g. newspaper headlines) is examined (see Berelson, 1952).

In qualitative research, small numbers of texts and documents may be analysed for a very different purpose. The aim is to understand the participants' categories and to see how these are used in concrete activities like telling stories (Propp, 1968; Sacks, 1974), assembling files (Cicourel, 1968; Gubrium and Buckholdt, 1982) or describing 'family life' (Gubrium, 1992).

The theoretical orientation of many qualitative researchers thus means that they are more concerned with the processes through which texts depict 'reality' than with whether such texts contain true or false statements. As Atkinson and Coffey put it:

> In paying due attention to such materials, however, one must be quite clear about what they can and cannot be used for. They are 'social facts', in that they are produced, shared and used in socially organized ways. They are not, however, transparent representations of organizational routines, decision-making processes, or professional diagnoses. They construct particular kinds of representations with their own conventions. (1997: 47)

The implications of this are clear:

> We should not use documentary sources as surrogates for other kinds of data. We cannot, for instance, learn through records alone how an organization actually operates day-by-day. Equally, we cannot treat records – however 'official' – as firm evidence of what they report ... That strong reservation does not mean that we should ignore or downgrade documentary data. On the contrary, our recognition of their existence as social facts alerts us to the necessity to treat them very seriously indeed. We have to approach them for what they are and what they are used to accomplish. (1997: 47)

What does it mean to approach texts 'for what they are'? Let us take a concrete example. In two of Harvey Sacks's lectures, he refers to a *New York Times* story about an interview with a navy pilot about his missions in the Vietnam War (1992, Vol. 1: 205–22, 306–11).

Sacks is specially interested in the story's report of the navy pilot's reported answer to a question in the extract below:

The navy pilot story

> How did he feel about knowing that even with all the care he took in aiming only at military targets someone was probably being killed by his bombs?
>
> 'I certainly don't like the idea that I might be killing anybody,' he replied. 'But I don't lose any sleep over it. You have to be impersonal in this business. Over North Vietnam I condition myself to think that I'm a military man being shot at by another military man like myself.' (Sacks, 1992, Vol. 1: 205)

Sacks invites us to see how the pilot's immediate reply ('I certainly don't like the idea . . .') shows his commitment to the evaluational scheme offered by the journalist's question. For instance, if the pilot had instead said 'Why do you ask?', he would have shown that he did not necessarily subscribe to the same moral universe as the reporter (and, by implication, the readers of the article) (1992, Vol. 1: 211).

Having accepted this moral schema, Sacks shows how the pilot now builds an answer which helps us to see him in a favourable light. The category 'military man' works to defend his bombing as a category-bound activity which reminds us that this is, after all, what military pilots do. The effect of this is magnified by the pilot's identification of his co-participant as 'another military man like myself'. In this way, the pilot creates a pair (military man and military man) with recognizable mutual obligations (bombing/shooting at the other). In terms of this pair, the other party cannot properly complain, or as Sacks puts it:

> there are no complaints to be offered on their part about the error of his ways, except if he happens to violate the norms that, given the device used, are operative. (1992, Vol. 1: 206)

Notice also that the pilot suggests 'you have to be impersonal in this business'. Note how the category 'this business' sets up the terrain on which the specific pair of military men will shortly be used. So this account could be offered by either part of the pair. However, as Sacks argues, the implication is that 'this business' is one of many where impersonality is required. For:

> if it were the case that, that you had to be impersonal in this business held only for this business, then it might be that doing this business would be wrong in the first instance. (1992, Vol. 1: 206)

Moreover, the impersonality involved is of a special sort. Sacks points out that we hear the pilot as saying not that it is unfortunate that he cannot kill 'personally' but rather that being involved in this 'business' means that one must not consider that one is killing persons (1992, Vol. 1: 209).

However, the pilot is only *proposing* a pair of military man and military man. In that sense, he is inviting the North Vietnamese to 'play the game' in the same way as a child might say to another 'I'll be third base'. However, as Sacks notes, in children's baseball such proposals can be rejected:

> if you say 'I'll be third base', unless someone else says 'and I'll be . . .' another position, and the others say they'll be the other positions, then you're not that thing. You can't play. (1992, Vol. 1: 307)

Of course, the North Vietnamese indeed did reject the pilot's proposal. Instead, they proposed the identification of the pilot as a 'criminal' and defined themselves as 'doing police action'.

As Sacks notes, these competing definitions had implications which went beyond mere propaganda. For instance, if the navy pilot were shot down then the Geneva Conventions about his subsequent treatment would only properly be applied if he indeed were a 'military man' rather than a 'criminal' (1992, Vol.: 307).

Sacks's analysis derives from his particular way of treating texts (like Atkinson and Coffey) as representations. Like Garfinkel (1967), Sacks wanted to avoid treating people as 'cultural dopes', representing the world in ways that some culture demanded. Instead, Sacks approached 'culture' as an 'inference-making machine': a descriptive apparatus, administered and used in specific contexts. The issue for Sacks was not to second-guess societal members but to try to work out:

> how it is that people can produce sets of actions that provide that others can see such things . . . [as] persons doing intimacy . . . persons lying, etc. (1992, Vol. 1: 119)

Given that many categories can be used to describe the same person or act, Sacks's task was:

> to find out how they [members] go about choosing among the available sets of categories for grasping some event. (1992, Vol. 1: 41)

So Sacks does not mean to imply that 'society' determines which category one chooses. Instead, he wants to show the active interpretive work involved in rendering any description and the local implications of choosing any particular category. Whether or not we choose to use Sacks's precise method, he offers an inspiring way to begin to analyse the productivities of any text.

TRANSCRIPTS

Like any kind of data, the analysis of tapes and transcripts depends upon the generation of some research problem out of a particular theoretical orientation.

As with the writing of fieldnotes, the preparation of a transcript from an audio-tape or a videotape is a theoretically saturated activity. Where there is more than one researcher, debate about what you are seeing and hearing is never just about collating data: it is data *analysis*. But how do you push the analysis beyond an agreed transcript?

The temptation is to start at line 1 of your transcript and to work your way down the page making observations as you go. However, the danger of proceeding in this way is that your observations are likely to be *ad hoc* and commonsensical. Moreover, if you are committed to an approach (like CA or DA) which looks at how the participants co-produce some meaning, then beginning with a single utterance gets you off on the wrong foot. How else can you proceed?

In Chapter Five, we came across Jennifer Mason's (1996) idea of formulating a research topic in terms of different kinds of puzzles. Identifying a puzzle can also be the way to kick-start the analysis of a transcript. Once you have found your puzzle, the best method is often to *work backwards and forwards* through your transcript to see how the puzzle arises and is resolved.

As in the other sections, let me take a concrete example. I was working on some transcripts of parent–teacher interviews gathered in Australian schools by Carolyn Baker and Jayne Keogh. The following examples involve a student, Donna (S), her parents (F and M) and her teacher (T). In Extracts 10.1 and 10.2 there are no audible responses from Donna or Donna's parents to a piece of advice from the teacher (> indicates turn-slots where receipts are absent):

Extract 10.1
T: that's the only way I can really (1.0) really help at the moment and (.) for Donna herself to um do a little bit more in class and not chat so much down the back with Nicky and (.) Joanne?
>   (1.0)
T: um (2.0)

Extract 10.2
T: [Or we maybe, if- our next unit of work, Donna? if it's (.) another group do you think you- you'd perform better not working with the same girls?
>   (1.0)
T: work with a different, with someone different in the class?
>   (2.0)
T: you'd prefer to work with the same girls

In Extract 10.3, Donna's father eventually responds after a pause in a turn-slot in which Donna might have spoken:

Extract 10.3
T: I- don't- know it's really the *three* of you got to pull up your socks sort of thing or (.) or you sit somewhere *diff*erent but
>   (2.0)
T: [(   )
F: [I think you should sit somewhere different

Finally, in Extract 10.4, Donna does not respond to her father's advice:

Extract 10.4
F: I[think you should sit somewhere different
M: Mm?
F: well think of your marks it's just (4.0) it's pretty rubbishy

The absence of (spoken) responses by students to their teacher's or parents' advice, such as in Extracts 10.1–10.4, gave us the puzzle which kick-started our analysis (Silverman et al., 1997). Such silence is a puzzle because it does not appear to fit with what we know about conversation where the absence of a response by someone selected for the next turn is remarkable and accountable (Sacks et al., 1974).

To try to solve this puzzle, we searched other data for comparable findings. In over 60 advice sequences in pre-HIV test counselling, I have only one example of such a silent response to advice (Silverman, 1997b). This is as follows (C = counsellor, P = patient):

Extract 10.5 (Silverman, 1997b: 118)
1   C: this is why we say hh if you don't know the person that
2   you're with (0.6) and you're going to have sex with them hh
3   it's *important* that you tell them to (0.3) use a condom
4   >   (0.8)
5   C: or to practise safe sex that's what using a condom means.
6   >   (1.5)
7   C: okay?
8   (0.3)
9   P: uhum
10   (0.4)
11 C: has your pa:rtner ever used a condom with you?

Notice the 1.5 second pause in line 6. Since this follows a possible turn-completion point as C concludes her advice, the pause can be heard as P's pause. Moreover, C demonstrates that she monitors it this way by going in pursuit of some response token (line 7) to indicate that at least P is listening. When, after a further pause, she obtains the continuer 'uhum' (line 9), C can now continue (line 11).

However, it is also worth noting C's explanation (or gloss) which follows 'use a condom' (line 3). Since that phrase could also have been heard as terminating C's advice, she seems to have inspected the 0.8 second pause that follows as representing an absent continuer and, therefore, a possible lack of understanding. So she provides her gloss (line 5) in order, unsuccessfully as it turns out, to create a stronger environment in which to get a continuer.

Extract 10.5 shares one further similarity with the teacher–pupil advice sequences. Here the patient is a 16-year-old person – by far the youngest of all the clients in our HIV counselling extracts.

On a non-analytic level, what we seem to be dealing with here is the social problem well known to both professionals and parents: namely, the common non-response of adolescents when told what to do by adults (or even when asked questions). This social problem is seen massively in hospital clinics run for adolescents and evokes continual, unsuccessful attempts to get the child to speak (see Silverman, 1987). In Extracts 10.6–10.8, taken from such clinics, we also find non-response to advice (D = doctor, P = patient and M = mother):

Extract 10.6 (diabetic clinic 1 (NH: 17.7))
D: What should we do about your diabetes? Because you've not been doing your testing
    (untimed pause)
D: I know at the moment you're feeling sod all this altogether
P: Don't know
D: Would it help if we got off your back?
    (untimed pause)

Extract 10.7 (diabetic clinic 2 (S: 12.2))
D: The blood sugar is really too high
    (untimed pause) [*P is looking miserable*]
M: We have to fight this all the way
D: One or two units, does this really upset you?
    (untimed pause) [*P is looking down and fiddling with her coat*]

Extract 10.8 (cleft-palate clinic (14.32–3))
D: Um (2.0) but you're satisfied with your lip, are you, we don't want anything done to that?
M: She doesn't (1.0) it doesn't seem to worry her
D: Heh heh don't want anything done about any[thing?
M: [heh heh
D: Not your nose?
    (3.0)

Throughout Extracts 10.5–10.8, adolescents fail to respond in the second-turn position to advice and questions. In Extracts 10.5 and 10.6, they eventually offer a minimal response after a second prompt. By contrast, in Extracts 10.7 and 10.8, when these young patients fail to take a turn when nominated as next speaker, their mothers speak for them, offering a commentary on their child's behaviour or feelings. Finally, in Extract 10.8, when D once more renominates the patient as next speaker, nothing is heard.

However, if we had stopped at the observation of a congruence between professional–client encounters involving young people in both medical and educational settings, we would only be restating a social problem well known to parents and professionals dealing with young people. I work on the assumption that the skills of social scientists arise precisely in their ability to look at the world afresh and hence hold out the possibility of offering insights to practitioners. The question is, then, how can we move from our commonplace observation to a social science analysis?

One familiar solution is to look *behind* our data in order to find explanations

133

for our observations. To this end, we might note various features of the apparent contexts in which communication is taking place here. For instance, we might expect that advice giving is more problematic in those service encounters, like health visiting, HIV-test counselling and diabetic and cleft-palate clinics, where the professional's advice is not necessarily sought by the client and where the professional's role is mainly that of gatekeeping (offering a blood test, supplies of insulin or cosmetic surgery).

By contrast, when parents attend interviews with teachers, they may be expected to be advice seekers and any gatekeeping aspect of the encounter is difficult to detect. However, there is nothing to suggest that the students at such interviews are there because they are themselves seeking advice or even information. Therefore, if the student rather than the parent is treated as the client, then these school interviews fall into line with the other settings where reluctant advice recipients are common.

If the student is constituted as the client, parent–teacher interviews are like health visiting, HIV counselling and consultations with adolescent diabetics where advice has not been sought by the client. Indeed, like the adolescent diabetic and the first-time mother, the student may hear a disciplinary intent behind the 'advice'.

This suggests another, more local, explanation of advice non-recipiency. A common feature of both teacher–parent and paediatric interviews, although not found in most pre-test counselling, is that there are potentially multiple clients. Therefore, we might speculate that one party (namely, a parent) might non-problematically claim the right to speak on behalf of another party (the student or patient). This allows parents to enter instead of the child and children to remain silent (after all, their parents can respond, as in Extracts 10.7 and 10.8). In this way, by working as a hearable 'team' (Goffman, 1961), they maintain the rules of turn-taking.

However, the danger is that we become so obsessed with finding an *explanation* of some phenomenon that we fail to investigate adequately whether there is, indeed, such a phenomenon and, if so, how it is locally 'put together'. This danger has been characterized as the problem of 'relevance' and 'procedural consequentiality' by Schegloff (1991) and as the 'explanatory orthodoxy' by Silverman (1997b: 23–6).

Our initial response was to shift the focus away from *explaining* our observation towards locating its interactional *achievement*. Thus we ask: how is questioning and advice giving interactionally managed, turn by turn, where the ostensible answerer or advice recipient is apparently non-responsive?

In multi-party professional–client settings, the recipient of a particular turn is not given by some institutional rule but is actively 'worked at' by the participants. Extract 10.8 is a very nice example of this, and is given again here:

Extract 10.8 (Cleft-palate clinic (14.32–3))
1   D: Um (2.0) but you're satisfied with your lip, are you, we don't want
2   anything done to that?
3   M: She doesn't (1.0) it doesn't seem to worry her

```
4    D:   Heh heh don't want anything done about any[thing?
5    M:                                            [heh heh
6    D:   Not your nose?
7         (3.0)
```

As I have already remarked, notice that, in lines 1–2, D appears to nominate as next speaker someone who might appropriately make an assessment about their 'lip'. However, although next speaker orients to this nomination (talking about 'she' and 'her' rather than 'I' and 'me' in line 3), she is not the next speaker so nominated. Moreover, when D appears to renominate M's daughter as next speaker (lines 4 and 6), although she is silent, M claims recipiency via her laughter at line 5.

Extract 10.8 shows that recipiency is constructed on a turn-by-turn basis. Moreover, even within a single turn, the recipient may be redefined. Notice, for instance, how D switches from the voice of 'you' to 'we' within line 1.

Such a switch is interactionally ambiguous. First, 'we' may be heard as no more than the patronising way of referring to organizational clients quite common in England (and, sometimes, the object of a sarcastic response, e.g. 'me and who else?'). Second, in this local context, it creates the possibility that D's question about 'lip satisfaction' is addressed to both or either mother and daughter. Indeed, it may be this very possibility that allows a parent to respond without a pause (in line 3) in a slot in which the child might have been expected to answer a question.

Extract 10.8, from a cleft-palate clinic, shows how the parties play with the ambiguity about who is the recipient of a particular question. Rather than treating ambiguity as a communication *problem*, the analysis has begun to show how the interactants can use ambiguity as a *resource*.

The same interpretation may be attached to the child's silence. Instead of treating this silence as indicating some *deficiency* on the part of the child, we argue that, faced with the ambivalence built into such questions and comments by teachers (and parents), silence can be treated as a display of interactional *competence*. We can speculate that this is because silence (or at least lack of verbal response) allows children to avoid implication in the collaboratively accomplished adult moral universe, and thus enables them to resist the way in which an institutional discourse serves to frame and constrain their social competencies.

CONCLUDING REMARKS

In this chapter I have shown how, using the four main kinds of qualitative data, you can begin data analysis. By generating a puzzle by early inspection of some data, whether your own or borrowed, you can kick-start any research project. In Chapter 11, we examine how data analysis can be developed after these first stages.

SUMMARY

Avoid spending the first period of your research without analysing any data. There are three ways to kick-start data analysis:

- Analyse data already in the public sphere.
- Beg or borrow other people's data.
- Analyse your own data as you gather them.

When analysing different kinds of qualitative data, the following issues arise:

- *Interviews* Is your aim to describe the 'gritty' reality of people's lives (realism) or to access the stories or narratives through which people describe their worlds (narrativism)?
- *Fieldnotes* You need to note what you can see (as well as hear) as well as how you are behaving and being treated.
- *Texts* Is your goal precise content analysis, in which you establish a set of categories and then count the number of instances that fall into each category? Or is your aim to understand the participants' categories and to see how these are used in concrete activities like telling stories, assembling files or describing 'family life'?
- *Transcripts* The preparation of a transcript from an audiotape or a videotape is a theoretically saturated activity. Where there is more than one researcher, sorting out what you are seeing and hearing is never just about collating data: it is data *analysis*.

Further reading

Harry Wolcott's little book, *Writing Up Qualitative Research* (Sage, 1990), especially Chapter 2, is a helpful, informal guide to beginning data analysis. Other relevant sources are: Amanda Coffey and Paul Atkinson, *Making Sense of Qualitative Data* (Sage, 1996), Chapter 2; and Jennifer Mason, *Qualitative Researching* (Sage, 1996), Chapter 6.

For further details of the case studies discussed in this chapter, see: Jody Miller and Barry Glassner, 'The "Inside" and the "Outside": finding realities in interviews', in David Silverman (ed.), *Qualitative Research* (Sage, 1997); my two monographs, *Communication and Medical Practice* (Sage, 1987) and *Discourses of Counselling* (Sage, 1997); and Harvey Sacks's *Lectures on Conversation* (Vol. 1, Blackwell, 1992), pp. 205–22 and 306–11.

Exercise 10.1

This gives you the opportunity to think about relevant datasets to which you may have early access.

1 Review relevant data already in the public sphere, for instance in the media (from newspapers to television and radio to the Internet). Select a dataset and begin to analyse it.
2 Ask your supervisor and/or fellow students about any relevant data that they might have which you could borrow, either as a preliminary exercise or possibly to develop long-term collaboration. Do a brief analysis of some of them.

Exercise 10.2

This gives you an opportunity to analyse your own data as soon as you obtain it.

1 Which questions does your preferred method of data analysis suggest? What interesting generalizations can you start to pull out of your data?
2 Do previous research findings seem to apply to your data? If not, why not? If so, how can you use your data to develop these findings?
3 How do particular concepts from your preferred model of social research apply to your data? Which concepts work best and hence look likely to be most productive?

11

Developing Data Analysis

Chapter 10 stressed the importance of early data analysis and showed how to kick-start such analysis. In this chapter, we will examine how you can develop your research after these beginnings. Although we will focus here just on observational and tape-recorded data, many of the suggestions equally apply to other kinds of qualitative data.

However, a checklist of 'suggestions' can appear somewhat anaemic and without substance. This chapter begins, therefore, with an account of how data analysis developed in one qualitative study.

A CASE STUDY: OBSERVING HEART CLINICS

In the early 1980s (see Silverman, 1987: Chs 1–6) I was directing a group of researchers studying a paediatric cardiology (child heart) unit. Much of our data derived from tape-recordings of an outpatient clinic that was held every Wednesday.

It was not a coincidence that we decided to focus on this clinic rather than upon, say, interaction on the wards. Pragmatically, we knew that the clinic, as a scheduled and focused event, lasting between two and four hours and tied to particular outcomes, would be likely to give us a body of good quality data. By contrast, on the ward, tape-recording would be much more intrusive and produce tapes of poorer quality because of multiple conversations and background noise. Even if these technical problems could be overcome, the (apparently) unfocused character of ward life meant that it would be far harder to see order than in the outpatient clinic. For instance, unlike the latter, there would be no obvious repetitive structures like scheduled meetings by appointment, physical examinations and announcements of diagnosis and prognosis.

Of course, this does not mean that a researcher should never study apparently unfocused encounters – from the hospital ward to the street corner. But it does mean that, if you do, you must be prepared for long vigils and apparently unpromising data before researchable ideas start to gel.

At our hospital clinic, we became interested in how decisions (or 'disposals') were organized and announced. It seemed likely that the doctor's way of announcing decisions was systematically related not only to clinical factors (like the child's heart condition) but to social factors (such as what parents would be told at various stages of treatment). For instance, at a first outpatients' consultation, doctors would not normally announce to parents the discovery of a major heart abnormality and the necessity for life-threatening surgery. Instead, they would suggest the need for more tests and only hint that major surgery might be needed. They would also collaborate with parents who produced examples of their child's apparent 'wellness'. This step-by-step method of information giving was avoided in only two cases. If a child was diagnosed as 'healthy' by the cardiologist, the doctor would give all the information in one go and would engage in what we called a 'search and destroy' operation, based on eliciting any remaining worries of the parent(s) and proving that they were mistaken.

In the case of a group of children with the additional handicap of Down's syndrome, as well as suspected cardiac disease, the doctor would present all the clinical information at one sitting, avoiding a step-by-step method. Moreover, atypically, the doctor would allow parents to make the choice about further treatment, while encouraging them to dwell on non-clinical matters like their child's 'enjoyment of life' or friendly personality.

We then narrowed our focus to examine how doctors talked to parents about the decision to have a small diagnostic test on their children. In most cases, the doctor would say something like:

> What we propose to do, if you agree, is a small test.

No parent disagreed with an offer which appeared to be purely formal – like the formal right (never exercised) of the Queen not to sign legislation passed by the British Parliament. For Down's syndrome children, however, the parents' right to choose was far from formal. The doctor would say things to them like the following:

> I think what we would do now depends a little bit on parents' feelings.

> Now it depends a little bit on what you think.

> It depends very much on your own personal views as to whether we should proceed.

Moreover, these consultations were longer and apparently more democratic than elsewhere. A view of the patient in a family context was encouraged and parents were given every opportunity to voice their concerns and to participate in decision-making.

In this subsample, unlike the larger sample, when given a real choice, parents refused the test – with only one exception. Yet this served to reinforce rather than to challenge the medical policy in the unit concerned. This policy was to discourage surgery, all things being equal, on such children. So the democratic form coexisted with (and was indeed sustained by) the maintenance of an autocratic policy.

TABLE 11.1   **Four ways to develop data analysis**

- Focus on data which are of high quality and are easiest to collect (tape-recordings of clinics)
- Focus on one process within those data (how medical 'disposals' are organized)
- Narrow down to one part of that process (announcing a small diagnostic test)
- Compare different subsamples of the population (Down's syndrome children and the rest)

The research thus discovered the mechanics whereby a particular medical policy was enacted. The availability of tape-recordings of large numbers of consultations, together with a research method that sought to develop hypotheses inductively, meant that we were able to develop our data analysis by discovering a phenomenon for which we had not originally been looking.

The lessons to be drawn from this study are summarized in Table 11.1.

In the second half of this chapter, I discuss the more general research strategies available to you when your data, as here, are in the form of tape-recordings of naturally occurring encounters. But perhaps you do not possess your data on tape. Does this mean that everything is lost?

In the next section, I attempt to show how you can shore up the quality of your fieldnotes. Even if, in the final analysis, fieldnotes can never rival the reliability of a good quality tape and transcript, thoughtfully constructed fieldnotes can provide the impetus for advanced data analysis.

FIELDNOTES AND DATA ANALYSIS

Two ways of systematizing fieldnotes

Where you do not have access to naturally occurring data – such as tape-recordings, texts or documents – you must attempt to transcribe as much as possible of what is said and done, and the settings in which it is said and done. Two practical rules have been suggested for making fieldnotes:

- Record what we can see as well as what we hear.
- Expand fieldnotes beyond immediate observations.

USING YOUR EYES

In a study of the social organization of a restaurant, W.F. Whyte (1949) reaped rich rewards by using his eyes to observe the spatial organization of activities. More recently, in a study of interaction in hospital wards, Anssi Peräkylä (personal correspondence) notes how spatial arrangements differentiate groups of people. There are the wards and patient rooms, which staff may enter anytime they need to. Then there are patient lounges and the like, which are a kind of public space. Both areas are quite different from areas like the nurses' room and doctors' offices where patients enter only by invitation. Finally, if there is a staff coffee room, you never see a patient there.

As Peräkylä points out, one way to produce different categories of human beings in a hospital is the allocation of space according to categories. At the same time, this allocation is reproduced in the activities of the participants. For instance, the perceptive observer might note the demeanour of patients as they approach the nurses' room. Even if the door is open, they may stand outside and just put their heads round the door. In doing so, they mark out that they are encroaching on foreign territory.

Unfortunately, we have all become a little reluctant to use our eyes as well as our ears when doing observational work. However, there are exceptions. Stimson has noted how 'photographs and diagrams are virtually absent from sociological journals, and rare in sociological books' (1986: 641). He then discusses a room set out for hearings of a disciplinary organization responsible for British doctors. The Professional Conduct Committee of the General Medical Council sits in a high-ceilinged, oak-panelled room reached by an imposing staircase. There are stained-glass windows, picturing sixteen crests and a woman in a classical Greek pose. As Stimson comments:

> This is a room in which serious matters are discussed: the room has a presence that is forced on our consciousness . . . speech is formal, carefully spoken and a matter for the public record. Visitors in the gallery speak only, if at all, in hushed whispers, for their speech is not part of the proceedings. (1986: 643–4)

In such a room, as Stimson suggests, without anything needing to be said, we know that what goes on must be taken seriously. Stimson aptly contrasts this room with a McDonald's hamburger restaurant:

> Consider the decorations and materials – plastic, paper, vinyl and polystyrene, and the bright primary colours. [Everything] signifies transience. This temporary character is further articulated in the casual dress of customers, the institutionally casualised dress of staff and the seating that is constructed to make lengthy stays uncomfortable. (1986: 649–50)

Stimson and Peräkylä show that ethnographers who fail to use their eyes as well as their ears are neglecting a crucial source of data. This lesson is most readily learnt if you imagine a sighted person being forced to make sense of the world while blindfolded!

EXPANDED FIELDNOTES

> Fieldwork is so fascinating and coding usually so energy-absorbing, that you can get preoccupied and overwhelmed with the flood of particulars – the poignant quote, the appealing personality of a key informant. You forget to *think*, to make deeper and more general sense of what is happening, to begin to explain it in a conceptually coherent way. (Miles and Huberman, 1984: 69)

In order to make 'deeper and more general sense of what is happening', Spradley (1979) suggests that observers keep four separate sets of notes:

1 short notes made at the time
2 expanded notes made as soon as possible after each field session
3 a fieldwork journal to record problems and ideas that arise during each stage of fieldwork
4 a provisional running record of analysis and interpretation (discussed by Kirk and Miller, 1986: 53).

Spradley's suggestions help to systematize fieldnotes and thus improve their reliability (see Chapter 13).

Like Spradley, Miles and Huberman offer systematic ways of expanding what gets recorded in fieldnotes. They suggest writing 'contact summary sheets' or extended memos after each observation (1984: 50–1, 69–71). An example of how to use a contact summary sheet to encourage analytic thinking is set out in Table 11.2.

TABLE 11.2 **Questions for contact summary sheets**

- What people, events or situations were involved?
- What were the main themes or issues in the contact?
- Which research questions did the contact bear most centrally on?
- What new hypotheses, speculations or guesses about the field situations were suggested by the contact?
- Where should the fieldworker place most energy during the next contact, and what sorts of information should be sought?

Source: Miles and Huberman, 1984: 50

Miles and Huberman suggest five reasons why such contact sheets are valuable:

1 to guide planning for the next contact
2 to suggest new or revised codes
3 to co-ordinate several fieldworkers' work
4 to serve as a reminder of the contact at a later stage
5 to serve as the basis for data analysis (adapted from Miles and Huberman, 1984: 51).

How we record data is important because it is directly linked to the quality of data analysis. In this sense, fieldnotes and contact sheets are, of course, only means to an end – developing the analysis.

Developing analysis of field data

> The move from coding to interpretation is a crucial one . . . Interpretation involves the transcendence of 'factual' data and cautious analysis of what is to be made of them. (Coffey and Atkinson, 1996: 46)

As Miles and Huberman (1984) point out, qualitative data come in the form of words rather than in numbers. The issue, then, is how we move from these words to data analysis. They suggest that data analysis consists of 'three concurrent flows of activity: data reduction, data display and conclusion drawing/verification' (1984: 21):

- *Data reduction* 'refers to the process of selecting, focusing, simplifying, abstracting, and transforming . . . "raw" data' (1984: 21). Data reduction involves making decisions about which data chunks will provide your initial focus.
- *Data display* is 'an organized assembly of information that permits conclusion drawing and action taking' (1984: 21). It involves assembling your data into displays such as matrices, graphs, networks and charts which clarify the main direction (and missing links) of your analysis.
- *Conclusion drawing* means 'beginning to decide what things mean, noting regularities, patterns, explanations, possible configurations, causal flows and propositions' (1984: 22).
- *Verification* means testing our provisional conclusions for 'their plausibility, their sturdiness, their "confirmability" – that is, their validity' (1984: 22).

Miles and Huberman demonstrate that in field studies, unlike much quantitative research, we are not satisfied with a simple coding of data. As I argued in Chapter 3, this means that qualitative researchers have to show how the (theoretically defined) elements that they have identified are assembled or mutually laminated. The distinctive contribution qualitative research can make is by utilizing its theoretical resources in the deep analysis of small bodies of publicly shareable data.

This means that coding your data according to some theoretical scheme should only be the first stage of your data analysis. You will then need to go on to examine how these elements are linked together. At this second stage, lateral thinking can help. For instance, you can attempt to give your chosen concept or issue a new twist, perhaps by pursuing a counter-intuitive idea or by noting an additional feature little addressed in the literature. In any event, as I show below, one way of achieving better data analysis is by a steadily more narrow focus.

Progressive focusing in fieldwork

We only come to look at things in certain ways because we have adopted, either tacitly or explicitly, certain ways of seeing. This means that, in observational research, data collection, hypothesis construction and theory building are not three separate things but are interwoven with one another.

This process is well described by using an analogy with a funnel:

Ethnographic research has a characteristic 'funnel' structure, being progressively focused over its course. Progressive focusing has two analytically distinct components. First, over time the research problem is developed or transformed, and eventually its scope is clarified and delimited and its internal structure explored. In this sense, it is frequently only over the course of the research that one discovers what the research is really 'about', and it is not uncommon for it to turn out to be about something quite remote from the initially foreshadowed problems. (Hammersley and Atkinson, 1983: 175)

Atkinson (1992) gives an example of such a redefinition of a research problem. Many years after completing his PhD, Atkinson returned to his original fieldnotes on medical education. He shows how the original data can be reread in a quite different way. Atkinson's earlier method had been to fragment his fieldnotes into relatively small segments, each with its own category. For instance, a surgeon's description of post-operative complications to a surgical team was originally categorized under such headings as 'unpredictability', 'uncertainty', 'patient career' and 'trajectory'. When Atkinson returns to it, it becomes an overall narrative which sets up an enigma ('unexpected complications') which is resolved in the form of a 'moral tale' ('beware, unexpected things can always happen'). Viewed in this way, the surgeon's story becomes a text with many resemblances to a fairytale!

Two studies of British medical clinics that I carried out in the 1980s also nicely illustrate Hammersley and Atkinson's funnel. As I showed above, my observation of a paediatric cardiology unit moved unpredictably in the direction of an analysis of disposal decisions with a small group of Down's syndrome children. Similarly, my research on cancer clinics, discussed in Chapter 10, unexpectedly led into a comparison of fee-for-service and state-provided medicine (Silverman, 1981; 1987).

These two cases had three features in common:

1   The switch of focus – through the 'funnel' – as a more defined topic arose.
2   The use of the comparative method as an invaluable tool of theory building and testing.
3   The generation of topics with a scope outside the substantive area of the research. Thus the 'ceremonial orders' found in the cancer clinics are not confined to medicine, while the 'democratic' decision-making found with the Down's syndrome children had unexpected effects of power with a significance far beyond medical encounters.

As I have noted elsewhere (Silverman, 1993), working this way parallels Glaser and Strauss's (1967) famous account of grounded theory. A simplified model of this involves these stages:

• an initial attempt to develop categories which illuminate the data
• an attempt to 'saturate' these categories with many appropriate cases in order to demonstrate their relevance
• developing these categories into more general analytic frameworks with relevance outside the setting.

Glaser and Strauss use their research on death and dying as an example. They show how they developed the category of 'awareness contexts' to refer to the kinds of situations in which people were informed of their likely fate. The category was then saturated and finally related to non-medical settings where people learn about how others define them (e.g. schools).

'Grounded theory' has been criticized for its failure to acknowledge implicit theories which guide work at an early stage. It is also clearer about the generation of theories than about their test. Used unintelligently, it can also degenerate into a fairly empty building of categories or into a mere smokescreen used to legitimize purely empiricist research (see my critique of four qualitative studies in Chapter 26; and see Bryman, 1988: 83–7). At best, 'grounded theory' offers an approximation of the creative activity of theory building found in good observational work, compared with the dire abstracted empiricism present in the most wooden statistical studies.

However, quantification should not be seen as the enemy of good field research. In the next section, I discuss one example of how simple tabulations were used to test an emergent hypothesis in the study of cancer clinics.

Using tabulations in testing fieldwork hypotheses

In the cancer study, I used a coding form which enabled me to collate a number of crude measures of doctor and patient interactions (Silverman, 1984). The aim was to demonstrate that the qualitative analysis was reasonably representative of the data as a whole. Occasionally, the figures revealed that the reality was not in line with my overall impressions. Consequently, the analysis was tightened and the characterizations of clinic behaviour were specified more carefully.

The crude quantitative data I had recorded did not allow any real test of the major thrust of this argument. Nonetheless, they did offer a summary measure of the characteristics of the total sample which allowed closer specification of features of private and NHS clinics. In order to illustrate this, let me briefly show you the kind of quantitative data I gathered on topics like consultation length, patient participation and the scope of the consultation.

My overall impression was that private consultations lasted considerably longer than those held in the NHS clinics. When examined, the data indeed did show that the former were almost twice as long as the latter (20 minutes as against 11 minutes) and that the difference was statistically highly significant. However, I recalled that for special reasons, one of the NHS clinics had abnormally short consultations. I felt a fairer comparison of consultations in the two sectors should exclude this clinic and should only compare consultations taken by a single doctor in both sectors. This subsample of cases revealed that the difference in length between NHS and private consultations was now reduced to an average of under 3 minutes. This was still statistically significant, although the significance was reduced. Finally, however, if I compared only *new* patients seen by the same doctor, NHS patients got 4 minutes more on average – 34 minutes as against 30 minutes in the private clinic. This last finding was not suspected and had interesting implications for the overall assessment of the individual's costs and benefits from 'going private'. It is possible, for instance, that the tighter scheduling of appointments at the private clinic may limit the amount of time that can be given to new patients.

As a further aid to comparative analysis, I measured patient participation in the form of questions and unelicited statements. Once again, a highly significant difference was found: on this measure, private patients participated much more in the consultation. However, once more taking only patients seen by the same doctor, the difference between the clinics became very small and was *not* significant. Finally, no significant difference was found in the degree to which non-medical matters (e.g. patient's work or home circumstances) were discussed in the clinics.

These quantitative data were a useful check on over-enthusiastic claims about the degree of difference between the NHS and private clinics. However, as I argued in Chapter 10, my major concern was with the 'ceremonial order' of the three clinics. I had amassed a considerable number of exchanges in which doctors and patients appeared to behave in the private clinic in a manner deviant from what we know about NHS hospital consultations. The question was: would the quantitative data offer any support to my observations?

The answer was, to some extent, positive. Two quantitative measures were helpful in relation to the ceremonial order. One dealt with the extent to which the doctor fixed treatment or attendance at the patient's convenience. The second measured whether patients or doctor engaged in polite small-talk with one another about their personal or professional lives. (I called this 'social elicitation'.) As Table 11.3 shows, both these measures revealed significant differences, in the expected direction, according to the mode of payment.

Now, of course, such data could not offer proof of my claims about the different interactional forms. However, coupled with the qualitative data, they provided strong evidence of the direction of difference, as well as giving me a simple measure of the sample as a whole which contexted the few extracts of talk I was able to use. I do not deny that counting can be as arbitrary as qualitative interpretation of a few fragments of data. However, providing researchers resist the temptation to try to count everything, and base their analysis on a sound conceptual basis linked to actors' own

TABLE 11.3 **Private and NHS clinics: ceremonial orders**

	Private clinic (*n* = 42)	**NHS Clinics** (*n* = 104)
Treatment or attendance fixed at patients' convenience	15 (36%)	10 (10%)
Social elicitation	25 (60%)	31 (30%)

Source: Silverman, 1993: 165

methods of ordering the world, then each type of data can inform the analysis of the other.

In Chapter 13, I return to the role of counting as an aid to validity in qualitative research. In the case of observational studies, such counting will often be based on the prior coding of fieldnotes. I now, therefore, turn to the issues that arise in such coding.

Limits in coding fieldnotes

The tabulations used in the cancer study derived from:

> that well-established style of work whereby the data are inspected for categories and instances. It is an approach that disaggregates the text (notes or transcripts) into a series of fragments, which are then regrouped under a series of thematic headings. (Atkinson, 1992: 455)

Such coding by thematic headings has recently been aided by computer-aided qualitative data analysis systems as discussed in Chapter 12. In larger projects, the reliability of coding is also buttressed by training coders of data in procedures which aim to ensure a uniform approach.

However, there remain two problems with coding fieldnotes. The first, and more obvious, problem is that every way of seeing is also a way of not seeing. As Atkinson points out, one of the disadvantages of coding schemes is that, because they are based upon a given set of categories, they furnish 'a powerful conceptual grid' (1992: 459) from which it is difficult to escape. While this 'grid' is very helpful in organizing the data analysis, it also deflects attention away from uncategorized activities. Therefore, as Clive Seale (personal correspondence) has noted: 'A good coding scheme would reflect a search for 'uncategorized activities' so that they could be accounted for, in a manner similar to searching for deviant cases.'

The second, less obvious, problem is that, as I pointed out in Chapter 3, 'coding' is not the preserve of research scientists. All of us 'code' what we hear and see in the world around us. This is what Garfinkel (1967) and Sacks (1992) mean when they say that societal members, like social scientists, make the world observable and reportable.

Put at its simplest, this means that researchers must be very careful how they use categories. For instance, Sacks quotes from two linguists who appear to have no problem in characterizing particular (invented) utterances as 'simple', 'complex', 'casual' or 'ceremonial'. For Sacks, such rapid characterizations of data assume 'that we can know that [such categories are accurate] without an analysis of what it is [members] are doing' (1992, Vol. 1: 429).

At this point, the experienced researcher might respond that Sacks has characterized conventional research as over-naive. In particular, most researchers are aware of the danger of assuming any one-to-one correspondence between their categories and the aspects of 'reality' which they purport to describe. Instead, following Weber (1949), many researchers claim that they are simply using hypothetical constructs (or 'ideal types') which are only to be judged in relation to whether they are *useful*, not whether they are *accurate* or *true*.

However, Sacks was aware of this argument. As he notes:

> It is a very conventional way to proceed in the social sciences to propose that the machinery you use to analyze some data you have is acceptable if it is not intendedly the analysis of real phenomena. That is, you can have machinery which is a 'valid hypothetical construct', and it can analyze something for you. (1992, Vol. 1: 315)

By contrast, the 'machinery' in which Sacks is interested is not a set of 'hypothetical constructs'. Instead, Sacks's ambitious claim is throughout 'to be dealing with the real world' (1992, Vol. 1: 316). The 'machinery' he sets out, then, is to be seen not as a set of more or less useful categories but as the *actual* categories and mechanisms that members use. In this sense, he points out:

> I intend that the machinery I use to explain some phenomenon, to characterize how it gets done, is just as *real* as the thing I started out to explain. (1992, Vol. 1: 315, my emphasis)

How should we respond to Sacks's radical critique of ethnography? The first point is not to panic! Sacks offers a challenge to conventional observational work of which everybody should be aware. In particular, Sacks's lecture 'Doing "being ordinary"' (1992, Vol. 2: 215–21) is essential reading for every fieldworker.

However, awareness does not mean that everybody has to follow Sacks's radical path. So one response is to state something like 'thanks but no thanks'. For instance, 'grounded theory' is an equally respectable (and much more popular) way of theorizing (about) fieldwork.

To this effective but essentially defensive manoeuvre, we can add two more ambitious responses. First, we can seek to integrate Sacks's questions about 'how' the social world is constituted with more conventional ethnographic questions about the 'whats' and 'whys' of social life (Gubrium and Holstein, 1997). Or, second, as I describe below, we can make this everyday 'coding' (or 'interpretive practice') the object of inquiry by asking 'how' questions about talk-in-interaction.

TRANSCRIPTS AND DATA ANALYSIS

The two main social science traditions which inform the analysis of transcripts of tapes are conversation analysis (CA) and discourse analysis (DA). For an introduction to CA, see ten Have (1998); for DA, see Potter and Wetherell (1987) and Potter (1997).

In this book we are, of course, more concerned with the practicalities of doing qualitative research. In the rest of this chapter I will, therefore, deal with two practical issues:

- the advantages of working with tapes and transcripts
- the elements of how to do analysis of such tapes.

Why work with tapes?

> The kind of phenomena I deal with are always transcriptions of actual occurrences in their actual sequence. (Sacks, 1984: 25)

The earlier ethnographers had generally relied on recording their observations through fieldnotes. Why did Sacks prefer to use an audio recorder?

Sacks's answer is that we cannot rely on our recollections of conversations. Certainly, depending on our memory, we can usually summarize what different people said. But it is simply impossible to remember (or even to note at the time) such matters as pauses, overlaps, inbreaths and the like.

Now whether you think these kinds of things are important will depend upon what you can show with or without them. Indeed, you may not even be convinced that conversation itself is a particularly interesting topic. But at least by studying tapes of conversations, you are able to focus on the 'actual details' of one aspect of social life. As Sacks put it:

> My research is about conversation only in this incidental way, that we can get the actual happenings of on tape and transcribe them more or less, and therefore have something to begin with. If you can't deal with the actual detail of actual events then you can't have a science of social life. (1992, Vol. 2: 26)

Tapes and transcripts also offer more than just 'something to begin with'. In the first place, they are a public record, available to the scientific community, in a way that fieldnotes are not. Second, they can be replayed and transcriptions can be improved and analyses taken off on a different tack unlimited by the original transcript. As Sacks told his students:

> I started to play around with tape recorded conversations, for the single virtue that I could replay them; that I could type them out somewhat, and study them extendedly, who knew how long it might take . . . It wasn't from any large interest in language, or from some theoretical formulation of what should be studied, but simply by virtue of that; I could get my hands on it, and I could study it again and again. And also, consequentially, others could look at what I had studied, and make of it what they could, if they wanted to disagree with me. (1992, Vol. 1: 622)

A third advantage of detailed transcripts is that, if you want to, you can inspect sequences of utterances without being limited to the extracts chosen by the first researcher. For it is within these sequences, rather than in single turns of talk, that we make sense of conversation. As Sacks points out:

> having available for any given utterance other utterances around it, is extremely important for determining what was said. If you have available only the snatch of talk that you're now transcribing, you're in tough shape for determining what it is. (1992, Vol. 1: 729)

It should not be assumed that the preparation of transcripts is simply a technical detail prior to the main business of the analysis. The convenience of transcripts for presentational purposes is no more than an added bonus.

As Atkinson and Heritage (1984) point out, the production and use of transcripts are essentially 'research activities'. They involve close, repeated listenings to recordings which often reveal previously unnoted recurring features of the organization of talk.

Such listenings can most fruitfully be done in group data sessions. As described by Paul ten Have (1998), work in such groups usually begins by listening to an extract from a tape with a draft transcript and agreeing upon improvements to the transcript. Then:

> the participants are invited to proffer some observations on the data, to select an episode which they find 'interesting' for whatever reason, and formulate their understanding or puzzlement, regarding that episode. Then anyone can come in to react to these remarks, offering alternatives, raising doubts, or whatever. (1998: 124).

However, as ten Have makes clear, such group data sessions should be rather more than an anarchic free-for-all:

> participants are, on the one hand, *free* to bring in anything they like, but, on the other hand, *required* to ground their observations in the data at hand, although they may also support them with reference to their own data-based findings or those published in the literature. (1998: *ibid*)

Analysing tapes

There is a strongly inductive bent to the kind of research that ten Have and Sacks describe. As we have seen, this means that any research claims need to be identified in precise analyses of detailed transcripts. It is therefore necessary to avoid premature theory construction and the 'idealization' of research materials which uses only general, non-detailed characterizations.

Heritage sums up these assumptions as follows:

> Specifically, analysis is strongly 'data-driven' – developed from phenomena which are in various ways evidenced in the data of interaction. Correspondingly, there is a strong bias against *a priori* speculation about the orientations and motives of speakers and in favour of detailed examination of conversationalists' actual actions. Thus the empirical conduct of speakers is treated as the central resource out of which analysis may develop. (1984: 243)

In practice, Heritage adds, this means that it must be demonstrated that the regularities described can be shown to be produced by the participants and attended to by them as grounds for their own inferences and actions. Further, deviant cases in which such regularities are absent must be identified and analysed.

However, the way in which CA obtains its results is rather different from how we might intuitively try to analyse talk. It may be helpful, therefore, if I conclude this section by offering a crude set of prescriptions about things to do and things to avoid in CA. These are set out in Tables 11.4 and 11.5.

TABLE 11.4 **How to do CA**

1 Always try to identify sequences of related talk
2 Try to examine how speakers take on certain roles or identities through their talk (e.g. questioner–answerer or client–professional)
3 Look for particular outcomes in the talk (e.g. a request for clarification, a repair, laughter) and work backwards to trace the trajectory through which a particular outcome was produced

Source: Silverman, 1998b

TABLE 11.5 **Common errors in CA**

1 Explaining a turn at talk by reference to the speaker's intentions
2 Explaining a turn at talk by reference to a speaker's role or status (e.g. as a doctor or as a man or woman)
3 Trying to make sense of a single line of transcript or utterance in isolation from the surrounding talk

Source: Silverman, 1998b

If we follow these rules, the analysis of conversations does not require exceptional skills. As Schegloff puts it, in his introduction to Sacks's collected lectures, all we need to do is to 'begin with some observations, then find the problem for which these observations could serve as ... the solution' (Schegloff in Sacks, 1992, Vol. 1: xlviii).

This means that doing the kind of systematic data analysis that CA demands is not an impossibly difficult activity. As Harvey Sacks once pointed out, in doing CA we are only reminding ourselves about things we already know. As Sacks remarks:

I take it that lots of the results I offer, people can see for themselves. And they needn't be afraid to. And they needn't figure that the results are wrong because they can see them ... [It is] as if we found a new plant. It may have been a plant in your garden, but now you see it's different than something else. And you can look at it to see how it's different, and whether it's different in the way that somebody has said. (1992, Vol. 1: 488)

CONCLUDING REMARKS

Using the examples of tapes and fieldnotes, we have seen how data analysis can be developed after the first stages. However, as I have implied throughout, good data analysis is never just a matter of using the right methods or techniques but is always based on theorizing about data using a consistent model of social reality. This commitment to theorizing about data makes the best qualitative research far superior to the stilted empiricism of the worst kind of quantitative research.

However, theorization without methodological rigour is a dangerous brew. In Chapter 12, we consider how computer software can aid qualitative research. Then, in Chapter 13, the issues of validity and reliability are discussed.

SUMMARY

Data analysis can be developed in five ways:

1 Focus on data which are of high quality and are easiest to collect.
2 Focus on one process within those data.
3 Narrow down to one part of that process.
4 Compare different subsamples of the population using the comparative method.
5 Generate topics with a scope outside the substantive area of the research.

Glaser and Strauss's (1967) famous account of grounded theory offers one way of developing analysis of observational data. It involves three stages:

1 an initial attempt to develop categories which illuminate the data
2 an attempt to 'saturate' these categories with many appropriate cases in order to demonstrate their relevance
3 developing these categories into more general analytic frameworks with relevance outside the setting.

Developing simple counting mechanisms can be a further useful way of identifying deviant cases and thereby developing generalizations. However, you should resist the temptation to try to count everything and try to base your analysis on a sound conceptual footing – often linked to actors' own methods of ordering the world.

If you want to try conversation analysis on transcripts, follow these rules:

1 Always try to identify sequences of related talk.
2 Try to examine how speakers take on certain roles or identities through their talk (e.g. questioner–answerer or client–professional).
3 Look for particular outcomes in the talk (e.g. a request for clarification, a repair, laughter) and work backwards to trace the trajectory through which a particular outcome was produced.

Further reading

Miles and Huberman's book *Qualitative Data Analysis* (Sage, 1984) provides a useful treatment of coding observational data. For a more recent discussion, see Robert Emerson et al.'s *Writing Ethnographic Fieldnotes* (University of Chicago Press, 1995). Hammersley and Atkinson's *Ethnography: Principles in Practice* (Tavistock, 1983), Chapters 7–8, is a classic discussion of how to analyse ethnographic data. A development of some of these ideas can be found in Martyn Hammersley's *What's Wrong with Ethnography? Methodological Explorations* (Routledge, 1992). A relatively recent treatment of 'grounded theory' is to be found in Strauss and Corbin's *Basics of Qualitative Research* (Sage, 1990). Sacks's work on conversation analysis is discussed in David Silverman, *Harvey Sacks: Social Science and Conversation Analysis* (Polity, 1998). The case studies of the cancer and heart clinics discussed here are found in David Silverman, *Communication and Medical Practice* (Sage, 1987), Chapters 6–7.

Exercise 11.1

This exercise is based on the various ways to develop data analysis discussed in this chapter. With reference to your own data:

1 Focus on one process within those data. Now narrow down your focus to one *part* of that process. Survey your data in terms of this narrow focus. What can you now find?
2 Compare different subsamples of your data in terms of a single category or process. What does this show?
3 Decide what features of your data may properly be counted and tabulate instances of a particular category. What does this tabulation indicate? Identify 'deviant' cases and explain what you will do with them.
4 Attempt to develop your categories into more general analytic frameworks with relevance outside the setting you are studying.

12

Using Computers to Analyse Qualitative Data

Clive Seale

The use of computers for basic content analysis of text became popular in the humanities from the 1960s onwards. Scholars of literature, for example, found that they could use the large mainframe computers of the time for counting the number of times particular words occurred in a text. A computer might have been used to count the frequency of Shakespeare's use of a particular word or phrase, to compare this with some other dramatist, or to compare it between Shakespeare's late plays and his early ones, or his comedies and his tragedies, or his plays and his poetry, and so on. The co-occurrence of particular words, or the incidence of particular phrases characteristic of particular writing genres, could be reported objectively, meaning that literary analysis could be based on apparently more rigorously reported evidence. Computers could do these things because of their capacity for rapidly processing large volumes of text (Miall, 1990).

Social researchers also exploited the advantages of computers for data analysis, but this was largely confined to statistical work until the early 1980s, when qualitative researchers began to catch up. There are several reasons for the delay. Before the widespread availability of personal computers, the use of mainframes was expensive and slow, requiring a degree of certainty about the analysis so that it could be pre-specified accurately. Statistical procedures could be programmed into computers because they were well described. They were planned on one day and often run on data during the night, the results being examined the following morning. By contrast, qualitative analysis was (and still is) far less formulaic, often requiring an approach to computing that gives quick feedback on the results of emergent questions, involving an interactive cycle of thinking and innovation only really made possible with the personal computer.

Additionally qualitative research, as a social movement like many others, emerged as an initially radical response to a dominant orthodoxy: that of quantitative research work. This involved a heartfelt rejection of the techno-logical appearance of statistical work, which smacked of dehumanization, over-control, obsession with technical puzzles rather than engagement with pressing social and political issues of the time. The computer symbolized these things, and many qualitative researchers remain distanced from this technology because of feelings that it may impose an alien logic on their analytic procedures. This, though, can impede a more balanced assessment of the advantages and disadvantages of the computer-assisted analysis of qualitative data (CAQDAS), which is, of course, not suitable for all of the things that qualitative researchers wish to do with data, but does offer significant benefits.

In this chapter I propose to show you how CAQDAS can be helpful in doing the kind of qualitative data analysis discussed in the previous two chapters – while also pointing out its limitations. I will describe features of programs which have been widely used by qualitative researchers since specialized packages were introduced from the early 1980s onwards. I will also discuss some of the less often used but more advanced features of packages, such as those involved in theory building. While particular packages will be mentioned, I do not aim to review all of them, or seek to describe the finer details of how particular packages work. Such information would probably become out of date quickly, since software developers continue to release new versions with extra features. At the end of the chapter is a section to help you gain access to the many free demonstration versions of the latest software that exist, so that this type of learning can occur. As in statistical analysis, you will learn best when you have a specific project in mind, and have time to explore how various available techniques might benefit what you want to do.

ADVANTAGES OF *CAQDAS*

The advantages of CAQDAS fall into four main categories:

1 speed at handling large volumes of data, freeing the researcher to explore numerous analytic questions
2 improvement of rigour, including the production of counts of phenomena and searching for deviant cases
3 facilitation of team research, including the development of consistent coding schemes
4 help with sampling decisions, be these in the service of representativeness or theory development.

Speed

Advantages are most obvious to the researcher faced with a large amount of word processed qualitative data, wanting to sort it into categories or coded segments which may then be filed and retrieved easily. For someone in this position, the speed at which programs can carry out sorting procedures on large volumes of data is remarkable. This saves time and effort which might otherwise be expended on boring clerical work, perhaps involving mounds of photocopied paper, colour coded, sorted into piles on the floor, cut up, pasted and so on. In turn, this gives the data analyst more time to think about the meaning of data, enabling rapid feedback on the results of particular analytic ideas so that new ones can be formulated. Qualitative data analysis then becomes more devoted to creative and intellectual tasks, less immersed in routine.

In the initial stages of analysis the rapidity with which CAQDAS can identify patterns in large volumes of text can be useful. Fisher (1997) gives an example using a feature similar to those used in the Shakespeare example above. This was from a project involving 244 interviews with children, parents and social workers about local authority child care procedures. The data had been analysed previously using manual methods. Fisher's analysis was done in order to assess the contribution which different CAQDAS software packages could make. He used a program (SONAR) to search for the word 'discipline' in the interviews and found that different family members appeared to have different meanings for the word, a feature that had been missed in the original manual analysis. This led to some creative thinking about what could have led to this and what it might mean for child care issues. In turn, this thinking led to the development of ideas for coding segments of text. Fisher likens this sort of pattern searching to an aerial view of a landscape. Patterns can sometimes be seen from the air which, to the person on the ground, are merely random features.

A further example is a project at the University of Ulm, Germany, by Mergenthaler (1996) in which some 2 million words of transcription from 300 hours of transcribed psychotherapy sessions were searched for the incidence of particular words. It was found that a high incidence of certain words used in sessions, selected because they related to the researcher-generated concepts of 'emotion' and 'abstraction', were associated with particular sessions evaluated by participants as 'good'. Of course, the issue of why there is this connection requires more meaningful analysis of the interactions, perhaps using a coding approach or conversational analysis, but as an initial finding generated by the simple word counting facilities of a CAQDAS program it helped focus the minds of the researchers on particular lines of enquiry rather than others.

Rigour

An additional advantage of CAQDAS is that it can help researchers demonstrate that their conclusions are based on rigorous analysis. This adds to the trust placed in research texts by readers, a matter with which most authors are still concerned in spite of some radical postmodern analyses of research texts (for example, Tyler, 1986; Denzin, 1997). This can involve counting the number of times things occur as well as demonstrating that you have searched for negative instances by examining the whole corpus of data rather than selecting only anecdotes supporting your interpretation. This is made relatively easy by CAQDAS.

Mention of counting is a reminder that the days of a great divide between qualitative and quantitative research work have now largely passed. The argument that each of these methodologies is inextricably linked to separate philosophical or theoretical positions (for example, Smith and Heshusius, 1986) is less and less convincing to most practising social researchers. The alternative position (for example, Bryman, 1988; Hammersley, 1992) is that for many purposes the two forms of analysis can be helpfully combined (see also Chapter 13).

CAQDAS helps you to make this combination. First, as already mentioned, events can be counted. These may be word strings in the text, as in the use made by literary scholars described above, or coded segments of text. I can give an example of this from my own work, where I had coded interviews with 163 people who had known elderly people living alone in private households in the year before their deaths. For this project I was using the ETHNO-GRAPH program. I wanted to show what the speakers had said about the elderly people's attitudes to receiving help from others and I wrote in the final report:

> It was very common for the people living on their own to be described either as not seeking help for problems that they had (65 instances covering 48 people), or refusing help when offered (144 instances in 83 people). Accounts of this often stressed that this reflected on the character of the person involved, although other associations were also made. In particular, 33 speakers gave 44 instances where they stressed the independence which this indicated:
>
> '[She] never really talked about her problems, was very independent.'
>
> '[She] was just one of those independent people who would struggle on. She wouldn't ask on her own.'
>
> 'She used to shout at me because I was doing things for her. She didn't like to be helped. She was very independent.'
>
> Being 'self sufficient', 'would not be beaten', and being said to 'hate to give in' were associated with resisting help. (Seale, 1996: 34)

As you can imagine, the 163 interviews generated a large amount of text. Because I had read through each interview, marking segments of text with code called *Help* to indicate when speakers had discussed the topic of the elderly person's attitude to help, which I had then entered on the computer, I was able to generate a listing of all these coded segments. Reading through this, I was able to code these into subcategories, distinguishing segments describing elderly people not seeking help in spite of problems, instances where a refusal of help was described, and within this, those segments that involved explicit reflections on the character of the person. A code called *Indep* marked segments where independence was mentioned. For all these things, the CAQDAS program which I was using allowed me to generate counts, some of which can be seen in the quote above. I could then select illustrative quotations that gave good, typical examples of the things I was talking about.

If I had wanted to take this analysis further, I could have asked the computer to show me quotations about women separately from men, or to compare what neighbours as opposed to adult children said about the elderly person's attitude to help. Such an analysis might have been done as part of a more general investigation of the effect of gender on the experience of living alone towards the end of life, or as a part of an investigation into kinship obligations in contemporary society. The computer would have generated lists of quotations separately, which might then have been subjected to more detailed scrutiny (for example, how women discuss 'independence' compared with men), but would also have enabled these to be counted. Such counts help the reader to see how widespread phenomena are, guarding against excessive emphasis on rare things that happen to suit the researcher's preferred arguments.

Durkin (1997) reports these benefits of CAQDAS too, in his study of people's experience of asbestosis litigation. For example, a comparison of interviews done in the USA with those done in the UK showed doctors and lawyers mentioning different issues. In the UK, there was an emphasis on the medical aspects of asbestosis claims; in the USA people were more likely to discuss the role of the media in encouraging claims, and the state of crisis which the volume of claims had produced. Lawyers had rather different views from doctors. These types of systematic comparison (between countries, or between professional perspectives) are greatly facilitated by the rapid retrieval of coded segments enabled by CAQDAS.

Team research

In addition, Durkin notes the impact of CAQDAS in the context of an international, collaborative research project where researchers needed to agree on the meaning of codes and so had to assess 'inter-rater reliability'. Some qualitative researchers who claim a separate ontological position from the majority have suggested that a concern with inter-rater reliability smacks of naive realism (see the review in Armstrong et al., 1997, for more details on this debate), preferring the view that all researchers will see a different reality in a given text. Most, however, feel that for collaborative work to proceed it is necessary to create some sort of shared agreement about the meaning of particular segments of data. Durkin found that CAQDAS helped the team check whether they were interpreting segments in the same way. This was particularly useful as coding moved from the more descriptive and mundane codes to ones that reflected broader theoretical concerns. Researchers could pass coded interviews between them, and compare the results of blind second coding rapidly, using the counting facilities made available by the computer. Lee and Fielding (1995), who have interviewed many researchers about their use of CAQDAS, note that in collaborative projects one of the major impacts has been the encouragement that this gives to agree shared meanings for codes, a matter that is easier to ignore without the discipline imposed by the use of computers.

Sampling

As well as counting, avoidance of anecdotalism and the encouragement of consistent coding of data, CAQDAS has been found helpful in relation to sampling issues. Durkin's (1997) project, like most qualitative work, did not involve representative random sampling of the type used to ensure external generalizability in statistical work. Instead, the project used snowball and volunteer sampling, as the people involved in the legal and medical networks of asbestosis litigation were mostly known to each other.

> [CAQDAS] made it . . . easier to keep track of which actors we had spoken to. It was simple enough to compare a list of mentioned names with the interview directory [made available by the CAQDAS program] . . . We knew we had reached near closure on the influential actors when the snowball sample question ('who else do we need to interview?') yielded only names of people we had already interviewed. (1997: 97)

I am now going to show you how CAQDAS can help a writer take an idea forward. I am writing about sampling and CAQDAS at the moment. Whenever I read an article or a book, I make notes of what I read in handwriting. Recently, I have been preparing a book on the quality of qualitative research (Seale, 1999), for which I have read a large number of books and articles over the past few months. First, I studied all my notes about this reading, typing the main ideas I had noted into my word processor, along with relevant code words to indicate the topics concerned. Two of the topics were CAQDAS and sampling issues, for which I have coded, although CAQDAS will not be a major preoccupation of the book and the level of detail I have given on this topic in my typed notes is fairly thin. However, I am now at the point in writing this chapter where I would like to say more about these two subjects. I can half remember that there are issues about representativeness that someone has written about in relation to CAQDAS, but I can't remember who it was or what they said. I am going to switch from my word processor into NUD•IST, the CAQDAS program which I have been using for this project. I am going to search for overlaps between the code words *caqdas* and *sample* and see what happens. Then I will show you the result.

OK, I have done this. I have used the 'copy' command of NUD•IST to paste the results into my word processing program. The whole thing took two to three minutes as I had to load the NUD•IST software. It looks like there are several references, so I will edit the output from NUD•IST to reduce this, showing just one 'hit' (Figure 12.1).

The figure shows that NUD•IST has given me a lot of extraneous information about the number of segments ('text units') I have found with this search. This sort of thing might have been useful were I using NUD•IST for analysis of data, but this usage is different: I just want a reference and I don't want to spend hours leafing through my notes to find it. The item of interest is Kelle (1995), an edited book on CAQDAS. The output tells me that on the third page of my notes about this book, Kelle discusses the work of Smith (as

Q.S.R. NUD•IST Power version, revision 3.0 GUI.
Licensee: Clive Seale.

PROJECT: VALREL.PRJ, User Clive, 11: 13 am, Jan 19, 1998.

****
(1 1)   /auton/IndSysSrch
*** Definition:
Search for (intersect (30) (57))
++
+++ ON-LINE DOCUMENT: DATA
+++ Retrieval for this document: 11 units out of 1034, =
1.1%

Kelle (1995) 3 – Smith style relat*ivism a waste of time.

                    482
Most research reports contain an implied realism (q).
R/I* Kerlinger a
positiv* ist at other extreme from Smith. Hammersley is
in the middle –
Reals* – though Denzin and Lincoln (postmod*) call him a
post-positivist.
You need to take a fallibilistic approach and try to
reduce error,
without going for perfect correspondence between text
and reality.
Neginst* Caqdas* can help with sample* issues and rel* of
coding .   483

++
+++ Total number of text units retrieved = 11
+++ Retrievals in 1 out of 1 documents, = 100%.
+++ The documents with retrievals have a total of 1034 text units,
so text units retrieved in these documents = 1.1%.
+++ All documents have a total of 1034 text units,
so text units found in these documents = 1.1%.
++

FIGURE 12.1   *An example of data analysis using NUD•IST*

in Smith and Heshusius, 1986, mentioned earlier), rejecting the relativistic philosophical position of this writer.

As you can see, my summary of the arguments here is pretty brief! If I wanted to see more on this topic, I would go back to the handwritten notes, or look again at the book. Then, there is a summary of the arguments of a number of writers concerning philosophical issues in social research, the topics indicated by the code words with asterisks next to them. Right at the end is 'Caqdas* can help with sample* issues' which indicates that this text contains material on these topics, though without specifying the detail of the argument.

Looking now at my handwritten notes I see that this is a reference to a chapter by Kelle and Laurie (1995) on 'Computer use in qualitative research and issues of validity' in a book edited by Kelle (1995). Here, they make the point that the rapid retrieval which CAQDAS makes possible can help in dealing with larger samples, so enhancing the confidence with which empirical generalizations are made. However, their main point is that theoretical sampling in qualitative research has a different purpose from random sampling. The aim is not so much to create empirical generalizations through large representative samples, but to develop theory. For example, this can be done by comparing cases where a phenomenon exists with those where it does not, seeing which other conditions appear to be associated with the phenomenon. This is the strategy of constant comparison described in the grounded theory approach of Glaser and Strauss (1967) (see Chapter 13). CAQDAS can help with this, say these authors, by ensuring that comparison of cases is systematic rather than impressionistic. If thorough coding has occurred across a number of cases, a CAQDAS program can rapidly indicate which cases show a phenomenon, as well as showing what other conditions are present in each case.

You can see from this example of my use of NUD•IST that as well as using CAQDAS for data analysis, programs can be adapted for other purposes too, often not envisaged by the original software developers. I use NUD•IST as a reference manager too. On the market at present are a number of such managers which promise to produce lists of references in a variety of conventional forms, suitable for the different demands of particular academic journals. These can create searchable databases, very similar to those available at computer terminals in libraries. My problem, though, was that I did not wish to key in afresh several hundred references that I had already in electronic form, from a variety of books and articles I had done over the years. NUD•IST has been helpful here, allowing me to import these files in the rough and ready formats in which they are typed, to which I have added code words for particular topics. When I was asked to write this chapter, my first step was to go to this database and search for a list of articles I had read on the topic of CAQDAS, which I could then retrieve from my paper files and use for a more thorough investigation of the academic literature that is now emerging on this topic.

LIMITATIONS AND DISADVANTAGES

My computer search tells me, in the objective and balanced way that computers generally do, that I must now restrain my personal enthusiasm for CAQDAS and attend to the documented disadvantages and limitations that have been reported in the literature and which I have found in my personal experience and duly jotted down in the CAQDAS database that now reports them to me. My computer-assisted survey tells me that there are three major subtopics here:

1   Do specialist CAQDAS packages do anything that cannot be done by a good word processor?

2 Do computers impose a narrowly exclusive approach to the analysis of qualitative data?
3 While clearly of use in analysing large volumes of data, CAQDAS packages are of little help in examining small data extracts, of the sort often examined by conversation analysts and some discourse analysts.

Using word processors for CAQDAS

Reid (1992) makes the first point, going on to describe ways in which word processors can help the qualitative data analyst. Most CAQDAS programs expect data to have been entered in a word processing package and this task, along with reading and coding large volumes of data, remains one of the major time-consuming elements of qualitative data analysis, which computers do not remove. The time-saving elements of CAQDAS occur at a later stage of data searching and retrieval. Having said this, data in the typed or printed form used in some qualitative projects (for example, newspaper articles, reports of political speeches) can be scanned into a computer using optical character recognition software (see Fisher, 1997, for an example of this).

Reid is helpful in pointing out a number of analytic tasks feasible with a word processor. For example, it is possible to search for strings of text. This feature can be exploited if the researcher enters code words near particular topics, which can subsequently be retrieved using the string search facility. Reid outlines a 'macro' (a sequence of key strokes contained in a command file) which will search for paragraphs in which a particular code word (say 'discipline') is embedded, saving each paragraph which it finds to a separate 'results' file. One can then repeat a similar macro on this results file to search and save only those paragraphs containing a second code word (say 'children'), in which case one will have retrieved data where the two codes ('discipline' and 'children') overlap. The file management capacities of most word processors mean that this can be done for separate files if need be, so that perhaps one could compare files for male with female interviewees. Not described by Reid, but also valuable for the qualitative data analyst, is a feature known as a 'spike' (available in Microsoft Word, for example). This feature enables a text to be visually inspected and segments of text extracted, to be temporarily stored in a clipboard, then added to by the contents of the next 'spiking' operation. All of the spiked material thus collected can then be copied to a separate document.

Clearly, then, word processors can do some of the things done by specialized packages. However, to an experienced user of CAQDAS programs, the procedures described by Reid appear unnecessarily time-consuming. In CAQDAS programs the complex macro-style instructions are already programmed in and available with just a few simple clicks or keystrokes. Additionally, they offer facilities not available on word processors, such as the export of counts to statistical packages, or visualization of conceptual maps. The cost of moving from a word processor is not a strong argument since CAQDAS programs are less expensive than, for example, most statistical software (for example, SPSS) and, indeed, most commercial word processing software.

A narrow approach to analysis

The second issue, concerning the possible imposition of a narrowly exclusive approach to analysis, has been raised most intelligently by Coffey and Atkinson (1996). I say 'most intelligently' because I think concerns about the computer imposing a particular analytic logic, alien to the spirit of qualitative research, can be fuelled by the slight paranoia about technology felt by some qualitative researchers, discussed at the start of this chapter. In contrast, Coffey and Atkinson begin from a description of a variety of analytic strategies used by researchers working within different qualitative genres. As well as the conventional and popular code-and-retrieve approach, typical of researchers working within the grounded theory approach, they also describe analysis of the formal structures of narratives (see also Riessman, 1993) and what they call 'domain analysis', which involves close examination of actors' use of language, seen through their choice of particular words, phrases and metaphors. Domain analysis involves a fine-grained attention to the way in which language constructs meaning, along the lines of a semiotic or discourse analytic approach (see, for example, Potter and Wetherell, 1994). This contrasts with the code-and-retrieve approach of grounded theory which relies on common-sense interpretations of the meaning of particular segments of text. Coffey and Atkinson's comment therefore reflects a balanced analysis of the extent to which CAQDAS packages support particular forms of analysis, though they do not discuss conversation analysis in any depth.

By now, you should be convinced that CAQDAS supports the code-and-retrieve operations of grounded theorizing adequately. Indeed, two of the leading packages (ETHNOGRAPH and ATLAS) were designed with this methodology in mind. For discourse analysts, concerned to discover how particular speakers use particular words and phrases, the capacity for rapid retrieval of word strings in large bodies of data will be attractive in a preliminary identification of areas of text likely to repay closer analysis. For such researchers it is useful, too, to make comparisons of different settings or speakers, to identify systematic differences in the language chosen. However, for the discourse analyst or semiotician CAQDAS would be pointless for detailed analysis of short data extracts and would not substitute for in-depth consideration of the meaning of particular, telling instances. Barthes (1973) would not have found CAQDAS particularly useful for *Mythologies*.

Coffey and Atkinson (1996) make the point that most CAQDAS software does not support analysis of the formal structure of narratives, but note that one program, ETHNO (Heise, 1988), is devoted to this. Heise shows this by using the software to analyse the formal structure of the Little Red Riding Hood story. The analyst identifies events in narratives and enters them into the computer. For example, there may be a point in most stories where the hero's task is outlined, another point where the first difficulty is overcome, another where good defeats evil, and so on. The computer generates diagrams of such events and allows the user to explore and test logical relationships between events across different narratives, as well as comparing different narrative structures. The formal structure of fairy stories, biographical accounts, observed rituals and so on can all be analysed and compared in this way.

Coffey and Atkinson observe that CAQDAS software 'generally is more valuable for the organization and retrieval of content than the discovery of form or structure' (1996: 176) and Heise's program clearly offers features unavailable in other packages, but it is worth considering how more conventional code-and-retrieve software could support the analysis of narrative form. Clearly, code words can refer to form as well as content. One might code what the wolf said to Red Riding Hood as being about big eyes, or big teeth, or hunger, or sexual terrorism, in which case we would be coding for content (though the last example relies on an underlying theory that might not be obvious or agreed by some readers). On the other hand we could use code words like *springing the trap* or *villain tricks victim* to indicate that a recurrent formal feature of fairy stories occurs at that moment in the text. Retrieval of all *springing the trap* moments in the Brothers Grimm or the Arabian Nights collections could be a part of an analysis of narrative form. Once coded one could search for co-occurring forms (for example, the presence of saviour figure in a fairy story) in order to test logical propositions about formal structures.

Small data extracts

The point I have been discussing merges with the third limitation of CAQDAS listed at the head of this section: the issue of small data extracts. This is not controversial. It has long been conventional advice to users of statistical packages that there is no point in spending time entering data from a ten-question interview schedule, done with ten people, in order to find out how many people answered 'yes' or 'no' to each question. You can work this out by hand more quickly. This advice also applies to CAQDAS. For the conversation analyst interested in reading and rereading a particular ten-second extract of talk, or the discourse analyst paying close attention to a single paragraph of text, there is no point in using CAQDAS.

Having said this, it is increasingly recognized that these more advanced and theory-driven modes of qualitative analysis have established a body of basic findings that can be extended by the comparative analysis of different data extracts. This can involve quite large bodies of data. For example, Silverman (1997a) presents a conversation analytic study of a large number of HIV counselling sessions, drawn from several different clinics. He finds that counselling sessions in this highly focused setting vary, for the most part, between a directive 'information delivery' (ID) format that has the virtue of

USING COMPUTERS TO ANALYSE QUALITATIVE DATA

being brief, but is not designed to elicit or address the particular concerns of clients, and an 'interview' (IV) format which takes longer, is more recognizable as being 'counselling' in the conventional sense implying elicitation of clients' concerns, and has the virtue of resulting in 'recipient designed' advice. The IV format is effective, in that it is accompanied by overt acknowledgement of the relevance of advice by clients, whereas the ID format sometimes shows clients resisting advice. These findings are based on an unusually large body of data, by comparison with most other CA studies. Clearly, it would be possible to build on these findings by examining data from a variety of other counselling settings, searching and marking transcribed extracts for the formal characteristics of ID or IV formats, perhaps as a part of some broader enterprise searching for the co-occurrence of particular formats and particular outcomes. For a study like this, CAQDAS would have some relevance in storing, retrieving and counting coded segments.

Like narrative analysis, though, the more popular CAQDAS packages are unable to support many of the things conversation analysts wish to do. This is particularly evident when it comes to transcription of talk from sound recordings. Here, it is useful to have software that can store and replay sound records, and time events within talk, such as the length of pauses. A program called CODE-A-TEXT (http://www.codeatext.u-net.com) allows the computer storage and replay of sound recordings. (ATLAS, reviewed in the next section, also allows the storage of audio recordings.) In CODE-A-TEXT, Hypertext links allow the user to work concurrently with transcript and sound or video. One can also add codes to audio segments without transcription. The transcription system of CODE-A-TEXT has a number of features useful for CA, including the automatic recording of the length of silences and the insertion of this into the transcript, as well as supporting the use of CA transcription symbols. The program can export counts of words or other letter strings, and counts of code words, to spreadsheets for numerical analysis. The existence of packages such as this has influenced some conversation analysts to advocate, cautiously, their use (for example, ten Have, 1999).

Using CAQDAS is no substitute for thinking hard about the meaning of data. This is often said in response to fears that computer technology will be used uncritically for data analysis. No doubt this fear is partly generated by the perception that just such a process has occurred too often in statistical research. However, experienced quantitative researchers have long been aware of the need to treat computers as instruments for pursuing arguments about data, rather than limiting thought to what the computer can do. Additionally, different packages offer different things, and if you think you want to do something that your package can't do, search for one that can and you will often find it. I hope the examples of ETHNO and CODE-A-TEXT in this section, neither of which are mainstream CAQDAS packages, will show you that this can result in some welcome finds. I'll now give you a brief description of three 'mainstream' packages, before discussing some more advanced analytic strategies supported by CAQDAS.

MAINSTREAM PACKAGES: *ETHNOGRAPH, NUD•IST* AND *ATLAS*

A full account of the range of CAQDAS packages is available in Miles and Weitzman (1995). As I've said, new versions continually emerge, and for the latest versions it is best to explore relevant Internet sites (see later) rather than read books which quickly lose their currency. These sites have the advantage of containing demonstration versions of the commercial packages, and free versions of shareware. There are also e-mail discussion groups where software developers will engage with issues users raise, as well as allowing users to communicate with each other from around the world. However, a brief review of the features of three mainstream packages is appropriate here in order to show you more about what such packages can support and illustrate the view that different programs suit different needs.

Ethnograph

ETHNOGRAPH (http://www.QualisResearch.Com) was one of the first CAQDAS programs and in the 1980s was the one most often used by qualitative researchers. Developed initially as a DOS program, it is easy to learn. Because of this I use it to teach CAQDAS to beginners, rather than any other package. The documentation is very explicit, and the continual prompts it offers the user to double check a chosen action is, while very helpful to beginners, a little irritating after a while. The core is a straightforward code-and-retrieve system. Version 5.0 for Windows is now released. This contains a number of welcome new features which overcome limitations of earlier versions. The number of data files no longer is limited to 80, for example, and it is possible to do on-screen coding with a mouse. For the first time it is possible to export counts of code words to files which can be read by statistical software.

The program, like all CAQDAS software, requires the user to enter text with another program (either a word processor or optical character recognition). Once imported, lines are numbered. Codes can be attached to the numbers associated with particular segments of text. Memoranda about the meaning of codes can be recorded so that their development is logged, and these and other memos can themselves be incorporated as elements of 'data' during searches (a feature which the developers of NUD•IST would call an instance of 'system closure'). Searching for segments of text has become more sophisticated in successive versions of the program. One can restrict searches to particular files, or to particular features of files recorded on attached 'facesheets' (for example, male or female interviewee; institutional or community setting; and so on). If data take the form of a conversation between several people, the capacity to restrict searches to particular speakers, or categories of speaker, is useful. 'Boolean' searches are feasible, so that overlaps of codes, and retrieval of segments coded with one word, but not with another, are supported. A new feature is the capacity automatically to scan data files for code words that were entered along with the data. This can be very useful if the researcher has a robust coding scheme developed before all data have been entered.

NUD•IST

NUD•IST (http://www.qsr.com.au) entered the scene somewhat later than ETHNOGRAPH, initially as a Macintosh program, but soon developing a PC Windows version which offered some of the more advanced features that ETHNOGRAPH version 5.0 is only now beginning to add. NUD•IST has been promoted energetically as a commercial package and has overtaken ETHNOGRAPH in popularity as a result, though ETHNOGRAPH's new version is clearly designed to adopt some of the features that have appealed to NUD•IST users. It is, for example, the first CAQDAS package to be commercially distributed by Sage Publications (http://www.sagepub.co.uk/scolari), though others have now been added to Sage's catalogue. NUD•IST offers more features than ETHNOGRAPH, but is a little harder to learn. The documentation is less explicit for the novice, and things that are quite simple in ETHNOGRAPH, such as printing out the results of a search, are made more complex in NUD•IST. As well as enabling just about everything that ETHNOGRAPH can do, NUD•IST offers more complex Boolean searches. The latest version has an online help screen as well.

Certain 'selling points' stressed by NUD•IST promoters can also be applied to other packages. The much vaunted idea of 'system closure' is an example. This refers to the fact that analytic memos, the ideas that a researcher has while interacting with data, can be recorded as 'data' and included in subsequent searches. Clearly, this is possible in any CAQDAS package that allows the input and coding of text. However, NUD•IST also stores the results of particular searches, and subsequent searches can search those results. This is a more advanced example of 'system closure' which is more difficult to find in other packages. Another feature is the coding of so-called 'offline' documents. Sometimes projects generate handwritten documents which the researcher may wish to use in the data analysis, including these in searches, but is unable to type into a computer because of time constraints. NUD•IST can search for references to such documents, so that the text they contain can be manually retrieved more efficiently. Once again, this is something logically possible in other packages, such as ETHNOGRAPH, where one can create dummy 'documents' without text, that can be numbered, coded and searched. The concept of an offline document is an idea rather than a software feature. Additionally, NUD•IST offers the user a visual display of coding (which NUD•IST calls 'indexing') in a hierarchical tree structure. This can be easily updated and changed as a coding scheme develops. NUD•IST is supported by an excellent user discussion group and website run by its developers.

Atlas

ATLAS (http://www.atlasti.de) was explicitly developed to enable a grounded theory approach, resulting in a program of considerable sophistication. Unlike the other two programs reviewed here, ATLAS allows graphics (pictures and so on) to be used as data. This means that, for example, handwritten documents can be electronically scanned as pictures, sections of which can be marked and coded for later retrieval. ATLAS also offers more extended features for theory development, including the capacity to create conceptual diagrams showing links between emerging ideas. These diagrams are themselves linked to instances of data, meaning that quotations illustrating theoretical statements can be gathered very quickly. This is an advance on the hierarchical structure imposed by NUD•IST's graphical display, although it is possible to export codes from NUD•IST to other conceptual mapping software. The appearance of ATLAS is initially rather complex, containing many buttons whose purpose is not easily apparent. Some users will feel that the ease with which ETHNOGRAPH is learned outweighs the sophisticated advantages offered by ATLAS. Coding and retrieving text segments will be all that many researchers wish to do. Others will find the new analytic possibilities opened up by ATLAS a considerable attraction. At this point it is appropriate to consider some more advanced analytic strategies, involving theory building and testing, which packages like ATLAS are designed to support.

THEORY BUILDING WITH *CAQDAS*

Most researchers who use CAQDAS confine their use to coding and retrieval of text segments, using the computer as an electronic filing cabinet (Lee and Fielding, 1995). Theory building is generally done in the mind, or with the aid of paper, if at all. Although in one sense all research studies, indeed all observations, are 'theory driven', not all research studies need to be explicitly 'theorized'. Much qualitative research is, in common-sense parlance, 'descriptive' and does not require the explicit elaboration of conceptual thought generally referred to as theory. However, CAQDAS does support theorizing and examples of this are available in the literature. Additionally, I use the term 'theory building' to incorporate both the generation of theory and its testing. It is in fact hard to discuss one without the other, and an important perception of later researchers responding to the original outline of grounded theory (Glaser and Strauss, 1967) has been that the testing of emerging ideas is important in contributing new theoretical ideas. Indeed, the constant comparative method for generating theory (see Chapter 13) can be understood as involving continual tests of ideas against data. The concept of 'abduction' (see Blaikie, 1993) is a helpful halfway house between the poles of induction and deduction, indicating this understanding of data analysis.

The capacity to map out ideas in diagrams or conceptual networks, supported particularly well by ATLAS, has already been mentioned. Software that is exclusively devoted to conceptual mapping is also available (such as Decision Explorer: http://www.banxia.co.uk/banxia). Links between concepts can be visually represented in a variety of forms, so that one type of link can mean 'X causes Y', another 'X is associated with Y', or 'X loves Y', 'X depends on Y', 'X is a property of Y' and so on. Since the network is linked to coded segments of data, instances of X and instances of Y, or instances of X where Y also occurs, or instances of Y where X is not present (and so on) can be generated by the application of Boolean search statements.

Let us imagine, for a moment, that CAQDAS had been available when Glaser and Strauss (1964) generated their grounded theory of social loss, an example of the use of the constant comparative method. These researchers recorded, amongst other things, instances of nurses talking about the care of patients who had died. Let us imagine that they searched through all of these stories, perhaps coded as *Nursetalk*, and discovered what, in the 1960s, they found through manual methods, that some of these were instances of 'social loss stories'. These were comments made that indicated the extent to which nurses felt a particular death constituted a serious loss or not. A code (let us imagine that it is called *Socialoss*) might have been attached to these stories, enabling their later retrieval and further analysis.

Glaser and Strauss report that the category 'social loss story' contained some variable examples, whose properties Glaser and Strauss were able to explore by comparing different incidents where nurses spoke about the deaths of patients. Thus a nurse might regretfully say of a 20-year-old man, 'he was to be a doctor', or of a 30-year-old mother, 'who will look after the children?', or of an 80-year-old widow, 'oh well, she had a good life'. This might have been established by close examination of these stories, retrieved by computer. Such an examination could have involved searches for word strings like 'age' or 'years'. Glaser and Strauss concluded that the age of a patient was a key factor in determining the properties of social loss stories, as well as the educational and occupational class of the person who died. Additionally, they found that nurses' 'composure' (itself a category with variable properties) was often disrupted at moments of high social loss. Thus relationships between two categories were mapped out. Eventually Glaser and Strauss were to incorporate this into a general theory of relationships between professionals and their clients, suggesting that clients of high social value were more likely to receive rapid attention from professionals.

The conceptual network that might then have helped this developing theory to emerge would have looked like that shown in Figure 12.2. The arrows indicate the features of patients considered in social loss stories, which can have two different outcomes, depending on the content of the story. At each stage, retrievals of data would have supported or refuted the emerging theory. Note too that further refinement is then possible. Glaser and Strauss (1964) suggest, for example, that the properties of social loss stories interact. If an elderly person of high education and social class status died, this would be less likely to result in loss of composure than a situation involving a younger person of high education and social class. Such relationships might

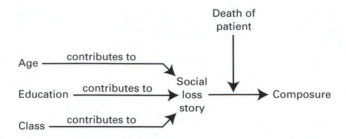

FIGURE 12.2   *Conceptual network of the type supported by ATLAS*

be indicated by further arrows indicating the conditions influencing particular outcomes. Other types of diagrams are possible for representing these ideas. For example, the hierarchical tree supported by NUD•IST could look as in Figure 12.3. If the researcher wishes to retrieve instances where the great age of a person was mentioned in a social loss story the 'address' of this 'node' for such a retrieval (to use the terms used in NUD•IST) would be 1, 1, 1. Note, though, that unlike Figure 12.2 the tree structure of Figure 12.3 does not allow lines of supposed influence to be shown, making it hard to distinguish the properties of social loss stories (patients' characteristics) from their consequences (composure outcomes).

This example can also help in understanding the theory-testing capabilities of CAQDAS. Before going into this, though, it is important to distinguish between two broad types of code. It is possible to code material *factually* rather than *heuristically*. Thus, for example, a segment of text might be described as being about 'composure' or about 'religion' or about 'alienation'. These are examples of heuristic codes, often reflecting the researcher's theoretical concepts, useful for retrieving segments of data so that examples of such talk can be thought about more deeply, subcategorized and so on. However, one might also want to code that composure, in a particular segment, has been retained or lost, that a person is a Catholic or a Protestant, or that someone is alienated or not. These are examples of factual codes. It is necessary to code 'factually' in this way in order to pursue the rigorous hypothesis testing supported by CAQDAS.

FIGURE 12.3   *Conceptual network of the type supported by NUD•IST*

Hesse-Biber and Dupuis (1995) give an example of hypothesis testing from a study of the causes of anorexia. Using factual coding with CAQDAS these researchers could test the proposition that weight loss related to certain antecedent conditions. A logical relationship between factual coding categories was written along the following lines: '*If* mother was critical of daughter's body image *and* mother–daughter relationship was strained *and* daughter experiences weight loss *then* count as an example of mother's negative influence on daughter's self-image.' Once particular interviews were identified as containing the codes involved, the text could be retrieved for further examination in order to see whether support for this causal interpretation could be justified for each case.

Clearly, the example from Glaser and Strauss could have been treated in a similar fashion. Selecting all examples of the loss of composure, the researchers could have examined to see whether these were accompanied by co-occurrences of codes for high education, class and low age, or particular combinations of these. This strategy would have searched out and retrieved negative instances, thus supporting an approach to data analysis that in, Chapter 13, we describe as analytic induction. Kelle (1995) contains a number of examples of these uses of CAQDAS, as well as references to programs that have been developed to support particular approaches to theory testing, such as AQUAD (Huber and Garcia, 1991).

HYPERLINKS TO POSTMODERN READINGS OF TEXT

The previous section may have made you feel that some of the fears that computers might take over analytic thought are justified. A technical fantasy seems to have emerged, uncomfortably close to quantitative work, with a language of counting, hypothesis testing and causal analysis that is alien to the interpretive freedom supported by qualitative approaches. Perhaps in response to these tendencies, Coffey et al. (1996) have outlined an approach to CAQDAS that is more in line with postmodern sensibilities, where deconstruction of a single authorial voice to enable multiple readings of text and data is enabled (the approach is also described in Coffey and Atkinson, 1996).

This approach makes use of a feature which I have not discussed so far, that of the hypertext link, whereby the analyst of data, or reader of a report, can click on a highlighted word or icon and go instantly to some link which has been previously made. Thus, a click on a code word might lead to an associated segment of text, or to a picture or sound file illustrating the concept. This feature will be familiar to users of the Internet. It has been promoted in certain CAQDAS packages (for example, HYPERSOFT: Dey, 1993) as avoiding the 'decontextualization' of data that can occur in simple code-and-retrieve approaches, such as those supported by ETHNOGRAPH. This is because the hypertext link does not retrieve the relevant segment, but shows it in its original location, surrounded, for example, by the rest of the interview in which the segment of speech occurs. Additionally, the analyst can attach explanations, interpretations and memos to particular links.

Coffey and Atkinson argue that, as an example, 'we might also attach additional details, such as career details of particular respondents, their family trees, or details about their domestic lives' (1996: 183). This means that the 'reader' of a research report will in fact interact with a computer rather than a book, with a research 'report' being written to a CD-ROM rather than paper. The reader will be able to explore original data in as much depth as is needed, thereby being free of the need to attend to an overarching and exclusive presentation by a single author.

The presentation of these ideas, like many new and interesting developments in qualitative research, has been couched initially in the form of a critique, to which the use of hypertext in these ways is offered as a solution. It seems that innovators often form their ideas as a response to perceived limitations of the dominant orthodoxy (or perhaps this is a rhetorical ploy to add to the persuasive appeal of the new idea). The ideas of Coffey et al. are presented as emerging in response to the limitations of the dominant grounded theory approach which they perceive to be supported by most CAQDAS software.

This critique has duly received a sophisticated reply from a representative of that approach, Udo Kelle (1997), who critiques the simple dichotomizing of hypertext versus coding, postmodernism versus grounded theory. Kelle draws on a learned and interesting discussion of the German hermeneutic tradition of biblical scholarship to show that both approaches can be fruitfully combined.

Here, we are in the realms of advanced methodological debate, a fascinating and somewhat self-sustaining arena of discourse which, however, is a little distanced from the practicalities faced by researchers grappling with particular research tasks. In the spirit of grounding the methodological debate, I would note that the ideas outlined by Coffey et al. seem like good and creative ones, that could benefit some researchers in what they want to do. In particular, they extend the topic of data analysis by pointing to the intimate links between data, analysis, interpretation and presentation to readers. In one sense, too, they have the potential to address more traditional concerns with reliability and validity, since a CD-ROM can contain a great deal more text and other data than a conventional book. This will enable one of the long-standing problems of qualitative researchers to be addressed, that of anecdotalism, since 'readers' will be able to examine the full corpus of data on which conclusions are based. This would, of course, still be an exhaustive task and it is likely that the single-paragraph abstract of findings will retain a greater appeal for readers concerned to survey a range of studies in order to extract the major research findings of a particular field.

SUMMARY

In this chapter I have introduced you to some of the basic features of CAQDAS, emphasizing the utility of many such programs for the electronic storage, filing and retrieval of large bodies of textual data. The time-saving element of this has been stressed, as well as the advantages that are gained in addressing issues of validity and reliability by the simple counting enabled by most such programs. The limitations of CAQDAS have also been discussed, including the issue of whether computer programs are likely to impose a narrowly exclusive approach to qualitative data analysis. As a result I hope that you will feel able to use CAQDAS for your own ends, rather than have it dictate an analytic strategy to you. There are many such programs available and if you find that a particular one does not support what you want to do, the odds are that another package will contain something more useful if you look hard enough. More elaborate uses of CAQDAS, for theory building and testing, were also described, as well as the more speculative use of hypertext and computer presentations in general, to create research reports that allow readers to engage in interpretive work relatively free from a dominant authorial interpretation.

Further reading

Kelle (1995) is a good collection of articles showing a variety of uses of CAQDAS. Fielding and Lee (1991) is an edited collection of similar pieces. Richards and Richards (1994), who are the producers of NUD•IST, have written an excellent review of the field. The CAQDAS and NUD•IST websites listed below contain up-to-date lists of references to books and articles on the subject.

Useful websites

ETHNOGRAPH (http://www.QualisResearch.Com)
NUD•IST (http://www.qsr.com.au)
ATLAS (http://www.atlasti.de)
Sage (http://www.sagepub.co.uk/scolari)
CAQDAS networking project at Surrey University, United Kingdom
(http://www.soc.surrey.ac.uk/caqdas)

Details of how to join user discussion groups are available at the above sites. The Sage Scolari site is included as Sage Publications distribute ETHNOGRAPH, NUD•IST, ATLAS and other CAQDAS products and the Scolari site contains links to the producers' websites.

Exercise 12.1

If you have an Internet connection, visit the websites listed in the 'Further reading' section of this chapter. Download a demonstration version of one of the mainstream programs described in the chapter (i.e. ETHNOGRAPH, NUD•IST or ATLAS). When you have spent some time getting to know the package and what it can do, jot down answers to the following questions:

1 How could I use this program to save time on my research project?
2 How could I use this program to improve the rigour of my study?
3 How could I use this program to develop the theoretical aspects of my study?
4 What are the limitations and disadvantages of using this for my study? Would another program overcome these, or should I opt for a 'manual' approach?

Exercise 12.2

Select a published qualitative research project that you already know quite well, which was done without the use of CAQDAS. It could, for example, be an early 'classic' study of Chicago School ethnography, or a well-known study relevant to your research topic. Examine the way in which the researcher appears to have collected and analysed the data and answer the following questions:

1 How might a CAQDAS program have been used to aid data collection in this study?
2 How might a CAQDAS program have been used to develop a coding scheme in this study?
3 How might the use of CAQDAS have improved the quality and rigour of data reporting in this study?
4 What other questions might have been asked of the data in the study, and could a CAQDAS program have helped in answering these?

13
Validity and Reliability

Unless you can show your audience the procedures you used to ensure that your methods were reliable and your conclusions valid, there is little point in aiming to conclude a research dissertation. Having good intentions, or the correct political attitude, is unfortunately never the point. Short of reliable methods and valid conclusions, research descends into a bedlam where the only battles that are won are by those who shout the loudest.

In Chapter 8, I was able to be reassuring about the scientific status of case studies based upon small amounts of data. However, I am less tempted to assure qualitative researchers that they need not be concerned about the reliability of their data or the quality of their interpretations. The reader has only to refer to Chapter 26 to see that my concerns about these matters extend to much published research.

In this chapter, I will attempt a diagnosis of the problem and suggest some practical solutions. But first it is important to be clear about the relevant terms – validity and reliability. For simplicity, I will work with the two straightforward definitions set out in Table 13.1.

Using examples of actual research studies, I review the pitfalls and opportunities that the demands of validity and reliability create for the novice researcher. Let me begin with validity.

VALIDITY

'Validity' is another word for truth. Sometimes one doubts the validity of an explanation because the researcher has clearly made no attempt to deal with

TABLE 13.1   **Validity and reliability**

Validity
By validity, I mean truth: interpreted as the extent to which an account accurately represents the social phenomena to which it refers. (Hammersley, 1990: 57)

Reliability
Reliability refers to the degree of consistency with which instances are assigned to the same category by different observers or by the same observer on different occasions. (Hammersley, 1992: 67)

contrary cases. Or sometimes, the demands of journal editors for shorter and shorter articles and the word limits attached to university courses mean that the researcher is reluctantly led only to use 'telling' examples.

Of course, such challenges to validity are not confined to qualitative research. The same sorts of problems can happen in the natural sciences. The demands of journal editors and university courses are little different in most fields. Nor is the temptation to exclude contrary cases unique to qualitative research. Moreover, the large research teams that sometimes collaborate in the natural sciences can unexpectedly threaten the credibility of findings. For instance, laboratory assistants have been shown to select 'perfect' slides for their professor's important lecture, while putting on one side the slides about which awkward questions might be asked (see Lynch, 1984).

It also should not be assumed that quantitative researchers have a simple solution to the question of validity. As Fielding and Fielding point out, some interpretation takes place even when using apparently 'hard' quantitative measures:

> ultimately all methods of data collection are analysed 'qualitatively', in so far as the act of analysis is an interpretation, and therefore of necessity a selective rendering. Whether the data collected are quantifiable or qualitative, the issue of the *warrant* for their inferences must be confronted. (1986: 12, my emphasis)

So, as you prepare your qualitative study, you should not be overly defensive. Quantitative researchers have no 'golden key' to validity.

Nonetheless, qualitative researchers, with their in-depth access to single cases, have to overcome a special temptation. How are they to convince themselves (and their audience) that their 'findings' are genuinely based on critical investigation of all their data and do not depend on a few well-chosen 'examples'? This is sometimes known as the problem of 'anecdotalism' (Silverman, 1993).

As Mehan (1979) notes, the very strength of ethnographic field studies – its ability to give rich descriptions of social settings – can also be its weakness. Mehan identifies three such weaknesses:

1 Conventional field studies tend to have an anecdotal quality. Research reports include a few *exemplary* instances of the behavior that the researcher has culled from field notes.
2 Researchers seldom provide the criteria or grounds for including certain instances and not others. As a result, it is difficult to determine the typicality or *representativeness* of instances and findings generated from them.
3 Research reports presented in tabular form do not preserve the materials upon which the analysis was conducted. As the researcher abstracts data from raw materials to produce summarized findings, the original form of the materials is *lost*. Therefore, it is impossible to entertain alternative interpretations of the same materials. (1979: 15, my emphasis)

Some years later, this problem was succinctly expressed by Bryman:

> There is a tendency towards an anecdotal approach to the use of data in relation to conclusions or explanations in qualitative research. Brief conversations, snippets from unstructured interviews . . . are used to provide evidence of a particular contention. There are grounds for disquiet in that the representativeness or generality of these fragments is rarely addressed. (1988: 77)

This complaint of 'anecdotalism' questions the *validity* of much qualitative research. Two common responses to it are to suggest method and data triangulation and/or respondent validation.

Triangulation refers to the attempt to get a 'true' fix on a situation by combining different ways of looking at it or different findings. In Chapter 3, I showed some of the difficulties that novice researchers can get into by attempting such triangulation. In Chapter 8, I discussed in more detail the analytical limitations of this approach.

Broadly, many of the models that underlie qualitative research are simply not compatible with the assumption that 'true' fixes on 'reality' can be obtained separately from particular ways of looking at it. Of course, this does not mean that you should not use different datasets or deploy different methods. The problem only arises when you use such multiplicity as a way of settling validity questions.

Respondent validation suggests that we should go back to the subjects with our tentative results and refine them in the light of our subjects' reactions (Reason and Rowan, 1981). Like triangulation, however, I fear it is a flawed method.

Of course, the subjects we study can, if we ask them, give us an account of the context of their actions. The problem only arises if we attribute a privileged status to that account (see Bloor, 1983; Bryman, 1988: 78–9). As Fielding and Fielding put it:

> there is no reason to assume that members have privileged status as commentators on their actions . . . such feedback cannot be taken as direct validation or refutation of the observer's inferences. Rather such processes of so-called 'validation' should be treated as yet another source of data and insight. (1986: 43)

Of course, this leaves on one side the ethics, politics and practicalities of the researcher's relation with subjects in the field (see Chapters 15 and 16). Nonetheless, these latter issues should not be *confused* with the validation of research findings.

If triangulation and respondent validation are fallible paths to validity, what more satisfactory methods remain? I discuss below five interrelated ways of thinking critically about qualitative data analysis in order to aim at more valid findings. These are:

- the refutability principle
- the constant comparative method

- comprehensive data treatment
- deviant-case analysis
- using appropriate tabulations.

The refutability principle

One solution to the problem of anecdotalism is simply for qualitative researchers to seek to refute their initial assumptions about their data in order to achieve objectivity. As Kirk and Miller argue:

> The assumptions underlying the search for objectivity are simple. There is a world of empirical reality out there. The way we perceive and understand that world is largely up to us, but the world does not tolerate all understandings of it equally. (1986: 11)

Following Kirk and Miller, we need to recognize that 'the world does not tolerate all understandings of it equally'. This means that we must overcome the temptation to jump to easy conclusions just because there is some evidence that seems to lead in an interesting direction. Instead, we must subject this evidence to every possible test.

The critical method implied here is close to what Popper (1959) calls 'critical rationalism'. This demands that we must seek to refute assumed relations between phenomena. Then, only if we cannot refute the existence of a certain relationship are we in a position to speak about 'objective' knowledge. Even then, however, our knowledge is always provisional, subject to a subsequent study which may come up with disconfirming evidence.

Popper puts it this way:

> What characterises the empirical method is its manner of exposing to falsification, in every conceivable way, the system to be tested. Its aim is not to save the lives of untenable systems but, on the contrary, to select the one which is by comparison the fittest, by exposing them all to the fiercest struggle for survival. (1959: 42)

Of course, qualitative researchers are not alone in taking Popper's critical method seriously. One way in which *quantitative* researchers attempt to satisfy Popper's demand for attempts at 'falsification' is by carefully excluding 'spurious' correlations (see Table 1.3 and associated text in Chapter 1).

To do this, the survey researcher may seek to introduce new variables to produce a form of 'multivariate analysis' which can offer significant, non-spurious correlations (see Mehan, 1979: 21). Through such an attempt to avoid spurious correlations, quantitative social scientists can offer a practical demonstration of their orientation to the spirit of critical inquiry that Popper advocates.

How can qualitative researchers satisfy Popper's criterion? The remaining four methods suggest an interrelated way of thinking critically during data analysis.

The constant comparative method

The comparative method means that the qualitative researcher should always attempt to find another case through which to test out a provisional hypothesis. In an early study of the changing perspectives of medical students during their training, Becker and Geer (1960) found that they could test their emerging hypothesis about the influence of career stages upon perceptions by comparing different groups at one time and also comparing one cohort of students with another over the course of training. For instance, it could only be claimed with confidence that beginning medical students tended to be idealists if several cohorts of first-year students all shared this perspective.

Similarly, when I was studying what happened to Down's syndrome children in a heart hospital, I tested out my findings with tape-recordings of consultations from the same clinic involving children without the congenital abnormality (Silverman, 1981). And, of course, my attempt to analyse the ceremonial order of private medical practice (Silverman, 1984) was highly dependent on comparative data on public clinics.

However, beginning researchers are unlikely to have the resources to study different cases. Yet this does not mean that comparison is impossible. The constant comparative method involves simply inspecting and comparing all the data fragments that arise in a single case (Glaser and Strauss, 1967).

While such a method may seem attractive, beginning researchers may worry about two practical difficulties involved in implementing it. First, they may lack the resources to assemble all their data in an analysable form. For instance, transcribing a whole dataset may be impossibly time-consuming – as well as diverting you from data analysis! Second, how are you to compare data when you may have not yet generated a provisional hypothesis or even an initial set of categories?

Fortunately, these objections can be readily overcome. In practice, it usually makes sense to begin analysis on a relatively small part of your data. Then, having generated a set of categories, you can test out emerging hypotheses by steadily expanding your data corpus.

This point has been clearly made by Anssi Peräkylä using the example of studies based on tape-recorded data:

> There is a limit to how much data a single researcher or a research team can transcribe and analyse. But on the other hand, a large database has definite advantages . . . a large portion of the data can be kept as a resource that is used only when the analysis has progressed so far that the phenomena under study have been specified. At that later stage, short sections from the data in reserve can be transcribed, and thereby, the full variation of the phenomenon can be observed. (1997: 206)

I employed this constant comparative method, moving from small to larger datasets, in my recent study of AIDS counselling (Silverman, 1997b). For instance, having isolated an instance of how a client resisted a counsellor's advice, I trawled through my data to obtain a larger sample of cases where advice resistance was present. This example is discussed in greater detail in the section below on 'deviant-case analysis'.

However, the constant comparative method, because it involves a repeated to and fro between different parts of your data, implies something much bigger. All parts of your data must, at some point, be inspected and analysed. This is part of what is meant by 'comprehensive data treatment'.

Comprehensive data treatment

Paul ten Have notes the complaint that in CA, as in other kinds of qualitative research, 'findings . . . are based on a subjectively selected, and probably biased, "sample" of cases that happen to fit the analytic argument' (1998: 135). This complaint, which amounts to a charge of anecdotalism, can be addressed by what ten Have, following Mehan (1979), calls 'comprehensive data treatment'. This comprehensiveness arises because, in qualitative research, 'all cases of data . . . [are] incorporated in the analysis' (1979: 21).

Such comprehensiveness goes beyond what is normally demanded in many quantitative methods. For instance, in survey research one is usually satisfied by achieving significant, non-spurious, correlations. So, if nearly all your data support your hypothesis, your job is largely done.

By contrast, in qualitative research, working with smaller datasets open to repeated inspection, one should not be satisfied until your generalization is able to apply to every single gobbet of relevant data you have collected.

The outcome is a generalization which can be every bit as valid as a statistical correlation. As Mehan puts it:

> The result is an integrated, precise model that comprehensively describes a specific phenomena (*sic*), instead of a simple correlational statement about antecedent and consequent conditions. (1979: 21)

Deviant-case analysis

Comprehensive data treatment implies actively seeking out and addressing deviant cases. Again Mehan makes the point:

> The method begins with a small batch of data. A provisional analytic scheme is generated. The scheme is then compared to other data, and modifications made in the scheme as necessary. The provisional analytic scheme is constantly confronted by 'negative' or 'discrepant' cases until the researcher has derived a small set of recursive rules that incorporate all the data in the analysis. (1979: 21)

Mehan notes that this is very different from the sense of 'deviant-case analysis' in quantitative, survey research. Here you turn to deviant cases in two circumstances:

- when the existing variables will not produce sufficiently high statistical correlations

- when good correlations are found but you suspect these might be 'spurious'.

By contrast, the qualitative researcher should not be satisfied by explanations which appear to explain nearly all the variance in their data. Instead, as I have already argued, in qualitative research, every piece of data has to be used until it can be accounted for.

Let me show you an example which uses deviant-case analysis with the aim of a comprehensive data treatment. The data in Extract 13.1 is drawn from a pre-HIV-test counselling interview between a patient (P) and a counsellor for HIV/AIDS (C) in a hospital clinic for sexually transmitted diseases. It is transcribed using CA transcription conventions (a more detailed treatment of this material is contained in Silverman, 1997b: 134–53).

As Extract 13.1 starts, C is offering a piece of advice about the importance of P thinking about how he might react if his test came out positive (i.e. showed that he had come into contact with HIV):

Extract 13.1 (Silverman, 1997b)

```
 1   C:   but you know it's important that you think about the
 2        fact that it might be positive hh though >in the
 3        majority of people< it comes back as totally negative
 4        (0.5)
 5   C:   but we have [to discuss that bit
 6   P:               [mm
 7   P:   (yes [I see)
 8   C:        [because in fact there there's nothing worse
 9        than than sort of hh umm someone saying >oh no no no
10        you haven't been at risk< and then (0.3) them having
11        a problem later on to face [occurring
12   P:                              [yeah
13   P:   um I mean I I should have thought let's cross
14        the bridge when we come to it heh is a better attitude
15        you know=
16   C:   =hh well:: everybody's different in their [attitudes
```

I was interested here in how P organized the statement of his resistance to C's advice. Note how P's explicit resistance to C's advice (in lines 1–3) about thinking about a positive test result is delayed for several turns and is only produced after a further ten lines of transcript. First, P does not take up an available turn-transition point (line 4 0.5 second gap). C can monitor the gap as implying a failure to affiliate to her advice. Indeed, there is evidence that she does hear it this way, because she temporarily abandons the advice for an agenda statement (line 5). P's subsequent utterances ('mm', 'yes I see') can now be heard as response tokens or continuers which acknowledge merely that he understands the agenda. Although such response tokens give the floor back to C, P has not so far affiliated to the advice.

However, when C uses her next turn (lines 8–11) to deliver information which might serve to underline her earlier advice, P now resists. Note, however, that not only does P delay his rejection across several turns but, within this turn, he hesitates, prefaces it and mitigates it by laughter. Moreover, although C marks the difference of views ('hh well', line 16), she does not contest her client's rejection of her advice. Instead, she backtracks in a way which, while not rejecting P's utterance, preserves some saliency in her original advice (as relevant to other people).

What is going on here? In an early paper, Erving Goffman (1959) suggested that a persistent consideration of interactants is to protect one another's public self-esteem, or 'face'. In doing whatever people are doing, they take into consideration the moral standing of themselves and their co-interactants that their doings project. In the ordinary course of events, this consideration entails the *protection* of the positive moral standing of the self and of others.

In CA's rigorous empirical approach, some important implications of Goffman's impressionistic concept of 'face' have been encapsulated in the concept of 'preference organization' (see also Heritage, 1984).

In CA, 'preference organization' basically entails the distinction between two formats of action. Certain actions – typically actions that occur in response to other actions, such as invitations, offers or assessments – can be marked as dispreferred, that is, problematic in one way or another. Thus, rejections of invitations or offers, or disagreements in response to assessments, can be performed in such a way that encodes their problematic status. Conversely, acceptance of invitation or offer, or an agreement with an assessment, can be performed in a way that does not exhibit such problematic status.

Conversation analytical research has identified a number of practices through which the dispreferred status of an action can be marked. According to Heritage (1984: 265–80), these practices include:

- The action is delayed within a turn or across a sequence of turns.
- The action is commonly prefaced or qualified within the turn in which it occurs.
- The action is commonly accomplished in mitigated or indirect form.
- The dispreferred action is commonly accounted for.

In Extract 13.1, where, as I have noted, the action that is marked as dispreferred, or problematic, is P's rejection of C's advice, we find all these features. Why is this so?

To put it in Goffman's terms, P's rejection might potentially threaten C's face as a potential helper (see also Brown and Levinson, 1987). Thereby, what is at issue in P's rejection of C's advice is no less than the local social solidarity between P and C. In enabling the participants to display the problematic status of this advice rejection, preference organization helps them to maintain C's face and to preserve social solidarity, while performing the action that potentially threatens these.

I now searched my corpus of sequences in which advice was rejected to try to identify a case where the participants did not mark advice rejection as dispreferred. In terms of preference organization, Extract 13.2 appeared to be my deviant case.

Just before Extract 13.2 begins, C had been reviewing P's many previous visits to the clinic, building up a case for viewing him as one of the 'worried well' who has 'created' his non-specific urethritis (NSU) 'by stress'. She then delivers her advice, clearly directed against this behaviour (lines 23–27), but gets an outright rejection (line 28) which does not appear to be delayed or mitigated (both canonical markers of dispreferred actions).

Extract 13.2 (Silverman, 1997b)
```
 1   C:   you can actually [create your own NSU by by stress
 2   P:                    [mm
 3   C:   and worry
 4   P:   mm I see I'm not the type of person to heh heh (    )
 5        [stress
 6   C:   [yes but it might be [something you're submerging up
 7   P:                        [get stressed
 8   C:   here you see
 9   P:   mm [hmm
10   C:      [and (.) mixed up with that is is (.) the worry
11        about (.) what you hear on TV and radio and (.) and
12        what you read in the news[papers
13   P:                            [mmm
14   C:   and magazines hh and so (0.5) mi there's a great
15        complete (.) mixmatch of of (.) what's actually
16        happening to human beings at the moment in (.) in GU
17        medicine because they're still worried [about
18   P:                                           [mm
19   C:   HIV as >a sexually transmitted disease< so so it might
20        be one of these you know=
21   P:   =mm
22   C:   that that's creating the problem (0.5) so hh um (1.0)
23        I think what you have to do is (.) when you've had
24        your clean bill of health this time
25        (0.4)
26   P:   yes
27   C:   is (.) [[softly]] get on with living
28   P:   I do live my life anyway so
```

In Extract 13.2 when, finally, C delivers the advice to which she has been leading (lines 23–27), she gets an outright rejection in which P points out that the advice is not suitable for him (line 28). P does not, in this extract, delay, preface, mitigate or account for his rejection of C's advice. Thus, one might suggest, P seems not to attend at all to the rules of preference organization.

However, we must bear in mind that, like any human rule system, preference organization does not determine behaviour but provides a way of making behaviour accountable. Therefore, rather than ignoring preference organization, P can be heard to express an extraordinarily strong rejection of

C's advice through expressing it in the *preferred* action format. It is the very lack of delay, preface, mitigation or account that constitutes this format; and thereby, it establishes the extraordinary strength of P's rejection.

It appears that the unfavourable environment of advice giving in Extract 13.2 makes relevant such extraordinary rejection. C's advice is embedded after a sequence in which P has formulated his own experience (line 4). However, this formulation has been resisted by C. Thereby, an environment has been created in which the participants disagree about what P's perspective is. As C's advice is embedded in her version of P – a version already refuted by P himself – a local environment now exists where C's advice can get rejected in the strongest available way.

Identification and analysis of this apparently deviant case thus led to greater knowledge about the circumstances in which people may not act in ways that considerations of 'face' might suggest. Therefore, I could conclude that it was not that preference organization was irrelevant here but rather that P displays, through his disattendance to some of the ordinary practices in using this organization, that something out of the ordinary has been going on.

The comparison between these two data extracts shows how the identification and further analysis of deviant cases can strengthen the validity of research. As implied here, it is important to underline the fact that such identification needs to stem from a theoretical approach to the data. Thus pieces of data are never intrinsically 'deviant' but rather become so in relation to the approach used – here CA's concept of preference organization. This theoretically defined approach to analysis should also properly apply to the compilation and inspection of data in tabulated form.

Using appropriate tabulations

It is usually mistaken to count simply for the sake of counting. Without a theoretical rationale behind the tabulated categories, counting only gives a spurious validity to research.

For instance, in the observation of classroom behaviour, Mehan (1979) suggests that many kinds of quantification have only limited value:

> the quantitative approach to classroom observation is useful for certain purposes, namely, for providing the frequency of teacher talk by comparison with student talk . . . However, this approach minimizes the contribution of students, neglects the interrelationship of verbal to non-verbal behavior, obscures the contingent nature of interaction, and ignores the (often multiple) functions of language. (1979: 14)

I do not attempt here to defend quantitative or positivistic research *per se*. I am not concerned with research designs which centre on quantitative methods and/or are indifferent to how participants construct order. Instead, I want to try to demonstrate some uses of quantification in research which is qualitative and interpretive in design.

To some extent, the tabulations I developed in my study of cancer clinics (see Table 11.3) fell foul of Mehan's criticisms. Although my comparison of clinics derived from Strong's (1979) discussion of 'ceremonial orders', the tabulation was based upon dubious, commonsensical categories. For instance, it is very problematic to count participants' questions when your only data are fieldnotes. Without being able to reinspect a tape-recording, my category of 'question' has an unknown relation to the participants' orientations.

An alternative is to count members' own categories as used in naturally occurring places. For instance, in my analysis of cardiac consultations with Down's syndrome children (see Chapter 11), I constructed a table, based on a comparison of Down's and non-Down's consultations, showing the different forms of the doctor's questions to parents and the parents' answers. This tabulation showed a strong tendency with Down's children for both the doctor and the parents to avoid using the word 'well' about the child, and this absence of reference to 'wellness' proved to be crucial to understanding the subsequent shape of the clinic consultation.

So there is no reason why qualitative researchers should not, where appropriate, use quantitative measures. Simple counting techniques, theoretically derived and ideally based on members' own categories, can offer a means to survey the whole corpus of data ordinarily lost in intensive, qualitative research. Instead of taking the researcher's word for it, the reader has a chance to gain a sense of the flavour of the data as a whole. In turn, researchers are able to test and to revise their generalizations, removing nagging doubts about the accuracy of their impressions about the data.

As Kirk and Miller remark:

> By our pragmatic view, qualitative research does imply a commitment to field activities. It does not imply a commitment to innumeracy. (1986: 10)

RELIABILITY

Counting based on members' own categories in the context of comprehensive data treatment is possible because, in principle, the quality of data should be high in qualitative research. By contrast, although quantitative researchers try to claim reliability by using pre-tested measures and scales, they can end up with highly unreliable tabulations. This is not because survey research questions are ambiguously worded but rather because asking and answering any question can never be separated from mutual interpretations which are inherently local and non-standardizable (see Antaki and Rapley, 1996).

By contrast with tabulated figures from survey research interviews, tapes and transcripts are open to further inspection by both researchers and readers. However, this opportunity is not always present in qualitative research. There are many observational studies where the reader has to depend on the researcher's depiction of what was going on. Indeed, perhaps the extended immersion in the 'field', typical of much qualitative research, leads to a certain

preciousness about the validity and reliability of the researcher's own interpretation of 'their' tribe or set of interview respondents.

As Bryman notes about such studies:

> field notes or extended transcripts are rarely available; these would be very helpful
> in order to allow the reader to formulate his or her own hunches about the per-
> spective of the people who have been studied. (1988: 77)

Earlier in this book, I have discussed two ways of strengthening the reliability of field data: fieldnote conventions (see Chapter 11) and inter-coder agreement (referred to in Chapter 10). In the remaining part of this chapter, I will
concretize this discussion of reliability by looking at an example of how
reliability was addressed in the context of one ethnographic study. I will then
examine practical issues of reliability in a study which worked with tapes
and transcripts of naturally occurring interaction.

Reliability in one ethnographic study

In their ethnographic study of adolescent drug users, first discussed in
Chapter 10, Barry Glassner and Julia Loughlin (1987) carefully tape-recorded
all their interviews. These tapes were then transcribed and coded by:

> identifying topics, ways of talking, themes, events, actors and so forth . . . Those
> lists became a catalogue of codes, consisting of 45 topics, each with up to 99
> descriptors. (1987: 25)

On the surface, such tabulation appears to involve the counting for the sake
of counting found in some quantitative research. However, the authors make
clear that their approach to data analysis is different from positivistic, survey
research studies:

> In more positivistic research designs, coder reliability is assessed in terms of agree-
> ment among coders. In qualitative research one is unconcerned with standardizing
> interpretation of data. Rather, our goal in developing this complex cataloguing and
> retrieval system has been *to retain good access to the words of the subjects*, without
> relying upon the memory of interviewers or data analysts. (1987: 27, my emphasis)

By retaining this access to subjects' own categories, Glassner and Loughlin
satisfy the theoretical orientation of much qualitative research while simul-
taneously allowing readers to retain some sort of direct access to raw data.

Moreover, Glassner and Loughlin suggest that their analysis fits conventional criteria of reliability. For instance:

*   The coding and data analysis was done 'blind': both the coding staff and
    the analysts of the data 'conducted their research without knowledge of
    [the] expectations or hypotheses of the project directors' (1987: 30).
*   The computer-assisted recording and analysis of the data meant that one

could be more confident that the patterns reported actually existed throughout the data rather than in favourable examples.

Reliability in a study of tape-recorded interaction

When people's activities are tape-recorded and transcribed, the reliability of the interpretation of transcripts may be gravely weakened by a failure to transcribe apparently trivial, but often crucial, pauses and overlaps. For instance, a recent study of medical consultations was concerned to establish whether cancer patients had understood that their condition was fatal.

In this study (Clavarino et al., 1995), we attempted to examine the basis upon which interpretive judgements were made about the content of a series of audiotaped doctor–patient interviews between three oncologists and their newly referred cancer patients. It was during this interview that the patients were supposedly informed that their cancer was incurable.

Two independent transcriptions were performed. In the first, an attempt was made to transcribe the talk 'verbatim' i.e. without grammatical or other 'tidying up'. Using the first transcription, three independent coders, who had been trained to be consistent, coded the same material. Inter-coder reliability was then estimated. Inconsistencies amongst the coders may have reflected some ambiguity in the data, some overlap between coding categories, or simple coding errors.

The second transcription was informed by the analytic ideas and transcription symbols of CA. This provided additional information on how the parties organized their talk and, we believe, represents a more objective, comprehensive and therefore more reliable recording of the data because of the level of detail given by this method.

By drawing upon the transcription symbols and concepts of conversation analysis, we sought to reveal subtle features in the talk, showing how both doctor and patients produced and received hearable ambiguities in the patient's prognosis. This involved a shift of focus from coders' readings to how participants demonstrably monitor each other's talk. Once we pay attention to such detail, judgements can be made that are more convincingly valid. Inevitably, this leads to a resolution of the problem of inter-coder reliability.

For instance, when researchers first listened to tapes of relevant hospital consultations, they sometimes felt that there was no evidence that the patients had picked up their doctor's often guarded statements about their prognosis. However, when the tapes were retranscribed, it was demonstrated that patients used very soft utterances (like 'yes' or more usually 'mm') to mark that they were taking up this information. Equally, doctors would monitor patients' silences and rephrase their prognosis statements.

CONCLUSION

Some social researchers argue that a concern for the reliability and validity of observations arises only within the quantitative research tradition. Because what they call the 'positivist' position sees no difference between the natural and social worlds, reliable and valid measures of social life are only needed by such 'positivists'. Conversely, it is argued, once we treat social reality as always in flux, then it makes no sense to worry about whether our research instruments measure accurately (e.g. Marshall and Rossman, 1989).

Such a position would rule out any systematic research since it implies that we cannot assume any stable properties in the social world. However, if we concede the possible existence of such properties, why shouldn't other work replicate these properties?

As Kirk and Miller argue about reliability:

> Qualitative researchers can no longer afford to beg the issue of reliability. While the forte of field research will always lie in its capability to sort out the validity of propositions, its results will (reasonably) go ignored minus attention to reliability. For reliability to be calculated, it is incumbent on the scientific investigator to document his or her procedure. (1986: 72)

Of course, exactly the same point may be made about the claims to validity, or truth status, of qualitative research studies. So, to underline the point with which this chapter began, unless you can show your audience the procedures you used to ensure that your methods were reliable and your conclusions valid, there is little point in aiming to conclude a research dissertation.

SUMMARY

Validity is another word for truth. We cannot say that the claims of a research study are valid when:

1   only a few exemplary instances are reported
2   the criteria or grounds for including certain instances and not others are not provided
3   the original form of the materials is unavailable.

Five ways of thinking critically about qualitative data analysis in order to aim at more valid findings were discussed:

• the refutability principle
• the constant comparative method
• comprehensive data treatment
• deviant-case analysis
• using appropriate tabulations.

Reliability refers to the degree of consistency with which instances are assigned to the same category by different observers or by the same observer on different occasions. For reliability to be calculated, it is incumbent on the scientific investigator to document his or her procedure and to demonstrate that categories have been used consistently.

Further reading

Clive Seale's recent book *The Quality of Qualitative Research* (Sage, 1999) offers an excellent overall treatment of the issues discussed in this chapter. A shorter but more specialized treatment is to be found in Peräkylä (1997). For a detailed discussion of 'analytic induction' see Becker (1998: 197–212).

Exercise 13.1

This is an exercise designed to help you think about the validity of your data analysis. It is best attempted when you have already written at least one substantial paper on your findings.

1 Choose any paper you have written on your data.
2 Explain on what grounds you chose those particular data extracts to report.
3 To what extent can you claim that these data were 'typical' or 'representative'?
4 To what extent have you investigated and reported 'deviant' cases?

Exercise 13.2

This exercise is meant to accustom you to the advantages and limitations of simple tabulations.

1 Select one dataset from your data corpus (e.g. a particular collection of interviews, observations or transcripts).
2 Count whatever seems to be countable in these data *according to your theoretical orientation*.
3 Assess what these quantitative data tell you about social life in this setting, e.g. what associations can you establish?
4 Identify deviant cases (i.e. items that do not support the associations that you have established). How might you further analyse these deviant cases, using either quantitative or qualitative techniques? What light might that throw on the associations which you have identified?

Exercise 13.3

I reproduce below a quotation from Barry Glassner and Julia Loughlin used earlier in this chapter:

> In more positivistic research designs, coder reliability is assessed in terms of agreement among coders. In qualitative research one is unconcerned with standardizing interpretation of data. Rather, our goal in developing this complex cataloguing and retrieval system has been *to retain good access to the words of the subjects,* without relying upon the memory of interviewers or data analysts. (1987: 27, my emphasis)

Now write a short piece (say 1000 words) explaining how your own data analysis provides the reader with good access to your original dataset. Check out this piece with your supervisor and other students. If they think it works, you may be able to use it as part of your final methodology chapter.

14

Keeping a Record

Record-keeping seems like a very dull activity. It may conjure up a picture of boring account books or even of Dickensian clerks with wing collars poring over ledgers in a gloomy nineteenth-century office.

In this short chapter, I will try to convince you that good record-keeping is not a dull and lonely activity but a fruitful, even enjoyable, way of establishing a dialogue with other people. It should be noted that these other people include yourself and your thoughts as they were a few years, months or even days ago.

The two principal areas of record-keeping discussed below are:

- a record of your reading
- a research diary.

RECORDING YOUR READING

By the time you begin a research degree, it is likely that you will have learned the habit of keeping your reading notes in a word processed file, organized in terms of (emerging) topics. I stress 'reading notes' because it is important from the start that you do *not* simply collate books or photocopies of articles for 'later' reading but read as you go. Equally, your notes should not just consist of chunks of written or scanned extracts from the original sources but should represent your ideas on the *relevance* of what you are reading for your (emerging) research problem.

So read critically. Don't just copy chunks of material. Strauss and Corbin (1990: 50–3, adapted here) suggest that the existing literature can be used for five purposes in qualitative research:

1 *To stimulate theoretical sensitivity* 'Providing concepts and relationships that [can be] checked out against [your] actual data.'

2 *To provide secondary sources of data* These can be used for initial trial runs of your own concepts and topics.
3 *To stimulate questions during data gathering and data analysis.*
4 *To direct theoretical sampling* To 'give you ideas about where you might go to uncover phenomena important to the development of your theory'.
5 *To be used as supplementary validation* To explain why your findings support or differ from the existing literature.

Following Strauss and Corbin, you should always approach any publication with a set of questions, for instance:

- What are the relevant findings?
- What are the relevant methodologies?
- What are the relevant theories?
- What are the relevant hypotheses?
- What are the relevant samples?
- What is the relevance to how I now see my research problem?
- What possible new directions for my research are implied?

Exercise 14.1 gives you an opportunity to test out your skills in using the existing literature to help you in your own research. It emphasizes that we should never read such literature without having formulated some prior set of questions.

It goes without saying that you should use a consistent system for referencing authors and other details of the material you are reading. The Harvard method of referencing is usually the system chosen in the humanities. This involves entering an author's surname, followed by date of publication and any page reference in your main text, as follows:

Abrams (1984: 2); Agar (1986: 84)

By using this method, you can save footnotes for substantial asides rather than for (boring) references. Detailed references are then appended in a bibliography in a form such as the following:

Abrams, P. (1984) 'Evaluating soft findings: some problems of measuring informal care', *Research Policy and Planning*, 2(2), 1–8
Agar, M. (1986) *Speaking of Ethnography*, Qualitative Research Methods Series, Vol. 2, London: Sage.

In Chapter 18, I discuss how such records of your reading can be integrated into the literature review chapter of your thesis. When you come to write that chapter, ideally towards the *end* of your research, you will have all the relevant material on file. But, just as important, you will also have a record of your changing thoughts about the literature and its relevance to your emerging research topic.

RESEARCH DIARIES

We commonly find the sense of the past in the present. Such 'rewriting of history' (Garfinkel, 1967) means that, unless you are careful, you may forget important aspects of your early thinking about your research which may be crucial to your readers' understanding. One way to ensure that you spell out your reasoning is to keep a research diary.

This will avoid presenting the reader with an apparently 'seamless web' of ideas which conceals the development of your thinking with all its set-backs and dead-ends. In this way, 'the text can be like a detective story, where one presents these kinds of "false leads" until they are revealed to be dead-ends' (Alasuutari, 1995: 192).

Another danger with the 'seamless web' picture of research is that it can conceal various tricks, sleights of hand and simple mistakes through which you reach your conclusions. Keeping proper records, including a research diary, helps to make your reasoning transparent – to yourself as well as to your readers. In this spirit, Huberman and Miles call for:

> careful retention, in easily retrievable form, of all study materials, from raw field notes through data displays and final report text. (1994: 439)

Keeping such careful records means that you will be amassing material that can form a substantial part of the methodology chapter of your thesis (see Chapter 19). It also implies an open-minded and critical approach to your research. This is what Huberman and Miles mean by 'a reflexive stance'. It involves:

> regular, ongoing, self-conscious documentation – of successive versions of coding schemes, of conceptual arguments . . . of analysis episodes – both successful ones and dead ends. (1994: 439)

In Table 14.1, I summarize the uses of a research diary.

TABLE 14.1 **Why keep a research diary?**

1   To show the reader the development of your thinking
2   As an aid to reflection
3   To help improve your time management
4   To provide ideas for the future direction of your work
5   To use in the methodology chapter of your thesis

Source: adapted in part from Cryer, 1996: 73

As an example of the kind of material that can be put into a research diary, here is an extract from Vicki's diary that we first came across in Chapter 2:

VICKI'S RESEARCH DIARY

SOLID PROGRESS (MARCH–MAY 1996)
Continued transcribing extracts. Also wrote chapter on natural history of the research process (to date), chapter on HIV counselling, chapter on offers, sent to DS for comments.

DISASTER (MAY 1996)
Hard disk crashed: lost two chapters and some data files that were not backed up!! Also lost draft chapter prepared on offers.

CONFERENCE (1–5 JULY 1996)
Went to 4th International Social Science Methodology Conference at Essex University. Set out framework for overall PhD and timetable.

WORKSHOP (19–21 SEPTEMBER 1996)
Went to CA weekend data workshop organized by Sarah Collins. This was a good experience for me. I came away feeling very confident about my data and the direction of my research.

DESPAIR (OCTOBER 1996)
Time spent trying to recover data and get transcript back to where had been six months previously – disheartened!!

TIME OUT (OCTOBER 1996 TO JANUARY 1997)
I felt I had achieved next to nothing since my hard disk crashed in May. I took time out and went to Australia to visit my sick brother.

STARTING UP AGAIN (JANUARY–MAY 1997)
Transcribed new data (transcripts 10, 14, 15) and identified other transcripts for transcription and identified extracts within these. Became interested in how doctors' clients responded to the offer to see the health adviser. Key themes: offers of screening tests for other STDs; offers to see the health adviser; and offers by doctors and health advisers.

This extract from Vicki's diary covers most of what a research diary should contain, namely (adapted in part from Cryer, 1996: 74):

- your research activities with dates
- your reading (see below)
- details of data collected
- directions of data analysis including 'special achievements, dead-ends and surprises'
- your own personal reactions
- your supervisor's reactions and suggestions.

It is also possible to write a research diary in a more structured form. For instance, in ethnographic research it may make sense to distinguish data analysis from the data itself, using square brackets for analytic observations (Hammersley and Atkinson, 1983: 164).

In a still more formalized approach, following Glaser and Strauss (1967), Laurel Richardson (1994) has suggested that you organize your notes into four different categories:

1 *Observation notes* (ON): 'fairly accurate renditions of what I see, hear, feel, taste, and so on'.
2 *Methodological notes* (MN): 'messages to myself regarding how to collect data'.
3 *Theoretical notes* (TN): 'hunches, hypotheses . . . critiques of what I am doing/thinking/seeing'.
4 *Personal notes* (PN): 'feeling statements about the research, the people I am talking to . . . my doubts, my anxieties, my pleasures' (1994: 526).

The truism that 'there is no one right method' applies to the keeping of research diaries as to so many other aspects of research. Whether you use a more or less structured method of diary-keeping, the most important thing about keeping a research diary is that it will encourage you to be *meticulous* in record-keeping and *reflective* about your data. As Hammersley and Atkinson comment:

> The construction of such notes . . . constitutes precisely the sort of internal dialogue, or thinking aloud, that is the essence of reflexive ethnography . . . Rather than coming to take one's understanding on trust, one is forced to question *what* one knows, *how* such knowledge has been acquired, the *degree of certainty* of such knowledge, and what further lines of inquiry are implied. (1983: 165)

SUMMARY

Keeping a record should involve both making an ordered record of your reading and keeping a research diary. In a research diary, you can show your readers the development of your thinking; help your own reflection; improve your time management; and provide ideas for the future direction of your work. As we see in Chapter 19, by keeping a research diary you can also be producing a substantial part of the methodology chapter of your thesis.

Further reading

On keeping a record of your reading, see Strauss and Corbin's *Basics of Qualitative Research* (Sage, 1990), Chapter 4. Pat Cryer's *The Research Student's Guide to Success* (Open University Press, 1996), Chapter 7, is a useful account of why and how to keep a research diary. On keeping more specialized notes about your data, see Richardson (1994) and Strauss and Corbin, Chapter 12.

Exercise 14.1

Below is an extract of around 300 words from my book
Discourses of Counselling: HIV Counselling as Social Interaction.

1 Read the passage and make notes from it (no more than 100 words) appropriate to a thesis on the nature of professional–client communication.
2 Now repeat the process on the assumption that your thesis topic is 'effective AIDS counselling'.
3 What relevance, if any, does this extract have to your own research? Note that such relevance can be methodological and theoretical as well as substantive. This means that a reading can be useful even if your substantive topic is very different.

Three major points have emerged from this discussion of a small number of post-test counselling interviews. First, following Peräkylä (1995), 'cautiousness' is seen, once more, to be a major feature of HIV counselling. This is true of the activities of both counsellors and clients. Thus, these counsellors seek to align their clients to the disclosure of their test-result, while clients, to whom the character of counselling is presumably 'opaque', often demur at taking any action which might demand an immediate telling of their test-result (or indeed, many other activities, like directly demanding clarification of the validity of HIV-tests) even when, as here, given the right to decide the agenda of their counselling interview. However, these agenda-offers, unlike the alignment strategies discussed by Maynard (1991) and Bergmann (1992), are being used in an environment where the upcoming diagnosis is likely to be heard as 'good'.

Second, we have seen how, when clients respond to agenda-offers by introducing other topics than the test-result (e.g. volunteering statements about themselves or asking, usually indirectly, about the validity of the HIV-test), they seem to 'kick in' standard counselling responses (e.g. information and requests for specification). While such responses are consonant with normative standards of good counselling practice, they are, once again, produced in an environment in which their positioning (prior to the telling of the test-result) may be problematic.

Finally, we have demonstrated that, for at least one client, this delay in telling is problematic. As Ex 7 (and its continuations) showed, this client analysed the delay in the delivery of his test-result as implying that C was about to deliver a 'positive' result – by referring to 'support groups' for HIV-positive people.

This apparent lack of fit between a delayed delivery of the test-result and its content (i.e. as HIV-negative) leads directly into some fairly clear practical implications. (Silverman, 1997a: 106)

15

Relations in the Field

Two French qualitative sociologists have recently reminded us of the close association between ethnographic research and a sense of the studied world as a 'field' with emergent properties. As they put it:

> Ethnographic studies are carried out to satisfy three simultaneous requirements associated with the study of human activities:
>
> (i)   the need for an empirical approach
> (ii) the need to remain open to elements that cannot be codified at the time of the study
> (iii) a concern for grounding the phenomena observed in the field. (Baszanger and Dodier, 1997: 8)

A whole series of practical questions about fieldwork now arise:

> what is the status of this 'specific' context in which the study takes place? How is it described? How is this framework delineated, since it is not a here-and-now situation, nor a situation in which mankind as a whole is characterized through the fundamental properties of every one of its activities? (1997: 11)

However, Baszanger and Dodier recognize that this concern for explaining observed activities in terms of social context does not apply to all qualitative research:

> this reference to field experience nevertheless distinguishes ethnographic studies from other observation methods that are not grounded in a specific field (analysis of conversation, situated cognition and ethnomethodology). (1997: 11)

So the meaning and significance of 'relations in the field' will vary according to the model of social research with which you are operating. For instance, as Gubrium and Holstein (1997) point out, while naturalists seek to understand social reality as 'it really is', using methods like prolonged observation and open-ended observation, this position is challenged from a range of directions by conversation analysts, feminists and postmodernists.

The obvious implication is that 'relations in the field' cannot simply be a technical issue to be resolved by technical means. Nevertheless, for ease of presentation, I will begin with some more practical questions, returning to the crucial analytic issues at the end of this chapter.

The following five practical questions are often asked about 'field' research:

• Are certain field settings more 'closed' to observation?
• Must access always be overt?
• What ethical issues lie in wait for me?
• Is feedback to research subjects necessary and/or useful?
• Can I learn anything from relations with subjects in the field?

I discuss below each of these questions. Each question will lead on to the discussion of possible 'solutions' and several case studies will be used in illustration of these points.

SETTINGS AND ACCESS

Textbooks (e.g. Hornsby-Smith, 1993: 53; Walsh, 1998: 224–5) usually distinguish two kinds of research setting:

• 'closed' or 'private' settings (organizations, deviant groups) where access is controlled by gatekeepers
• 'open' or 'public' settings (e.g. vulnerable minorities, public records or settings) where access is freely available but not always without difficulty, either practical (e.g. finding a role for the researcher in a public setting) or ethical (e.g. should we be intruding upon vulnerable minorities?).

Depending on the contingencies of the setting (and the research problem chosen) two kinds of research access may be obtained:

• 'covert' access without subjects' knowledge
• 'overt' access based on informing subjects and getting their agreement, often through 'gatekeepers'.

The impression you give may be very important in deciding whether you get overt access:

> Whether or not people have knowledge of social research, they are often more concerned with what kind of *person* the researcher is than with the research itself. They will try to gauge how far he or she can be trusted, what he or she might be able to offer as an acquaintance or a friend, and perhaps also how easily he or she could be manipulated or exploited. (Hammersley and Atkinson, 1983: 78)

Five ways of securing and maintaining overt access have been noted.

IMPRESSION MANAGEMENT
Impression management is to do with the 'fronts' that we present to others (see Goffman, 1959). It involves avoiding giving an impression that might

pose an obstacle to access, while more positively conveying an impression appropriate to the situation (see Hammersley and Atkinson, 1983: 78–88). For instance, I have failed to gain access, despite initial expressions of interest, in two settings. In a paediatric clinic in the early 1980s, a very conservatively dressed physician, spotting my leather jacket, said I was being 'disrespectful of his patients' and threw me out! Fifteen years before that, as a novice researcher, I let slip over lunch that I was thinking of moving from the UK to North America when I had completed my PhD. This attitude was apparently viewed as improperly 'instrumental' by my host organization and the promised access was subsequently refused. The implication of this latter incident is that there is no 'time out' in field relations and that the most apparently informal occasions are times when you will often be judged.

OBTAINING 'BOTTOM-UP' ACCESS

This can sometimes be forgotten at great cost. For instance, in the early 1970s, the access granted by the head of personnel at a large organization was put in danger by the fact that I had not explained my aims properly to his subordinates. This underlines the point that access should not be regarded as a once and for all situation.

BEING NON-JUDGEMENTAL

Being non-judgemental is often a key to acceptance in many settings, including informal subcultures and practitioners of a particular trade or profession. While the relativist tendencies of many social sciences may allow the researcher sincerely to profess non-judgementality on particular groups' values and practices, this is not always the case when you are studying certain forms of professional practice. Indeed to the researcher who thinks they know something about 'professional dominance' or even just basic communication skills, it is very easy to appear judgemental. However, this not only endangers field relations but also espouses a dangerous orthodoxy.

The 'divine orthodoxy' is that people are 'dopes' (see Silverman, 1997b: 23–6). Interview respondents' knowledge is assumed to be imperfect: indeed they may even lie to us. In the same way, practitioners (like doctors or counsellors) are assumed always to depart from normative standards of good practice.

Under the remit of the divine orthodoxy, the social scientist is transformed into a philosopher-king (or queen) who can always see through people's claims and know better than they do. Of course, this assumption of superiority to others usually guarantees that access will not be obtained or, if obtained, will be unsuccessful!

OFFERING FEEDBACK

Some research subjects will actually want your judgements – providing they are of an 'acceptable' kind. For instance, business organizations will expect some 'pay-off' from giving you access. I discuss what this might involve shortly.

ESTABLISHING A CONTRACT
Establishing a contract with the people researched may vary from an information sheet, read and agreed by an individual, to a full-blown contract (but see Punch, 1986, on post-contract problems).

I have so far avoided discussing 'covert' access, i.e. access obtained without subjects' knowledge. We should not assume that 'covert' access always involves possible offence. For instance, on a course I am currently teaching, students have been asked to engage in a small exercise where they observe people exchanging glances in an everyday setting (see Sacks, 1992, Vol. 1: 81–94). Providing the students are reasonably sensitive about this and refrain from staring at others, I do not envisage any problems arising.

However, in other cases, covert observation can lead to severe ethical problems as well as physical danger to the researcher. For instance, Fielding (1982) obtained permission to research a far right British political party but still felt it necessary to supplement official access with covert observation.

In this new situation, he put himself at some potential risk as well as creating ethical dilemmas relating to how much he revealed to his subjects and to outside authorities. It is such ethical issues which I will discuss in the next section.

ETHICS IN QUALITATIVE RESEARCH

As the German sociologist Max Weber (1946) pointed out in the early years of this century, all research is contaminated to some extent by the values of the researcher. Only through those values do certain problems get identified and studied in particular ways. Even the commitment to scientific (or rigorous) method is itself, as Weber emphasizes, a value. Finally, the conclusions and implications to be drawn from a study are, Weber stresses, largely grounded in the moral and political beliefs of the researcher.

From an ethical point of view, Weber was fortunate in that much of his empirical research was based on documents and texts that were already in the public sphere. In many other kinds of social science research, ethical issues are much more to the fore. For instance, both qualitative and quantitative researchers studying human subjects ponder over the dilemma of wanting to give full information to subjects but not 'contaminating' their research by informing subjects too specifically about the research question to be studied.

Moreover, when you are studying people's behaviour or asking them questions, not only the values of the researcher but the researcher's responsibilities to those studied have to be faced.

Jennifer Mason (1996: 166–7) discusses two ways in which such ethical issues impinge upon the qualitative researcher:

1   The rich and detailed character of much qualitative research can mean intimate engagement with the public and private lives of individuals.
2   The changing directions of interest and access during a qualitative study mean that new and unexpected ethical dilemmas are likely to arise during the course of your research.

Mason suggests that one way to confront these problems is to try to clarify your intentions while you are formulating your research problem. Three ways of doing this are to:

1   Decide what is the purpose(s) of your research, e.g. self-advancement, political advocacy etc.
2   Examine which individuals or groups might be interested or affected by your research topic.
3   Consider what are the implications for these parties of framing your research topic in the way you have done (1996: 29–30).

Ethical procedures can also be clarified by consulting the ethical guidelines of one's professional association. All such guidelines stress the importance of 'informed consent' where possible (see Punch, 1994: 88–94). The nature of 'informed consent' is set out in Table 15.1.

However, initial consent may not be enough, particularly where you are making a recording. In such cases, it often is proper to obtain further consent to how the data may be used (see Table 15.2).

I have now responded to three of the five questions with which I began, namely:

•   Are certain field settings more 'closed' to observation?
•   Must access always be overt?
•   What ethical issues lie in wait for me?

However, so far, I have provided fairly general answers to these questions. I now want to slow the pace down and give you an example of a case study. I hope this will 'flesh out the bare bones' of these important issues.

TABLE 15.1   **What is informed consent?**

•   Giving information about the research which is relevant to subjects' decisions about whether to participate
•   Making sure that subjects understand that information (e.g. by providing information sheets written in subjects' language)
•   Ensuring that participation is voluntary (e.g. by requiring written consent)
•   Where subjects are not competent to agree (e.g. small children) obtaining consent by proxy (e.g. from their parents)

Source: adapted from Kent, 1996: 19–20

TABLE 15.2   **A sample consent form for studies of language use**

As part of this project, we have made a photographic, audio and/or video recording of you. We would like you to indicate below what uses of these records you are willing to consent to. This is completely up to you. We will only use the records in ways that you agree to. In any use of these records, names will not be identified.

1   The records can be studied by the research team for use in the research project
2   The records can be used for scientific publications and/or meetings
3   The written transcript and/or records can be used by other researchers
4   The records can be shown in public presentations to non-scientific groups
5   The records can be used on television or radio

Source: adapted from ten Have, 1998: Appendix C, based on a form developed by Susan Ervin-Tripp, Psychology Department, University of California at Berkeley

A CASE STUDY: OPEN ACCESS TO A PUBLIC SETTING

This case study is drawn from my work on HIV counselling (Silverman, 1997b: 226–8) and has already been referred to in Chapter 7. It illustrates the changing trajectory of one qualitative research project according to the nature and kind of access and funding and my relations with people 'in the field'.

In 1987, I was given permission to sit in at a weekly clinic held at the genito-urinary department of an English inner-city hospital (Silverman, 1989a). The clinic's purpose was to monitor the progress of HIV-positive patients who were taking the drug AZT (Retrovir). AZT, which seems able to slow down the rate at which the virus reproduces itself, was then at an experimental stage of its development.

Like any observational study, the aim was to gather first-hand information about social processes in a 'naturally occurring' context. No attempt was made to interview the individuals concerned because the focus was upon what they actually did in the clinic rather than upon what they thought about what they did. The researcher was present in the consulting room at a side angle to both doctors and patient.

I set out below some of the things that happened during this research using indicative headings.

MAKING CONCESSIONS
Patients' consent for the researcher's presence was obtained by the senior doctor who preferred to do it this way (this was effective but was it ethical?). Given the presumed sensitivity of the occasion, tape-recording was not attempted. Instead, detailed handwritten notes were kept, using a separate sheet for each consultation. Because observational methods were rare in this area, the study was essentially exploratory.

GIVING FEEDBACK
Along the way, I also discovered how an ethos of 'positive thinking' was central to many patients' accounts and how doctors systematically concentrated on the 'bodies' rather than the 'minds' of their patients. This led on to

some practical questions about the division of labour between doctors and counsellors.

GOOD LUCK

About the time I was writing up this research, Kaye Wellings, who then was working for the publicly funded Health Education Authority (HEA), approached me about the possibility of extending my research to HIV counselling. Until that time, the HEA had been funding research on the effectiveness of 'safer sex' messages carried in the mass media. In the light of the explosion in the number of HIV tests in the UK in the late 1980s, Kaye thought it might be useful to take a longer look at the effectiveness of the health promotion messages being delivered in counselling people around the HIV antibody test.

I was interested in such a study for two reasons. First, it was the logical development of my study of medical interviews with AIDS patients. Second, it offered the opportunity to pursue my interest in looking at how communication between professionals and their clients worked out in practice – as opposed to the injunctions of textbooks and training manuals. Consequently, I submitted a research proposal and received funding from the HEA for 30 months beginning in late 1988.

TROUBLES WITH ACCESS

As it turned out, receiving the funding was only the first part of what became a battle to recruit HIV-testing centres for the research. It must be remembered that the late 1980s was a time when AIDS health workers were being flooded by patients and by requests from researchers anxious to study AIDS care. Apart from such overload, two other factors complicated access. First, obviously, were the multiple ethical issues involved in studying consultations where patients were asked to reveal the most intimate aspects of their behaviour. Second, extra patients and government worries about the AIDS 'pandemic' had brought sudden huge increases in resources to the previously 'Cinderella' branch of medicine treating patients with sexually transmitted diseases. Following the usual pattern, these resource changes produced 'turf' battles between different professions and different centres involved in the AIDS field (see Silverman, 1990).

All this meant that many months were taken in obtaining research access. One leading British centre turned me down, offering the understandable reason that they were already overloaded with researchers. At another such centre, a doctor gave me access but the counsellors subsequently proved very resistant to me observing or tape-recording their HIV consultations. Eventually, a compromise was reached whereby I myself was required to request patients to agree to participate in the research. Predictably, very few agreed in these circumstances.

MORE LUCK

Just as I thought that I had been funded for a study that I could never carry out, my luck began to turn. Riva Miller and Robert Bor agreed to offer me access to their counselling work with respectively haemophiliacs and the general population at the Royal Free Hospital (RFH) in London. This was a major breakthrough in two respects. First, Miller and Bor had just produced a major book (Miller and Bor, 1988) on using 'systemic' method in AIDS counselling. Second, Miller and Bor had a video archive of the work of their clinics going back to the early 1980s.

On the basis of my access at the RFH, a major pharmaceuticals company, Glaxo Holdings PLC (now Glaxo Wellcome), agreed to fund a two-year study (subsequently increased to three years) of the video archive. I was then lucky enough to recruit Anssi Peräkylä from Finland as Glaxo Research Fellow to work on this archive. Anssi had already conducted distinguished ethnographic work in hospital settings. Following his appointment, he more or less taught himself conversation analysis (CA) and had finished his PhD on the RFH data in three years, as well as publishing many articles both jointly with me and/or Bor and on his own. Gradually, other centres joined the project and data were also obtained directly from centres in the USA and Trinidad, as well as from Douglas Maynard's US HIV counselling materials.

ETHICAL ISSUES AGAIN

As the research started to take off, great attention had to be paid to the ethical issues involved. We ended up with a method of recruitment whereby counsellors themselves explained the research to patients (often with the aid of written materials) and invited them to participate. Consent was sought on the understanding that the anonymity of all patients would be strictly protected by concealing their names (and other identifying information) in reports or publications. In addition, only Peräkylä, myself and a limited number of trained researchers and transcribers would have access to the audiotapes. The RFH videotapes were given additional protection: Peräkylä himself transcribed them, so access to them was limited to the two of us and the videos were never to be publicly shown or indeed to leave the premises of the RFH.

THE CONTINGENCY OF METHODOLOGY

In a multiple centre study, I could not, as in my earlier work, be physically present as all the data were gathered. Instead, the audiotapes were simply sent to me by each of the centres for analysis. Soon we were inundated by data to be passed on to our main transcriber, Dr David Greatbatch, himself a distinguished CA researcher.

However, given the high quality of transcription required and our limited resources, it became totally impractical to transcribe all the tapes. Instead, a few interviews were transcribed from each centre. On this basis, what I can best call 'candidate hypotheses' were developed about particular features in the talk, for instance how health advice was delivered and received. Peräkylä and I would then transcribe multiple instances from many more interviews where relevant phenomena seemed to occur.

In this way, the initial hypotheses were refined and subject to the test of 'deviant cases' which we actively sought out in our data. Overall, our method had much in common with the traditional method of 'analytic induction' commonly used by anthropologists and ethnographers (see Silverman, 1993: Ch. 7).

Let us now return to the two remaining questions:

- Is feedback to research subjects necessary and/or useful?
- Can I learn anything from relations with subjects in the field?

As we shall see, my case study bears on both these questions.

FEEDBACK: CASE STUDIES

> The bottom line for practitioners is always, 'So what?' A qualitative researcher's efforts to convey nonjudgmental objectivity is likely to be perceived instead as a typical academic cop-out. (Wolcott, 1990: 59)

In order to address practitioners' 'So what?' question, during and after the research described above, I held many workshops for AIDS counsellors – including many who had not participated in the study. To give some idea of the extent of this 'feedback', between 1989 and 1994 I ran four workshops on the research for counsellors in London (two at hospitals, one at Goldsmiths' College and one at The Royal Society of Medicine), as well as three workshops in Australian centres, three in Trinidad and Tobago, and one each in the USA, Finland and Sweden. In addition, each participating centre was given a detailed report of our findings.

At these workshops, we did not shield behind a posture of scientific neutrality. But neither did we seek to instruct counsellors about their presumed 'failings'. Instead, we spoke about the ways in which our data showed that all communication formats and techniques had mixed consequences. We then invited our audience to discuss, in the light of their own priorities and resources, the implications for their practice. Moreover, when asked, we were not afraid to suggest possible practical options.

In my judgement, these meetings were successful, not least because our detailed transcripts showed features of counselling of which the practitioners themselves were often unaware. Often such features revealed how these people were cleverer than they had realized in following their own theoretical precepts and achieving their desired goals.

However, less experienced researchers may be more hesitant to offer feedback to practitioners and organizations. In this case, Wolcott (1990) offers the three ideas set out in Table 15.3.

Of course, not all qualitative research is concerned with organizations or professional practitioners. What kind of feedback is possible when you are studying non-work-related activities?

It is important that you try to offer feedback to all parties that are under

TABLE 15.3   **Giving appropriate feedback to practitioners**

1   Ask for the kind of additional information required for you to make a recommendation (e.g. what exactly the organization is trying to accomplish)
2   Identify seeming paradoxes in the pursuit of goals (e.g. doctors who encourage their patients to communicate and to make choices may be the most autocratic)
3   Identify alternatives to current practices and offer to assess these

Source: Wolcott, 1990: 60

study. So, if your target is, say, the activities of counsellors or doctors, then you have not finished your task without offering some degree of feedback to their clients or patients. One way to do this is to utilize already existing networks, for example patients' or community groups. So during my work on paediatric clinics in the early 1980s, I spoke to parents' groups at heart and diabetic clinics. For instance, I used my clinic data to show mothers of diabetic adolescents that their feelings of inadequacy were common and probably inevitable given the guilt-provoking character of diabetic control and the usual rebelliousness of teenagers.

Where it is difficult to find such community groups, you may well find that participants in a study welcome receiving their own transcript of relevant data. For instance, a transcript of your own medical interview may work as a useful reminder of what the doctor said. And a transcript of a life-history interview may give a respondent a tangible autobiographical record.

I now want to move from ethical and practical matters to the methodological issue suggested by my final question:

• Can I learn anything from relations with subjects in the field?

One way of answering this question is to think through how your own identity was viewed by the participants. As my case study showed, my identity and aims as a researcher were viewed differently, in various contexts, by different professionals such as counsellors and doctors and by research funding bodies. However, this was viewed not just as a 'trouble' for the smooth running of the research but also as a source of data about how organizations worked (see also Peräkylä, 1989).

The second case study below shows how another identity, that of gender, can be relevant to field research.

A CASE STUDY: GENDER IN THE FIELD

Almost all the 'classics' of the Chicago School were written by men, and those researchers who rose up the academic hierarchy to become full professors were also mostly men (see Warren, 1988: 11). Increasingly, the gender of fieldworkers themselves was seen to play a crucial factor in observational research. Informants were shown to say different things to male and female researchers. For instance, in a study of a nude beach, when approached by someone of a different gender, people emphasized their interest in 'freedom and naturalism'. Conversely, where the researcher was the same gender as the informant, people were far more likely to discuss their sexual interests (Warren and Rasmussen, 1977, reported by Warren, 1988).

In studies which involved extended stays in 'the field', people have also been shown to make assumptions based upon the gender of the researcher. For instance, particularly in rural communities, young, single women may be precluded from participating in many activities or asking many questions. Conversely, female gender may sometimes accord privileged access. For instance, Oboler (1986) reports that her pregnancy increased her rapport with her Kenyan informants, while Warren (1988: 18) suggests that women field-workers can make use of the sexist assumption that only men engage in 'important business' by treating their 'invisibility' as a resource. Equally, male fieldworkers may be excluded or exclude themselves from contact with female respondents in certain kinds of situation (see McKeganey and Bloor, 1991).

One danger in all this, particularly in the past, was that fieldworkers failed to report or reflect upon the influence of gender in their fieldwork. For instance, in a study of a large local government organization, we discussed but did not report the different kinds of situations to which the male and female researchers gained easy access (Silverman and Jones, 1976). Moreover, even as the role of doing fieldwork as a woman has become more addressed, hardly any attention has been paid by researchers to questions of male gender (McKeganey and Bloor, 1991: 198).

Nonetheless, as fashions change, it is possible to swing too far and accord gender issues too much importance. As McKeganey and Bloor (1991: 195–6) argue, there are two important issues relevant to the significance of gender in fieldwork. First, the influence of gender may be negotiable with respondents and not simply ascribed. Second, we should resist 'the tendency to employ gender as an explanatory catch-all' (1991: 196).

For instance, McKeganey and Bloor suggest variables other than gender, like age and social class, may also be important in fieldwork. Equally, I would argue, following Schegloff (1991), that we need to demonstrate that participants are actually attending to gender in what they are doing, rather than just work with our intuitions or even with statistical correlations. None of this should imply that it would be correct to swing full circle and, like an earlier generation, ignore gender issues in research. It is incumbent upon fieldworkers to reflect upon the basis and status of their observations. Clearly, how the researcher and the community studied respond to their gender can provide crucial insights into field realities. Indeed, we would do well to become conscious that even taken-for-granted assumptions may be culturally and historically specific. For instance, Carol Warren suggests that:

> The focal gender *myth* of field research is the greater communicative skills and less threatening nature of the female fieldworker. (1988: 64, my emphasis)

207

As Warren notes, the important thing is to treat such assumptions not as 'revealed truths' but as 'accounts' which are historically situated.

This second case study shows how gender may help you learn something from relations with subjects in the field. Another way in which researchers have attempted to use field relations as data is by seeking and responding to comments made by participants about research conducted upon them. Returning to an issue I first raised in Chapter 13, can responses to feedback be used as a means of validating your research findings?

FEEDBACK AS A VALIDATION EXERCISE?

Reason and Rowan (1981) criticize researchers who are fearful of 'contaminating their data with the experience of the subject'. On the contrary, they argue, good research goes back to the subjects with the tentative results, and refines them in the light of the subjects' reactions.

This is just what Michael Bloor (1978; 1983) attempted in his research on doctors' decision-making. Bloor (1978) discusses three procedures which attempt respondent validation:

1   The researcher seeks to predict members' classifications in actual situations of their use (see Frake, 1964).
2   The researcher prepares hypothetical cases and predicts respondents' responses to them (see also Frake, 1964).
3   The researcher provides respondents with a research report and records their reactions to it.

In his study of doctors' decision-making in adeno-tonsillectomy cases, Bloor used the third method, hoping for 'a sort of self-recognition effect' (1978: 549). Although Bloor reports that he was able to make some useful modifications as a result of the surgeons' comments, he reports many reservations. These centre around whether respondents are able to follow a report written for a sociological audience and, even if it is presented intelligibly, whether they will (or should) have any interest in it (1978: 550). A further problem, noted by Abrams, is that 'overt respondent validation is only possible if the results on the analysis are compatible with the self-image of the respondents' (1984: 8).

Bloor's point has been very effectively taken up by Fielding and Fielding (1986) (respondent validation is also criticized by Bryman, 1988: 78–9). The Fieldings concede that subjects being studied may have additional knowledge, especially about the context of their actions. However:

> there is no reason to assume that members have privileged status as commentators on their actions . . . such feedback cannot be taken as direct validation or refutation of the observer's inferences. Rather such processes of so-called 'validation' should be treated as yet another source of data and insight. (1986: 43)

I can only add that, if feedback is a highly problematic part of validating research, this does *not* mean that it should be ignored as a way of maintaining contact with subjects in the field. However, this issue should not be *confused* with the validation of research findings.

Moreover, as Bloor points out, the problematic research status of this activity need not mean that attempts at respondents' validation have *no* value. They do generate further data which, while not validating the research report, often suggest interesting paths for further analysis (Bloor, 1983: 172).

Of course, in referring to the function of 'accounts', we are already entering into an analytical perspective on how social reality operates. This is because, as noted at the outset of this chapter, the issue of 'relations in the field' is riddled with theoretical assumptions.

SUMMARY

In this chapter, I have discussed how to respond to *five* practical questions in doing fieldwork:

1   Are certain field settings more 'closed' to observation?
2   Must access always be overt?
3   What ethical issues lie in wait for you?
4   Is feedback to research subjects necessary and/or useful?
5   Can you learn anything from relations with subjects in the field?

Throughout, I have emphasized that 'relations in the field' are theoretically saturated. This cannot, therefore, be simply a technical issue to be resolved by technical means.

Further reading

Hammersley and Atkinson (1983: 54–76) provide a useful discussion of the practicalities of obtaining access to individuals, groups and organizations. A more introductory account of these issues, appropriate to the undergraduate researcher, is found in Walsh (1998). Nigel Fielding (1982) is a very interesting account of the perils of observational research. Issues of ethics in qualitative research are well discussed in Jennifer Mason's *Qualitative Researching* (Sage, 1996), Chapters 2, 4 and 8. Peräkylä (1989) and McKeganey and Bloor (1991) provide revealing accounts of the negotiation of identity in fieldwork. Before you contemplate taking your findings back to your subjects, you should read Michael Bloor (1978; 1983).

Exercise 15.1

Consult your research notes on your contacts 'in the field'. Now answer the following questions:

1 What 'successes' and 'troubles' have occurred during your fieldwork?
2 How can you treat such events as data?
3 What theoretical ideas can you use to help you (if you need help, consult Peräkylä, 1989, and McKeganey and Bloor, 1991)?

Exercise 15.2

Make a list of the ethical problems that you have detected in your research. Now explain how you have resolved them.

Then give your account, together with your research diary, to your supervisor or a fellow student. Ask them whether they are satisfied with how you have (a) identified and (b) handled ethical issues.

16
Getting Feedback

Analysing research data and writing up our findings are never solitary activities – although this is certainly how they can seem as we labour in front of our PC screen in the small hours. In practice, researching involves entering a series of social relationships. These include those between student and supervisor; student and fellow student; student and members of the wider academic community; and student and research subjects in 'the field'.

As we saw in the previous chapter, such relationships need not just be viewed as potential or real sources of 'trouble'. Instead, they can and should be treated as important sources of insight into how well we are practising our research skills. Effective feedback is an essential resource for effective research. As two psychologists have put it:

> Adults learn best in situations where they can practise and receive feedback, in a controlled, non-threatening environment. So a good principle to aim for is: no procedure, technique, skill, etc., which is relevant for your thesis project should be exercised by you there for the first time. (Phillips and Pugh, 1994: 52)

In this short chapter, I will discuss two means of obtaining feedback on your research:

- by writing draft papers
- by giving oral presentations.

WRITING

Delivering papers on agreed topics at regular intervals to your supervisor is the standard university method of working towards a final piece of assessed research. Constructive feedback from your supervisor can encourage you to scale new heights. By contrast, where that feedback is minimal or even destructive, your whole enterprise may be threatened.

So, if your supervisor is very critical of a paper you have submitted, you should expect to be told how you can improve your work and to be offered practical suggestions rather than woolly generalities. For instance, being told to think 'more critically' or to 'be more rigorous' is unlikely to be helpful. By contrast, specific advice about a new topic or a different way of pursuing one of your existing topics should give you some useful impetus.

But your supervisor is not the only person who can give you useful feedback on your work. Your fellow students, particularly those working in similar areas, should be delighted to give you feedback. In return, they will learn about related work and have the opportunity to test their ideas out on you.

Sometimes you will need to take the initiative to form such a student support group. Sometimes, as I do with my own research students, your supervisor will organize workshops for students working on similar topics or using similar methods to present and discuss their data. In either case, you will gain the opportunity to test out preliminary ideas in a non-threatening environment.

Writing for your peers or speaking to them is wonderful practice at getting the correct level for your thesis. The great temptation in writing up what may be your first piece of serious research is to try to achieve an exalted level of technical language in order to impress your supervisor. Unfortunately, this attempt often leads to clumsy jargon which clouds your real line of argument and confuses your readers.

In discussing writing a thesis, Wolcott wisely addresses this issue of the level at which you write:

> Write for your peers. Pitch the level of discussion to an audience of readers who do *not* know what you are talking about. Write your dissertation with fellow graduate students in mind, not your learned committee members. Address your subsequent studies to the many who do not know, not the few who do. (1990: 47)

Contrary to appearances, Wolcott's injunction 'write for your peers' is *not* a cop-out. For most researchers, the most difficult thing to do is to write with such clarity that they can be understood and enjoyed by non-specialists. Indeed, for some researchers, the hardest thing to grasp is that writing should always be tailored for as big an audience as possible and that this means thinking about what that audience may know already and expect from you. Naturally, the same applies to oral presentations.

SPEAKING

Early on in my academic career, I was invited to talk about my research at a seminar at another university. I had already grasped the need to tailor my remarks to a particular audience and so had prepared two different talks on my research. One was highly specialist, the other was non-technical. Unfortunately, on that day, I had misjudged my audience and brought with me what turned out to be the 'wrong' talk. Faced with a heavyweight group of specialists, I was insufficiently experienced to improvise and was forced to present the 'Mickey Mouse' version of my research!

I still cringe when I think of this experience. However, although I failed embarrassingly on this occasion, I had at least been partially correct in my method: I had attempted to prepare a talk with an audience in mind (see Cryer, 1996: 133). Just as we design our ordinary conversation for particular recipients (children, colleagues etc.) so 'recipient design' should always go into your oral presentations. As Gary Marx comments:

> Try to remember who you are talking to, and the differential stake you and your audience have in your topic. Gear your talk to your audience. (1997: 107)

Following Marx, you will clearly want to give different kinds of talks to experts in your field, to participants in your research and to general but non-specialist academic audiences. For each audience, you should choose a particular focus (e.g. theory, method, substance) and an appropriate vocabulary (see Strauss and Corbin, 1990: 226–9).

However, such 'recipient design' is insufficient. You must all have had the experience of speakers who only have time to get through a small part of their material or who overrun and use up the time for questions. Good time management is a quality possessed by effective speakers. If you think you will not have the confidence to improvise to beat the clock, then it is wise to try out your talk beforehand with a watch nearby.

The usual experience is that it takes far longer to get through your material than you expect. So take the minimum of material in one file and, if necessary, bring a 'comfort blanket' of additional material in another file to use in the unlikely event that you need it.

Finally, never read out a talk. I know having your full script is a source of comfort. As Gary Marx puts it:

> The fact that you get only one chance with a live audience may engender anxiety and the written word is a safety net. But it has a pre-determined, even stultifying quality, which denies the fluid and interactive nature of live presentations. (1997: 107)

But think back to all those boring talks you have attended in which the speaker had his head buried in his script. Do you really want to inflict that on your audience? More positively, 'You will never know what verbal riffs lie buried in your consciousness if you always cling to the security of the page' (1997: 107). Instead, try to present your points through uncluttered visual aids (slides, overhead projector transparencies). Where you need to provide extensive material (e.g. long transcripts or tables), then distribute handouts.

Above all, try to grab your audience's attention at the outset. There are many tactics you can use at the start of your talk:

- Begin with a puzzle, as in a detective novel.
- Start with an interesting data extract.

- Start with a personal anecdote about how you became interested in your topic.
- If you are not the first speaker, try to relate what you have to say to what has gone before.
- Tell an apposite witty story (but only if this comes naturally!).

Let me now illustrate these suggestions by some examples.

THE ART OF PRESENTING RESEARCH

You will have gathered already that, in my view, even the most astounding research can sound dull if not properly presented. Unfortunately, this does not mean that poor research can be retrieved if you are a witty and effective speaker, because you will eventually be found out! But effective presentation of good research should be your aim.

To flesh out the bare bones of my argument, I have taken extracts from my reports on presentations by research students completing their first year in my own department. Naturally, to protect the innocent, I have given these students false names.

Each student was allowed up to fifteen minutes to make a presentation to their fellow students on their progress during their first year and their plans for further work. Then ten to fifteen minutes were allowed for questions.

Just as we tend to preface 'bad' news by 'good' news when giving information in everyday life, let me begin with some reports of 'good' practice. Below are some extracts from my reports.

Good practice

Pat's talk was lively and clear, making good use of overhead transparencies. She responded well to questions. This was a well-focused presentation, lively and interesting. The handouts were helpful and the video data were fascinating.

Derek gave a lively and relatively clear talk, making good use of his overheads. He spoke with some humour, gave an 'agenda' to his audience and explained the difficulties of his project.

This was highly professional with good use of overheads and handouts. Hazel used her limited time well, managing to accommodate her talk to the fifteen minutes available. Her answers to questions were most effective, giving me the impression that she is already in control of her topic.

This was a well-focused presentation, lively and interesting. Sasha's answers to questions were good. Overall, I felt this was an excellent presentation based upon a piece of highly professional research. My views seem to be

214

shared by the students present, one of whom remarked that she hoped her own work would be up to this standard in a year or two's time. Congratulations are due to Sasha and her supervisor.

This was a well-focused presentation, lively and interesting and improvised rather than read. The audience's attention was held throughout. Ray's answers to questions were thoughtful and helpful. In particular, he was able to establish a dialogue with students from a range of backgrounds and was at home responding to theoretical and practical issues. I especially liked Ray's attempt to derive methodological issues from the data analysis. There were time problems from which Ray will have learned something. Overall, I felt this was an excellent presentation based upon a piece of highly professional research.

SUMMARY
The following are the qualities that impressed me in these presentations:

- liveliness
- not reading out a prepared text
- recipient design for the audience
- clarity
- effective visual aids
- humour
- explaining your agenda
- not minimizing your difficulties
- good time management
- good response to questions.

Now for the 'bad' news!

Bad practice

John was hampered by lack of preparation. His extempore presentation may have confused the audience by introducing too many topics and using too many examples which were not fully explained. His habit of turning his back on the audience to address the (empty) blackboard was unfortunate and, I am afraid, added to the impression of a non-user-friendly talk. This is disappointing given John's breadth of reading and excellent understanding. I think the only solution is to work harder on trying to relate his concerns to the interests and knowledge of particular audiences.

This was an interesting presentation. However, Bruce made things a little difficult for his audience by offering no initial agenda, by not using overheads and by having only one copy of some data extracts. He also ran into time problems which better planning could have obviated. This presentation will have given him the opportunity in future talks to think through his objectives and to offer more user-friendly methods.

215

This was probably too specialized for a mixed audience, although Larry responded clearly to questions. The talk improved when Larry departed from his script and gave an example (about record production) which brought to life the abstract concepts he was using. I strongly suggest that, in future, for such an audience, he uses more overheads and then talks around them, using such helpful examples.

SUMMARY
The following qualities concerned me in this group of presentations:

- lack of preparation
- too much material
- not looking at the audience
- lack of recipient design
- no agenda
- no visual aids
- poor time planning.

Most presentations fell between these extremes. I will conclude with some 'mixed' examples.

Mixed practice

Maurice gave a clear presentation using handouts and overheads. His delivery was good and appropriately recipient designed. My only suggestion is that he should try to type overheads and put less material on each sheet.

Stan had taken the trouble to prepare handouts. However, it was disappointing that, perhaps because of time limitations, he had not analysed the data provided. I would also have preferred him not to read out a paper. It is important to practise the art of talking using only a few props, like overheads, if you want to keep the audience's attention. Nonetheless, Stan's talk was well organized and timed and he offered interesting responses to questions, showing a pleasing ability to admit when he was unsure about a point.

As in an earlier talk, this was very professional, combining good overheads with helpful illustrations from video and audiotape. My only suggestion for Dean is that it might be helpful to give more guidance to the audience about the issues to look for before offering data.

Mary gave a confident, well-prepared talk based on a handout. She responded well to questions. My only suggestion is that, in future, she works more on integrating any handout with her talk so that her audience are not confused about what they should be attending to at any one time.

Yoko had thoughtfully prepared overheads but these were not as clearly related to her talk as they might have been. Although it is always very difficult to speak in one's second language, it is hard to keep the audience's attention when a paper is read. In my view, it is worth Yoko practising at giving presentations simply by talking around her overheads. One way to do this would be to focus on the nice examples of texts and images that she presented and to pull out her analytic and methodological points from them rather than to attempt to read a rather abstract paper.

Julia gave an engaging, lively presentation which held her audience throughout. I liked her explanation of the personal reasons behind her research and admired her ability to speak without notes. Her overheads were useful. Some minor suggestions for future talks: remember to avoid turning away from the audience to look at the screen; think about using other information sources as well as overheads (handouts of definitions would have been useful); and try out a talk beforehand so as to avoid time problems.

This was an interesting talk which carefully explained the issues involved for a non-specialist audience. Jane's account of how her interest in the topic 'coalesced' was very useful, as were her overhead transparencies (although, in future, she should note that these can be most effectively used by covering up parts until she gets on to them). She ran into some time difficulties and this is also something to watch in future. Overall, a good account of a fascinating topic.

Luigi made a good attempt to explain a difficult topic to a non-specialist audience. I particularly liked his account of his intellectual and personal background. In future, he will need to pay more attention to explaining his concepts and to time constraints.

SUMMARY
The following were the 'good' and 'bad' news about these presentations:

- using visual aids *but* these are poorly prepared
- well organized *but* reading out a prepared text
- giving examples of data *but* not explaining what to look for
- using handouts *but* not integrating them in the talk
- explaining the background *but* not explaining your concepts
- using overheads *but* turning away to look at them or having too much material on the screen.

Good and bad presentations

Take your oral presentations as seriously as you do your writing. Speak to your audience with clarity, logic, vigour, and examples that will grab them. (Marx, 1997: 107)

In Table 16.1, I set out what we have learnt about making an effective oral presentation of your research.

TABLE 16.1   Giving a talk: problems and solutions

Problem	Solution
Losing your audience	Recipient design
Overrunning	Don't prepare too much material
Boring your audience	Use visual aids: don't read out a talk

CONCLUSION: WHY DOES FEEDBACK MATTER?

There are two reasons why student researchers write papers and give talks:

- to pass some internal assessment
- to get feedback on their work.

Unfortunately, in our assessment-obsessed university culture, students tend to forget that feedback from peers and advanced scholars serves both normative and instrumental ends.

In a normative sense, offering material for feedback recognizes the community of scholars to which scientific work aspires. Instrumentally, such feedback will undoubtedly help improve your thesis. If you have long-term academic ambitions, it will also help you to improve your teaching skills and, perhaps, to plant the seeds of future journal articles!

So never think of this as 'mere' presentation or the 'boring' bit that has to be got through in order to get your degree. If we cannot use our research to engage others in dialogue, maybe we are in the wrong business!

SUMMARY

Effective feedback is an essential resource for effective research. This chapter has discussed two means of obtaining feedback on your research:

- by writing draft papers
- by giving oral presentations.

Writing should always be tailored for as big an audience as possible, and this means thinking about what that audience may know already and expect from you. So get feedback from fellow students as well as your supervisor.

Attempt to give a talk on your research before you write a final version of your thesis. In this talk, avoid losing your audience (recipient design your presentation); set a time limit and never overrun; and use visual aids to avoid boring your audience.

Further reading

Harry Wolcott's *Writing Up Qualitative Research* (Sage, 1990) covers feedback as well as many other practical matters. Pat Cryer's *The Research Student's Guide to Success* (Open University Press, 1996), Chapter 13, discusses giving presentations on your work. Gary Marx's paper 'Of methods and manners for aspiring sociologists: 37 moral imperatives' (*The American Sociologist*, Spring 1997, 102–25) is a lively and extremely helpful guide for the apprentice researcher.

Exercise 16.1

Select two articles in your area of research from two different journals or books. Work out the audience(s) at which the journal or book is aimed by reading the journal's 'instructions to contributors' or a book's introductory editorial chapter.

Then go through the steps below:

1 In what way does each article attempt to reach its appropriate audience(s)?
2 How successful is it in doing so?
3 How could it be improved to appeal more to its target audience(s)?
4 How could it be rewritten to appeal to other audiences?

Exercise 16.2

Get invited to give a talk on your research and make sure that somebody attends who is prepared to give you good feedback. Plan the talk to reach the audience (e.g. students, staff, laypeople or a mixture). Having given your talk, ask the attending person for feedback on the success of your talk. Then consider how you could have improved the talk to appeal more to its target audience.

17

The First Few Pages

Pertti Alasuutari describes writing a thesis as rather like learning to ride a bicycle through gradually adjusting your balance:

> Writing is first and foremost analyzing, revising and polishing the text. The idea that one can produce ready-made text right away is just about as senseless as the cyclist who has never had to restore his or her balance. (1995: 178)

Alasuutari reminds us that 'writing up' should never be something left to the end of your research. Instead, writing should be a continuous process; you will be learning as you go from your supervisor, your peers and your own mistakes.

In this and the following four chapters, we will examine how this writing up can be accomplished efficiently if rarely painlessly.

Nearly all dissertations begin with four elements:

- a title
- an abstract
- a list of contents
- an introduction.

If you follow my advice and devote most attention to your data analysis chapters, then you may tend to treat these beginnings as routine matters, speedily disposed of. However, the impression you create at the start of your dissertation is very important and the writing of the first few pages should never be regarded as 'busy work', i.e. as a triviality.

In this short chapter, I offer some practical advice about each of these beginning sections of your dissertation.

THE TITLE

In the early stages, you will probably be asked to give a short title to your research for administrative purposes. You will almost certainly change this title before long, so do not attach too much importance to it. However, as Harry Wolcott suggests, it is a good idea to be thinking about an effective final title and to keep notes about your ideas (1990: 70–1).

Titles should catch the reader's attention while properly informing them about the main focus of your research. My own preference is for a two-part title: a snappy main title, often using a present participle to indicate activity; and a more descriptive subtitle.

For illustration, two of my books were entitled:

Reading Castaneda: a Prologue to the Social Sciences
Interpreting Qualitative Data: Methods for Analysing Talk, Text and Interaction

Among my papers, you will find the following titles:

'Describing sexual activities in HIV counselling: the co-operative management of the moral order'
'Unfixing the subject: viewing "bad timing"'
'Policing the lying patient: surveillance and self-regulation in consultations with adolescent diabetics'

Of course, using a present participle in the main title is merely my preference, intended to stress the *active* nature of the research as well as the fact that I study people's *activities*. Nor do I always follow my own rule. For instance, my 1997 book on AIDS counselling was entitled:

Discourses of Counselling: HIV Counselling as Social Interaction

But titles do matter and need careful thought, as any marketing person will tell you. So give this matter thought and discuss it with your supervisor. Then try Exercise 17.1.

THE ABSTRACT

This should succinctly cover the following:

* your research problem
* why that problem is important and worth studying
* your data and methods
* your main findings
* their implications in the light of other research.

There is usually a word limit for abstracts (100 words is common). Within the word limitations, try to make your abstract as lively and informative as possible. Read the abstracts of other dissertations in your area and try out drafts on other students and see if they find your abstract clear and pithy. Know what your audience is likely to be most interested in and 'emphasize your problem and content, not your fieldwork techniques' (Wolcott, 1990: 81).

Harry Wolcott nicely sums up what makes a good abstract:

> An abstract can offer a valuable opportunity to inform a wide audience, to capture potential readers, and to expand your own interactive professional network. Whether others will pursue their reading may depend largely on their assessment of your abstract, including its style. (1990: 81)

THE LIST OF CONTENTS

You may think this is a very trivial matter. Not so! A scrappy or uninformative list of contents (or, worse still, none at all) will create a terrible impression.

In order to be user-friendly, recipient design the list to achieve two ends:

1 to demonstrate that you are a logical thinker, able to write a dissertation with a transparently clear organization
2 to allow your readers to see this at once, to find their way easily between different parts of the dissertation and to pinpoint matters in which they have most interest.

One useful device which helps to achieve these two things is to use a double-numbering system. So, for instance, a 'review of the literature' chapter may be listed as:

Chapter 3: Review of the literature
3.1   The background studies
3.2   The core readings
3.3   The study closest to my own

Of course, this is only an illustration. More detailed discussion of what a literature review should contain is provided in the next chapter of this volume.

THE INTRODUCTION

Anne Murcott (1997: 1) says that the point of an introduction is to answer the question: what is this thesis about? She suggests that you answer this question in four ways by explaining:

1 why you have chosen this topic rather than any other, e.g. either because it has been neglected or because it is much discussed but not properly or fully
2 Why this topic interests you

3 the kind of research approach or academic discipline you will utilize
4 Your research questions or problems.

Like this chapter, there is no reason why your introduction should be any longer than two or three pages, particularly if your 'methods' chapter covers the natural history of your research (see Chapter 19). The role of the introduction, like your abstract, is to orientate your readers. This is best done clearly and succinctly.

SUMMARY

The impression you create at the start of your dissertation is very important. Your title should catch the readers' attention while properly informing them about the main focus of your research.

An abstract should describe your research problem; why that problem is important and worth studying; your data and methods; your main findings and their implications in the light of other research.

Your list of contents should allow your readers to find their way easily between different parts of the dissertation and to pinpoint matters in which they have most interest. Your introduction should explain why you have chosen this topic rather than any other; why this topic interests you; the kind of research approach or academic discipline you will utilize; and your research questions or problems.

Further reading

Harry Wolcott's *Writing Up Qualitative Research* (Sage, 1990), pp. 70–82 has an excellent discussion of how to present student dissertations. A further useful source is Pat Cryer's *The Research Student's Guide to Success* (Open University Press, 1996), Chapter 12.

Exercise 17.1

This is an exercise to encourage you to find a good title and abstract for your dissertation.

1 Make a list of three or four possible titles for your dissertation. Try to make the main title intriguing and the subtitle descriptive.
2 Now reverse the order, putting the subtitle first. Which works best? Why?
3 Try out your titles on students working in similar areas or using similar methods or data. Which do they think works best? Why?
4 Now try out two different abstracts in the same way.

Exercise 17.2

Show the introduction to your dissertation to a range of fellow students. Encourage them to tell you whether they feel tempted to read more. If not, why not? If so, why?

Now use their response to revise your introduction.

18

The Literature Review Chapter

There are four common misconceptions of the literature review chapter:

- It is done just to display that 'you know the area'.
- It is easier to do than your data analysis chapters.
- It is boring to read (and to write).
- It is best 'got out of the way' at the start of your research.

Later in this chapter, all these assertions will be questioned. In contrast I will argue that a literature review:

- should combine knowledge with critical thought
- involves hard work but can be exciting to read
- should mainly be written *after* you have completed your data analysis.

I will begin, however, by trying to answer some practical questions about writing a literature review. Namely, what should it contain? Where will you find what you need to read? How should you read?

PRACTICAL QUESTIONS

What should a literature review contain?

In part, a literature review should be used to display your scholarly skills and credentials. In this sense, you should use it:

> To demonstrate skills in library searching; to show command of the subject area and understanding of the problem; to justify the research topic, design and methodology. (Hart, 1998: 13)

Such justification also means, as I remarked in Chapter 6, that any literature review connected with a piece of research has as much to do with the issue of generalizability as with displaying your academic credentials. This involves addressing the questions set out in Table 18.1.

Once you start to see your literature review as dialogic rather than a mere replication of other people's writing, you are going in the right direction.

TABLE 18.1   **Contents of a literature review**

- What do we already know about the topic?
- What do you have to say critically about what is already known?
- Has anyone else ever done anything exactly the same?
- Has anyone else done anything that is related?
- Where does your work fit in with what has gone before?
- Why is your research worth doing in the light of what has already been done?

Source: adapted from Murcott, 1997

Conceived as an answer to a set of questions, your reading can immediately become more directed and your writing more engaging and relevant.

Where will I find the literature?

There are many potential sources of information about what literature you need to read and where to find it:

- your supervisor
- the subject librarian in your university library
- bibliographies in the literature you read
- online searches on the World Wide Web
- newsgroups on the Internet
- your fellow students (past and present).

There is no need to worry about admitting your lack of knowledge. Indeed the American sociologist Gary Marx recommends taking 'short cuts': 'learn how to use computer searches, encyclopaedias, review articles. Ask experts for help' (1997: 106). Once you start looking, you will speedily find that you have the problem not of too little literature but of too much! Getting away from the books and towards your data is a leap that most of us need to make as early as possible. As Marx cautions: 'Don't become a bibliophile unless it suits you' (1997: 106).

There's so much: how will I find the time?

Before you panic, you need to remember that you would not have reached this stage of your academic career without learning the tricks of the reading trade. These tricks go beyond the skills of speed reading (although these help): your aim is usually to 'fillet' a publication in terms of your own agenda (not the author's!).

Again, Marx makes the point well:

Sample! Learn how to read by skimming, attending to the first and last sentence, paragraph or chapter. Read conclusions first, then decide if you want the rest. Most social science books probably shouldn't be books; they have only a few main (or at least original) ideas. (1997: 106)

If these are some answers to the usual 'nuts and bolts' questions, we still need to tackle the underlying principles behind a literature review. As my earlier discussion of 'misconceptions' suggested, these principles are not always obvious or clear-cut.

PRINCIPLES

This is how the best recent book on the topic defines a literature review:

> The selection of available documents (both published and unpublished) on the topic, which contain information, ideas, data and evidence written from a particular standpoint to fulfil certain aims or express certain views on the nature of the topic and how it is to be investigated, and the effective evaluation of these documents in relation to the research being proposed. (Hart, 1998: 13)

Chris Hart's term 'effective evaluation' means, I believe, attending to the following principles.

Show respect for the literature

Your single-minded pursuit of your (ideally) narrow research topic should not lead you to show disrespect for earlier research or to disconnect your work from the wider debate in which it figures. Your dissertation will be assessed in terms of its scholarship, and being 'scholarly' means showing 'respect' as well as striking out on your own. In Marx's words:

> Even producers of literature must know the literature, and a major criterion for evaluating work is whether or not it is put in a context of prior scholarship. We are not only creators of new knowledge, but protectors and transmitters of old knowledge. Our inheritance is the astounding richness of the work of prior scholars. Beyond that, one has a strategic interest in the peer reciprocity inherent in the citing system. (1997: 106)

Be focused and critical

Respect can only get you so far. Scholarship also means advancing knowledge – although the level of the advance required will vary according to the degree at which you are aiming. Such advance involves a strict focus and a critical perspective on what you read:

> After some initial grovelling, know what you are looking for. Approach the literature with questions and remember that your goal is to advance it, not simply to marvel at its wonders. Seek an appropriate balance between appreciation and advancement of the literature. (1997: 106)

Avoid mere description

Any academic has horror stories of literature reviews which were tediously and irrelevantly descriptive. Rudestam and Newton characterize well such failing reviews:

> [they consist of] a laundry list of previous studies, with sentences or paragraphs beginning with the words, 'Smith found...', 'Jones concluded...', 'Anderson stated...', and so on. (1992: 46)

In this vein, Gary Marx recommends avoiding writing 'a literature summary without an incisive critique that will help your peers to view the world differently' (1997: 106). Instead, you need to focus on those studies that are relevant for defining *your* research problem. By the end of the literature review:

> the reader should be able to conclude that, 'Yes, of course, this is the exact study that needs to be done at this time to move knowledge in this field a little further along.' (Rudestam and Newton, 1992: 47)

This entails giving different amounts of attention to what you read according to how central it is to your topic. Background literature can just be described in a sentence. By contrast, the most relevant studies 'need to be critiqued rather than reported' (1992: 49). Such critique can focus on failings of theory or method (see Chapter 26).

Write up after your other chapters

The common version of a student research trajectory suggests that a major early aim is to complete a literature review. This version is supported in the 'time checklist' provided by British Research Councils for PhD students. This includes the following recommendation: 'First year ... student to complete a literature survey' (British Research Councils, 1996). Elsewhere the same publication gives less dogmatic advice:

> In some subjects a *literature survey* forms an important starting portion of the work, and this should be carried out in the early stages. Before the end of the first year, the student should have a good idea of relevant work carried out by others, but it will be necessary to keep up with new literature throughout the period, so that the thesis takes account of the latest developments in its subject area.

This more considered advice hints at the problems of completing your literature review at an early stage. These problems may include:

- Completing the literature survey in year one and writing it up can mean a lot of wasted effort: until you have done your data analysis, you do not know what will be relevant.
- You may be tempted to regard the literature review as a relatively easy

task. Since it tests skills you have already learned in your undergraduate career, it may become potential 'busy work'. If so, it only will delay getting down to the data analysis on which you should be judged.

• As I asked in Chapter 5, can you ever get out of the library in order to write your thesis? One book will surely have a list of further 'crucial' references and so on, *ad infinitum*. Anybody who thinks a library PhD is a 'quick fix' would be well advised to ponder whether they have the willpower to stop reading.

These considerations mean that the bulk of your reading is usually best done in and around your data collection and analysis. In the end, this will save you the time involved in drafting your literature review chapter before you can know which literature will be most relevant to your treatment of your topic. It will also force you out of the library. As Marx comments: 'searching the literature must not become an end in itself or a convenient way to avoid the blank page' (1997: 106).

So: read as you do the analyses. By all means write notes on your reading but don't attempt to write your literature review chapter early on in your research.

However, as researchers, we should be critical and innovative. In this regard, how far is the literature review chapter simply an unconsidered relic of an out-of-date version of scholarship? Do we need such a chapter?

DO YOU NEED A LITERATURE REVIEW CHAPTER?

The major unorthodox figure here is the American ethnographer Harry Wolcott. Wolcott argues that student researchers often mistakenly assume a need to defend qualitative research in general as well as the particular approach or method you are using. But, as he suggests after a century of qualitative research (and several decades of more specific qualitative approaches):

There is no longer a call for each researcher to discover and defend [qualitative methods] anew, nor a need to provide an exhaustive review of the literature about such standard procedures as participant observation or interviewing. Instead of having to describe and defend qualitative approaches, as we once felt obligated to do, it is often difficult to say anything new or startling about them. Neophyte researchers who only recently have experienced these approaches first-hand need to recognize that their audiences probably do not share a comparable sense of excitement about hearing them described once again. (1990: 26)

Wolcott also points to some positive gains of avoiding the statutory review chapter. As he puts it:

I expect my students to know the relevant literature, but I do not want them to lump (dump?) it all into a chapter that remains unconnected to the rest of the study. I want them to draw upon the literature selectively and appropriately as needed in the telling of their story. (1990: 17)

This means that you can bring in appropriate literature as you need it, not in a separate chapter but in the course of your data analysis:

> Ordinarily this calls for introducing related research toward the end of a study rather than at the beginning, except for the necessary 'nesting' of the problem in the introduction. (1990: 17)

Wolcott's radical suggestion is, no doubt, too radical for most students (and their supervisors!). Nevertheless, even if you decide to write the conventional literature review chapter, what he has to say is a salutary reminder that, in writing a research dissertation, you should cite other literature only in order to connect your narrow research topic to the directly relevant concerns of the broader research community. Making wider links should properly be left to your final chapter (see Chapter 21).

SUMMARY

In this chapter, I have argued that a literature review should: combine knowledge with critical thought; involve hard work but be exciting to read; and mainly be written *after* you have completed your data analysis.

A literature review should contain answers to the following questions:

- What do we already know about the topic?
- What do you have to say critically about what is already known?
- Has anyone else ever done anything exactly the same?
- Has anyone else done anything that is related?
- Where does your work fit in with what has gone before?
- Why is your research worth doing in the light of what has already been done?

Further reading

The essential book on this topic is Chris Hart's *Doing a Literature Review: Releasing the Social Science Imagination* (Sage, 1998). This covers in detail all the issues discussed in this brief chapter as well as addressing the different requirements of literature reviews for BA, MA and PhD dissertations (1998: 15).

For shorter, livelier discussions see Harry Wolcott's *Writing Up Qualitative Research* (Sage, 1990) and Gary Marx's paper 'Of methods and manners for aspiring sociologists: 37 moral imperatives' (*The American Sociologist*, Spring 1997, 102–25).

Exercise 18.1

Select what you regard as the two or three most relevant pieces of literature. Now:

1 Make notes on each, attempting to use each one to answer the questions found in Table 18.1.
2 Incorporate these notes in a short literature review chapter which only refers to these two or three works.
3 Discuss this review with your supervisor.

Exercise 18.2

When you complete each data analysis chapter, look back over the literature you have discussed. Now ask yourself these questions:

1 Is there sufficient discussion of each reference to render further discussion (in a literature review chapter) redundant?
2 If not, practise writing about these references in a way that adds to how you have described them in your data analysis chapters. Again, you may use Table 18.1 as a guide.

19
The Methodology Chapter

In writing up research, we tell (structured) stories about data. It is only natural, then, that our readers should expect to be told how we gathered our data, what data we ended up with and how we analysed them. This is why all research reports seem to have a methodology chapter or at least a section devoted to 'data and methods'. Within that rubric, however, as I show later, there are many different formats we can use to give an account of our data and methods.

Moreover, not all research reports will have the same objective. Indeed, we can distinguish three different kinds of student dissertation: theoretical, methodological and empirical. Each of these demands different discussion of 'methods'.

1   *Theoretical*   Here you claim to develop some theoretical insights by means of a critical review of a body of literature. In the theoretical dissertation, your methodology chapter will need to discuss your rationale for selecting your corpus of literature and any illustrative examples. It will also need to show how you have attempted to produce a systematic analysis e.g. by considering the arguments for positions that you reject.
2   *Methodological*   Here you are mainly concerned to develop a method (e.g. focus groups or textual analysis) or to compare and contrast the use of several different methods. Here the whole thesis may be devoted to methodological matters and so a separate chapter called 'methodology' may be redundant or simply devoted to explaining why you have chosen certain methods to compare and/or which data you choose to use for this exercise.
3   *Empirical*   In this, the most common form of research report or dissertation, you will analyse some body of data. Here you will be expected to show that you understand the strengths and weaknesses of your research strategy, design and methods. Hence a 'methodology' chapter is appropriate.

WHAT SHOULD THE METHODOLOGY CHAPTER CONTAIN?

In a quantitative study, there is a simple answer to this question. You will have a chapter usually entitled 'Data and methods'. As Table 19.1 shows, this chapter will typically contain four elements.

The straightforward character of a quantitative methods chapter unfortunately does not spill over into qualitative research reports. At first sight, this simply is a matter of different language. So, in reporting qualitative studies, typically we do not talk about 'statistical analysis' or 'research instruments'.

These linguistic differences also reflect broader practical and theoretical differences between quantitative and qualitative research. More particularly, in writing up qualitative research, we need to recognize:

- the (contested) theoretical underpinnings of methodologies
- the (often) contingent nature of the data chosen
- the (likely) non-random character of cases studied.

Each of these three features raises issues which should not be concealed or generate guilt. Your research training courses and your reading should have made you aware of the theories on which your methods rest. So the rule here, in writing your methods chapter, is simply: *spell out your theoretical assumptions.*

Everybody realizes that contingent events related to personal interest, access or even simply being in the right (wrong) place at the right (wrong) time often determine which data you are able to work upon. So be straightforward: *spell out the (sometimes contingent) factors that made you choose to work with your particular data.*

Finally, everybody knows that qualitative researchers can work fruitfully with very small bodies of data that have not been randomly assembled. If this is the case, *explain how you can still generalize from your analysis.* For example, in Chapter 8, I discussed four different but positive answers to this question of how we can obtain generalizability:

- combining qualitative research with quantitative measures of populations
- purposive sampling guided by time and resources
- theoretical sampling
- using an analytic model which assumes that generalizability is present in the existence of *any* case.

So, when writing your methodology chapter avoid over-defensiveness. Many great researchers will have used similar methods with few qualms. So draw from their strength.

TABLE 19.1 **The method chapter in a quantitative thesis**

1 Subjects studied
2 Research instruments used
3 Procedures used in applying these instruments to these subjects
4 Statistical analysis

Source: adapted from Rudestam and Newton, 1992: 61

On the other hand, self-confidence should not mean lack of appropriate self-criticism. Your literature review chapter will already have considered other studies in terms of 'the strengths and limitations of different research designs and techniques of data collection, handling and analysis' (Murcott, 1997: 2).

Treat your methodology chapter in the same way as a set of cautious answers to questions that another researcher might have asked you about your work. Anne Murcott suggests that you try to answer the kinds of questions set out in Table 19.2.

In practice, this will usually mean describing the following:

- the data you have studied
- how you obtained those data (e.g. issues of access and consent)
- what claims you are making about the data (e.g. as representative of some population or as a single case study)
- the methods you have used to gather the data
- why you have chosen these methods
- how you have analysed your data
- the advantages and limitations of using your method of data analysis.

To answer Murcott's four questions in Table 19.2, in the context of my elaborations above, may now look to be a pretty tall order, particularly if you feel you have to devote a long section to each of these issues.

However, the methodology chapter of a qualitative study can be a much more lively, interesting affair than this suggests. In this context, there are three issues to bear in mind. First, a highly formal chapter can be dull to read as well as to write. Many is the time I have ploughed through a desperately boring methodology chapter, usually written in the passive voice. I often get the feeling that the chapter is there for purely formal purposes. In the words of a British song about the war, 'because we're here, because we're here, because we're here'! In such cases, I can hardly wait to get on to the (more lively) heart of the study.

Second, 'methodology' has a more flexible meaning in qualitative research than in its quantitative sister. In Chapter 6, I defined 'methodology' as 'a general approach to studying research topics'. As such, your readers will be more interested in a methodological discussion in which you explain the actual course of your decision-making rather than a series of blunt assertions in the passive voice (e.g. 'the method chosen was . . .').

TABLE 19.2 **Questions for the qualitative methodology chapter**

1 How did you go about your research?
2 What overall strategy did you adopt and why?
3 What design and techniques did you use?
4 Why these and not others?

Source: Murcott, 1997

Third, a research study submitted for a university degree, even up to the PhD level, is principally evaluated in terms of how far you can demonstrate that you have the makings of a competent researcher. Hence your examiners will be interested to know something about the history of your research, including your response to the various difficulties and dead-ends that we all experience.

As Alasuutari argues, false leads and dead-ends are just as worth reporting as the method eventually chosen:

> It is precisely for this reason that taking 'fieldnotes' about the development of one's thinking is needed . . . The text can be like a detective story, where one presents these 'false leads' until they are revealed to be dead-ends. (1995: 192)

Alasuutari's version of the history of research as a 'detective story' is incompatible with a formal methodology chapter in the passive voice. Instead of a formal, impersonal chapter, one offers the reader 'fieldnotes about the developments of one's thinking'. One way to do this is to rename the 'methodology' chapter 'The natural history of my research'.

In Chapter 2, we saw how some of my research students used their field diaries to write lively natural histories. These informed the reader, among other things, about:

- the personal context of their research topic
- their trials and errors
- their highs and lows.

Examples of how these topics can be treated in your 'natural history' chapter are set out in Table 19.3.

The more informal 'natural history' style of methodology chapter that I recommend should not be taken to mean that 'anything goes'. On the contrary, by asking readers to engage with your thinking *in process*, they are in a far better position to assess the degree to which you were self-critical. Moreover, an autobiographical style is only appropriate to the extent that it allows you to address properly the kind of crucial methodological questions set out in Table 19.2. Clearly, your readers will not want to hear needlessly and endlessly about how your personal life impinged upon the process of obtaining your degree!

CONCLUDING REMARKS

Some universities (like some academic journals) still have a pretty fixed idea of what a methodology chapter (or section) should contain. Therefore, it is probably worth discussing with your teachers whether a 'natural history' format is appropriate to describe the methodology that you have chosen. But even if you do not write your chapter in this way, you will still gain by keeping dated fieldnotes about the trajectory of your project.

TABLE 19.3 **Topics for a natural history of a research study**

The personal context
Like most human activities, this research started in the midst of experiences and events which make more sense in retrospect than they did at the time. (Georgia)

My interest in developing a research study in the field of alcoholism came about naturally as I had been working in this field for many years. (Seta)

Developing through trial and error
At first, I was disappointed with what I found. I was to become familiar with dismay: many times, I was to look at a piece of text and feel: 'there's nothing here, I'm on the wrong track'. (Georgia)

I started thinking of a new study with a qualitative methodology which I was introduced to on my [part-time] MA course in sociology [at Goldsmiths'] in 1985–6. On this course, I became aware of the relevance of the status of interview data, how naturally occurring data or unstructured interview data can be treated as analysable texts which do not need to be considered as being true or false. (Seta)

Highs and lows
As in Vicki's research diary: from analytic breakthroughs to having your hard disk crash. The travails of a part-time student etc.

However, if you do write a 'natural history' chapter, it is much more likely that you will avoid boring your readers (and yourself). It is also more likely that you will overcome the common problem of failing to explicate to the reader what is now 'obvious' to you. As Alasuutari puts it:

> Researchers always become more or less blind to their texts and thoughts, so that they do not notice that they have failed in spelling out certain premises or starting points without which an outsider has a hard time understanding the text. (1995: 192)

A 'natural history' chapter, based on contemporary fieldnotes, will be more likely to make your readers 'insiders' and to avoid you being an 'outsider' in relation to your own text.

SUMMARY

All research reports have a methodology chapter or at least a section devoted to 'data and methods'. In it, you will be expected to show that you understand the strengths and weaknesses of your research strategy, design and methods. In this chapter you should explain:

• your theoretical assumptions
• the factors that made you choose to work with your particular data
• how you can generalize from your analysis.

However, a highly formal methodology chapter can be dull to read as well as to write. Instead, it is often right to offer the reader fieldnotes about the developments of one's thinking called 'the natural history of my research'.

Further reading

The most helpful comments on writing a methodology chapter are to be found in Pertti Alasuutari's *Researching Culture: Qualitative Method and Cultural Studies* (Sage, 1995), Chapters 13 and 14.

Exercise 19.1

Assemble the various memos you have written during your research. Now write 500 words on each of the following topics related to your research:

1 the main things that have helped you finish and the main things that have held you back
2 what you have learned about your research topic
3 how you have improved your knowledge of (a) methodology and (b) theory
4 what lessons your research has for other students at your level.

Note: if you have not finished your research yet, do Exercise 2.1 instead.

20
Writing your Data Chapters

We have already seen how many supervisors and funding bodies suggest that doing a research study falls into three equal phases. These phases are commonly defined as:

- reviewing the literature
- gathering your data
- analysing your data.

Faced with this convention, it may be necessary to restate the obvious. Assuming that you are writing an empirically based study, your data analysis chapters are (or should be) the key basis on which your dissertation will be judged. Unlike coursework essays, where knowledge of the literature and an ability to analyse it critically will stand you in good stead, dissertations that involve research count as nothing without good data analysis. Moreover, as I have said several times already, in my view there are usually no Brownie points awarded for successfully gathering your data. Whether or not such data gathering involved discomfort, danger or the need to learn another language is, ultimately, neither here nor there. In the final assessment, everything comes down to what you do with your data.

This situation implies two clear messages. First, as I have stressed throughout this book, you cannot begin too early in your data analysis. Second, when you write it up, you need to develop the skills to present your analysis clearly and cogently to your readers.

This is why, as Jay Gubrium (personal correspondence) has commented, students need advice on the actual writing up of their data analysis. They need to understand 'what to say first, next, where to place things, how to introduce extracts and what to say in relation to them, how to draw conclusions'. In this chapter, I offer advice addressed at Gubrium's recommendations.

It will be useful at once to make a distinction between how you write up your analysis of particular sets of data and how you craft your overall argument. Alasuutari (1995) calls the former area the 'microstructure' of a thesis and the latter its 'macrostructure'. This is how he explains the difference between the two levels:

> The difference between the two could be compared to different dimensions of the architecture of a house. At the macrolevel one thinks how the rooms and different activities are placed in relation to each other, whereas at the microlevel one considers the furnishing and interior decoration of different rooms. (1995: 179)

This is a helpful distinction because, as Alasuutari suggests, different issues arise in relation to the organization of individual chapters (the 'microstructure') and the overall organization of your thesis ('the macrostructure'). In the rest of this chapter, I will consider each structure separately.

THE MACROSTRUCTURE

> The macrostructure is how the investigation proceeds from one chapter to another so that it forms a logical and sound whole. (1995: 179)

How do you ensure that your data analysis chapters form 'a logical and sound whole'? I discuss below two answers to this question:

- plan your table of contents at an early stage and continually revise it
- in the final write-up, decide the form of the 'story' you want to tell about your research.

Early planning of list of contents

Plan what you may put into your data chapters as early as you can and then keep revising your list. As Harry Wolcott suggests, projecting a list of contents provides for:

> an orderly progression, a clear identification of major points and subordinate ones, and an overview . . . to assess whether the structure I have designed accommodates the data to be presented and provides an appropriate sequence for the presentation. (1990: 18)

By such early planning of the structure of your thesis you can help to clarify your research design and identify upcoming problems:

> Insurmountable problems in finding a sound macrostructure may be a sign of weaknesses in the research design: problems which have to be sorted out first. (Alasuutari, 1995: 179)

Alasuutari gives the example of a set of chapters which veer unpredictably between different themes – a good indication of an unclear research design. This means that, if you have difficulty in working out your list of contents, then you are exhibiting symptoms of a confused research design.

SOME PRACTICAL ILLUSTRATIONS

To show you how lists of contents can be projected, in this section I set out examples from three of my current research students: Sally Hunt, Kay Fensom and Vicki Taylor (whose 'natural history' I discussed in Chapter 2). In each case, these research students started to project a list of contents at an early stage.

Sally has gathered audio recordings of case conferences of a community health team seeking to house mentally ill, homeless people. Her work is ethnographic in focus. This is how her present draft list of contents reads:

Producing single homelessness: descriptive practice in community mental case-work

1	Introduction: aims of the study
2	Natural history of the research
3	Literature used in the analysis
4–6	The ethnographic context
7	Constructing the case
8	Constructing the client
9	Gender as an interpretive framework
10	Constructing the mental health team
11	Conclusion: limitations and implications

Kay is analysing crime stories in local newspapers in London and Northern Ireland. To do this, she is using Harvey Sacks's membership categorization device (MCD) analysis (see Chapter 10 in relation to the story about the navy pilot). This is her draft list of contents:

Locating newsworthiness in newspaper headlines: reading inference and 'motive'

1	Natural history: stages, directions and influences
2	Theoretical framework
3	The media, 'newsworthiness' and the activity of reading
4–7	Data chapters (each on a separate crime headline)
8	Dealing with critiques of MCD analysis
9	Conclusions: what has the analysis achieved?

Finally Vicki, as we saw in Chapter 2, is analysing audio recordings of HIV-test counselling, focusing on offers of other medical tests and services. Her approach is derived from conversation analysis (CA) (see Chapter 11). This is her current draft list of contents:

Making and receiving offers in HIV-test counselling

1	Pre-test counselling: the UK context
2	Why CA?
3	Data and methods
4	The overall trajectory of the counselling interview
5–8	Making and receiving offers: different formats of the offer, the organization of acceptances and rejections, post-response tag components
9	Conclusion: implications for future research

More than a year before each of these students will finish their dissertation, they are already planning these drafts. Planning is important because your research dissertation will probably be the longest piece of writing you have ever done. BA or MA research essays are commonly 10,000 words and PhDs are usually between 70,000 and 100,000 words. However, it is important not to focus upon your own difficulties in writing at this length, for I guarantee that in nearly every case you will find you have too *little* space.

Instead, think of how the reader needs a guide to follow a long story. Provide that guide at the start and repeat it, as appropriate, in every chapter (see Alasuutari, 1995: 180). This will mean providing regular 'signposts' to help the reader understand what you are going to do (or have done) and how these relate to your overall theme. It also means planning the form of the 'story' you wish to tell.

Planning your story

There are at least three models to choose from in working out the macrostructure of your thesis:

- the hypothesis story
- the analytic story
- the mystery story.

Each is discussed briefly below.[1]

THE HYPOTHESIS STORY
This is how many journals require you to organize your paper. It follows a standard three-part way of writing up research reports derived from quantitative studies, namely:

1 State your hypotheses.
2 Test them.
3 Discuss the implications.

As Alasuutari (1995: 181) points out, there are two reasons why you are unlikely to want to use this model for writing up your qualitative dissertation. First, you may well be proceeding inductively, developing and testing hypotheses in the course of your data analysis. If so, then clearly you cannot state a prior hypothesis. Second, however, there are reasons to be suspicious of the hypothesis story because, even in quantitative studies, it often represents not the 'actual' logic of the research but a reconstructed logic fitted to how your cross-tabulations of variables actually worked out (1995: 181–3).

THE ANALYTIC STORY
The hypothesis story usually demands a passive voice format (for example,

'it was hypothesized that. . .' or 'the findings were . . .) which can be difficult to write and still more painful to read! Telling an analytic story is a more conversational way of writing. It involves deciding 'the main analytic story line that you wish to tell' (Strauss and Corbin, 1990: 230). As Strauss and Corbin put it:

> think intently about the *analytic logic* that informs the story. Every research mono-graph, indeed every research paper, will have such a logic . . . In a sense the entire thesis or monograph will represent a spelling out of this analytic story. (1990: 230)

To write this story, you need to ask yourself questions like:

- What are the key concepts that I have used in this study?
- How do my 'findings' shed light on these concepts and, through them, on the substantive topics I studied?
- What, therefore, has become of my original research problem and the literature regarding it?

Rather than hope that the reader will eventually find out these matters, telling an analytic story lays everything out on a plate at the outset.

There is much to be said for this model, for it helps the readers who can settle back knowing what they will find in the rest of your thesis. Some readers, however, may actually want to be surprised. Such surprises can be planned rather than the mere outcome of sloppy design. This is where the mystery story comes in.

THE MYSTERY STORY

Alasuutari refers to an approach to writing that 'proceeds by pointing out mysteries and by gradually developing questions and answers' (1995: 183). In this approach, one:

> starts directly from empirical examples, develops the questions by discussing them, and gradually leads the reader to interpretations of the material and to more general implications of the results. (1995: 183)

Beginning one's data analysis in the form of a mystery story has at least two advantages. First, it may well capture your readers' attention, as like the readers of detective stories, they want to stay with you in order to find 'who-dunnit'. Second, it more accurately mirrors the inductive form of much quali-tative research where findings (and even topics) are only gradually revealed.

Set against this, you must remember that writing a mystery story requires many craft skills. Should you fail, you will certainly lose your readers' inter-est. So, in practice, many writers of good qualitative dissertations follow Strauss and Corbin's idea of telling an analytic story to lead their readers through the data analysis chapters.

In a sense, whichever story form you choose can be safely left to personal choice. More important is whether you are telling *some* coherent story. For, despite their differences, all three models share one important feature in common: they give the study focus and point. This means that the structure of your thesis should only rarely flow from the chronological order in which you happened to find out things. As Pat Cryer puts it: 'the final version of the thesis should be written, with hindsight, knowing where one has been' (1996: 178).

Telling the story in the order in which things happened is only appropriate for a natural history chapter (see Chapter 19). If the overall structure of your thesis just reflects the order in which you discovered things, then your examiners are unlikely to praise you for your verisimilitude. They are much more likely to criticize you for being too lazy to work out a coherent structure for your argument.

As Alasuutari puts it, returning to the motif of a 'mystery story':

> A good investigation is indeed like a murder mystery in that it does not contain much irrelevant text: themes or details that have nothing to do with the solution revealed in the end . . . One could talk about the *economy principle* of a study: everything included must be related and tied in with the argumentation developed and presented in the investigation. (1995: 186, my emphasis)

Now attempt Exercise 20.1.

THE MICROSTRUCTURE

With a clear 'macrostructure', you are well set up to write well-organized and well-argued data chapters. Whether it is a matter of setting out an overall argument (the macrostructure) or developing an analysis of a particular topic (the 'microstructure'), you should always write in a way that helps the reader. As Gubrium (personal communication) notes, this is not always something that comes easily to inexperienced researchers:

> many students don't take their readers into account; they don't know how to 'teach' their readers what they should be reading into the empirical material present. Many just throw stuff into the text and expect the reader to get the point.

Thinking about your reader(s) turns out to be an excellent way of answering perennial problems that arise when you first write up a qualitative study. For instance, you may ask yourself: how much depth is needed in my data analysis? How much is enough? Strauss and Corbin suggest a good way of answering such questions:

> The answer is first that you must know what your main analytic message will be. Then you must give enough conceptual detail to convey this to readers. The actual form of your central chapters should be consonant with the analytic message and its components. (1990: 232–3)

So the answer to these questions is found in how you have depicted the main message of your thesis (the 'macrostructure'). The point here is: know your message and stick to it!

Normally, each data analysis chapter will have three sections:

- an introduction in which you explain what you are going to do in advance
- the main section in which you work through your data in terms of what you have already said
- a conclusion in which you summarize what you have shown and connect it to the next chapter.

I set out below some suggestions for writing each of these sections with an audience in mind.

Introduction

Never spring anything on your readers. Even if you have decided to tell a mystery story (see above), your audience should always know what the mystery is about and what kind of 'clues' they should be looking for.

So at the outset, preface each data analysis chapter with an explanation of how its topic relates to your thesis as a whole and how the chapter will be organized. As a broad rule, no sub-heading should ever appear in a chapter without it having received a prior explanation of its nature and logical place in your argument.

Along these lines, Pat Cryer suggests four components of a good introduction to a chapter. These are set out in Table 20.1.

Main section

Now that your readers know the areas that this chapter will discuss, it is important that you initially pull apart these areas and discuss each one separately. The golden rule for writing data analysis is to *make one point at a time*. So, if you find yourself veering off in another direction, cut out the offending material and put it in another section. Sometimes this will mean returning to the same data but from a different perspective. Sometimes it will mean getting rid of some data altogether.

Your readers will find their life much easier if they are not distracted by too many different arguments. And it is also much more likely that you will be able to recognize gaps in your argument if it is stripped to the bone.

If you are making just one point at a time, it is, of course, crucial that your

TABLE 20.1 **Components of a data chapter introduction**

1	Scene-setting for the chapter, i.e. explaining the general area(s) that the chapter considers
2	Locating the gap in knowledge which the chapter addresses
3	Explaining how the chapter fills that gap
4	Providing a brief overview of what is in the chapter

Source: adapted from Cryer, 1996: 182

readers should immediately grasp what that point is. Therefore, a second rule is: *top and tail each data extract*. This means writing a sentence or two before every extract to context it in your argument. This way your readers will know what to look for while they read it.

Follow that up with a more detailed analysis of the extract in terms of the single point you are using it to make. If the extract is inconclusive, then admit to it. So, a third rule is: *always show that you understand the limitations of both your data and your analysis of them*.

For your readers to be able to follow your analysis, they will need to be able to locate the extract(s) to which you are referring and where to find the relevant part of that extract. So a fourth rule is: *always number your extracts*. One effective way to do this is to give each extract two identifying numbers: the first will be the number of the chapter in which it appears, and the second the order in which it is placed in the chapter. So the first data extract in Chapter 3 of your thesis should be numbered Extract 3.1.

Line numbers should also be used for any extracts over two lines in length. In this way, for instance, you can refer to Extract 3.1, lines 5–7, without having to reprint the passage.

A fifth rule is: *convince the reader*. Not only must your readers be able to see why you interpreted your data in the way you did, they must be convinced by your interpretation. As Anne Murcott suggests: 'the basis for saying that the data say "x" rather than "y" has to be made apparent' (1997: 2). Murcott suggests that the way to display that your analysis has this kind of critical component is to 'discuss candidate interpretations and make the case for judging, and so discarding, alternatives as inferior or inadequate' (1997: 2).[2]

Conclusion

When you reach the end of a tight piece of data analysis, you may feel that nothing further needs to be done. Not so! You owe it to your readers to tie the whole chapter together again. Not only will this remind them of what you (and they) have learnt in the preceding pages but it will also prepare them for the chapter(s) to follow.

Table 20.2 sets out what the conclusion of a data chapter might contain:

TABLE 20.2 **Components of a data chapter conclusion**

1	Explain what the chapter has done
2	Describe the new questions the chapter has identified
3	Explain where these questions will be addressed (e.g. in the next chapter or in the overall conclusions)

Source: adapted from Cryer, 1996: 183

It is worth remembering that it is unlikely that you will achieve a well-argued, reader-friendly thesis at one go. I conclude this chapter, therefore, with some suggestions about moving to a final draft or what Harry Wolcott calls 'tightening up' (1990: 47).

TIGHTENING UP

'Make sure all parts are properly in place before tightening' (directions for assembling a new wheelbarrow, reported by Wolcott, 1990: 47). Wolcott's analogy of assembling a wheelbarrow reminds us that no subtle change of detail will work if the macrostructure of your thesis is not properly in place. As he puts it:

> Before you start tightening, take a look at how the whole thing is coming together. Do you have everything you need? (And do you need everything you have? Remember, you're only supposed to be tightening up that wheelbarrow, not filling it!). (1990: 48)

You are likely to be too close to your work to tell easily whether everything is properly in place. As Pat Cryer suggests, the author of a thesis:

> will know it inside and out and back to front. So the link between its components may be clear to you, while not being as clear to those who have met your work only recently. (1996: 186)

There are two ways of giving yourself the critical distance necessary to see whether all the parts of your thesis are in place. First, if time allows, put it on one side for a while. After a time on the back burner, Wolcott notes:

> I do a better job of strengthening the interpretation, spotting discrepancies and repetitions, locating irregularities in sequence or logic, and discovering over-worked words, phrases, and patterns after periods of benign neglect. (1990: 52)

Locating what Wolcott calls 'irregularities' can mean deleting particular points to which you may have become attached but which detract from your overall argument (Seale, personal correspondence).

A second strategy to obtain distance is to give a talk on your research during the writing-up stage, or to find:

> someone new to your work who will listen to you explaining it or will read the draft thesis and tell you where they have trouble following. (Cryer, 1996: 186)

Once the macrostructure is in place, it is time to tighten up the microstructure. Among the things to look at here are:

* unclear or infelicitous language
* over-large claims about your data or analysis
* needless repetition
* insufficient detail (see Wolcott, 1990: 49–50).

When you have done all of these things, you must recognize that the tightening-up period is nearly over. Certainly, you can ask yourself: 'Have I really got the last details in? Got them right?' (Strauss and Corbin, 1990: 235).

247

To check this out, you can ask your supervisor and/or fellow students to have one final read and then respond to their comments. But remember: the revision process is potentially endless! The real cop-out is not submitting a less than perfect thesis but being stuck in a process of endless revisions:

> Part of an increasing maturity as a research-writer is to understand that no manu-script is ever finished. (1990: 235)

Just as parents eventually realize that their children have become adults and will leave home, now is the time to make the break with your manuscript. Like 'empty nest' parents, you should be ready to strike out in new directions. But first you must 'let go'.

SUMMARY

Your data analysis chapters are (or should be) the key basis on which your dissertation will be judged. However, different issues arise in relation to the organization of individual chapters (the 'microstructure') and the overall organization of your thesis ('the macrostructure').

Good overall organization is based upon planning your list of contents at an early stage and continually revising it. You also need to decide the form of the 'story' you want to tell about your research and structure your data chapters accordingly.

Individual data analysis chapters will have a microstructure based on three sections: an introduction in which you explain what you are going to do in advance; the main section in which you work through your data in terms of what you have already said; and, finally, a conclusion in which you summarize what you have shown and connect to the next chapter. Ways of writing each of these sections were provided, as well as suggestions on the final 'tightening up'.

NOTES

1 As we shall see, the ideas of the hypothesis story and the mystery story derive from Alasuutari (1995).
2 See Chapter 13 for a discussion of these issues in terms of 'validity' and 'reliability', and Chapter 11 for an explanation of how diagrams and charts may illustrate your rigorous thinking. On this latter point, see also Mason (1996: 131–3) and Strauss and Corbin (1990: 131–7).

Further reading

Harry Wolcott's *Writing Up Qualitative Research* (Sage, 1990) is a marvellous account of how to write up data. Useful, shorter treatments are: Pat Cryer, *The Research Student's Guide to Success* (Open University Press, 1996), Chapter 18; Pertti Alasuutari, *Researching Culture: Qualitative Method and Cultural Studies* (Sage, 1995), Chapter 14; and Anselm Strauss and Juliet Corbin, *Basics of Qualitative Research* (Sage, 1990), Chapter 13.

Exercise 20.1

Try organizing your data analysis in two chapters. Don't do this arbitrarily but find a logical way.
Now try reordering this material into five shorter chapters with a different logic.
Consider which format works best and why.

Exercise 20.2

Select a coherent piece of your data analysis which might become a chapter. Give the chapter a title that fits what you are trying to do there. Using Tables 20.1 and 20.2, now:

1 Write an introduction for this chapter.
2 Write a conclusion.
3 Add in your data analysis and show the whole chapter to a colleague. Ask her to what extent your introduction and conclusion helped her to see what you were getting at. If so, why? If not, why not?
4 Now revise and repeat the process.

21
The Final Chapter

In the previous chapter, I concluded with the recommendation to 'let go'. However, since all research reports (including dissertations) seem to end with a set of 'conclusions', you cannot finally let go until your concluding chapter is written.

Having cycled painfully to the top of the hill, the great temptation at this point is to relax and freewheel down to the finish. In practice, such relaxation of effort is reflected in the all too common 'summaries' found in the final chapter of dissertations.

Although summaries are often quite useful devices at the end of data analysis chapters, I suggest that you should never write a summary as your concluding chapter. If your readers need a summary at this point, then your 'macrostructure' (Alasuutari's concept discussed in the previous chapter) is not in place. If it is in place, then what you have said should already be crystal clear. So resist the temptations of a final downhill freewheel.

But do you even need a final chapter? Cannot your thesis stop after you have finished your data analysis?

Think of a musical example. Classical symphonies typically end with a fast movement marked 'allegro' or 'presto'. Rather than a mere recapitulation of earlier themes, they take them up and develop them still more. As such, they seem designed to provide listeners with some of the most stimulating material in the composition. So your final chapter is, indeed, necessary. But it should function to stimulate your readers by demonstrating how your research has stimulated you.

WHY THE FINAL CHAPTER IS NECESSARY

Part of that stimulation arises in linking the particularities of your own research back to the more general issues that arise within (your part) of your discipline. As the authors of the standard British text on PhDs comment:

> You are not doing some research for its own sake; you are doing it in order to demonstrate that you are a fully professional researcher, with a good grasp of what is happening in your field and capable of evaluating the impact of new contributions to it – your own as well as others. (Phillips and Pugh, 1994: 60)

This defines what you must set out to demonstrate in your final chapter:

> It is here that you underline the significance [to your discipline] of your analysis, point out the limitations in your material, suggest what new work is appropriate, and so on. (1994: 59)

Phillips and Pugh's remarks suggest part of the answer to the practical question: what exactly should your final chapter contain?

WHAT EXACTLY SHOULD YOUR FINAL CHAPTER CONTAIN?

> In the most general terms it [your final chapter] is a discussion as to why and in what way . . . the theory that you started with [is] now different as a result of your research work. Thus your successors (who include, of course, yourself) now face a different situation when determining what their research work should be since they now have to take account of your work. (1994: 59–60)

A helpful way of looking at this is in terms of Anne Murcott's question: 'What does the candidate want the reader to make of all this?' (Murcott, 1997: 3). As Table 21.1 shows, the final chapter gives you the opportunity to give your own twist to the wider implications of your research. Such implications must, of course, reflect your own critical sense of what is good and not so good in your own research. Always remember: unless you define your own sense of the limitations (and implications) of your work, your readers will do it for you!

WHAT'S GOOD AND NOT SO GOOD

As Harry Wolcott (1990) notes, in assessing your thesis, your examiners will recognize that chance happenings as well as your research design have limited (as well as improved) your research. Be upfront about these matters. So, in your final chapter, write:

TABLE 21.1 **Suggested contents for your final chapter**

- The relation between the work done, the original research questions, previous work discussed in the literature review chapter and any new work appearing since the study began
- Some answer to the classic examiner's question: 'if you were doing this study all over again, is there anything you would do differently? Why so?', i.e. the lessons to be learned from the conduct of the study
- Any implications for policy and practice
- Further research that might follow from your findings, methods or concepts used

Source: adapted from Murcott, 1997: 3

a broad disclaimer in which [you] make quite clear [your] recognition of all the limitations of the study (e.g. that it occurred in a particular place, at a particular time, and under particular circumstances; that certain factors render the study atypical; that limited generalization is warranted; etc.). (1990: 30)

However, what Wolcott calls 'this litany of limitations' should be coupled with a stress on what you believe you have achieved. So, as in life, be realistic but don't undersell yourself! This can be in the form of:

a conservative closing statement that reviews succinctly what has been attempted, what has been learned, and what new questions have been raised. (1990: 56)

Wolcott's helpful suggestion is, in my view, somewhat undermined by his use of the adjective 'conservative'. Beware of employing so much caution that you bore the reader! If you can effectively show why you have been stimulated, then you are much more likely to stimulate your audience.

Stimulation requires an active imagination. And, in science, it is theory which feeds the imagination.

Theory has been extensively discussed in the first three parts of this volume. Here I want to suggest a practical sense of theorizing which can help in writing an effective final chapter.

THEORIZING AS THINKING THROUGH DATA

An imaginative conclusion will move on from the careful description and analysis of your earlier chapters to a stimulating but critical view of the overall implications of your research. Without this, your research may amount to no more than a set of descriptions of data achieved by some mechanical use of a method.

Since much qualitative research works inductively, generating and testing hypotheses during data analysis, your final chapter is often the best place to present theoretical linkages and speculations. As Pertti Alasuutari comments, in qualitative data analysis:

One preferably starts directly from empirical examples, develops the questions by discussing them, and gradually leads the reader into interpretations of the material and to more general implications of the results. If one feels like discussing and constructing them, the best position for grand theoretical models is *in the final pages*. (1995: 183, my emphasis)

'Grounded theory' is a term used to describe a way of inducing theoretically based generalizations from qualitative data. However, it is crucial that, if grounded theory is your 'thing', you use it imaginatively rather than as a label to dress up a largely pedestrian study.

As I argue in Chapter 26, some 'grounded theory' studies fall short of imagination. This possibility is recognized in a leading text on grounded theory:

> It is entirely possible to complete a grounded theory study, or any study, yet not produce findings that are significant. If the researcher simply follows the grounded theory procedures/canons without imagination or insight into what the data are reflecting – because he or she fails to see what they are really saying except in terms of trivial or well-known phenomena – then the published findings can be judged as failing on this criterion [i.e. of being significant]. (Strauss and Corbin, 1990: 256)

The final chapter is likely to be the place where your examiners will discover whether your theoretical pretensions are, as implied by Strauss and Corbin, merely mechanical. But, if theory must never be mere window-dressing, this does not mean that theory is ultimately more important than research. Theory without data is empty; data without theory say nothing.

This reciprocal relationship between theory and data is well captured by Coffey and Atkinson. As they put it:

> Data are there to think with and to think about . . . We should bring to them the full range of intellectual resources, derived from theoretical perspectives, substantive traditions, research literature and other sources . . . [this means] that methods of data collection and data analysis do not make sense when treated in an intellectual vacuum and divorced from more general and fundamental disciplinary frameworks. (1996: 153)

The problem is that you may become so immersed in your highly specific research topic that you are ill-prepared to step back and to think about what Coffey and Atkinson call 'more general and fundamental disciplinary frameworks'. As I suggested in Chapter 6, you can give your research this broader perspective by forcing yourself to think about how what you have discovered may relate to broader issues than your original research topic. In this way, a very narrow topic may be related to much broader social processes. As we saw in Chapter 6, this was how Mary Douglas's anthropological study of an African tribe took us from a very narrow issue (how the Lele perceive the pangolin) to a very broad social process (how societies respond to anomalous entities).

In this way, argue Coffey and Atkinson:

> qualitative data, analysed with close attention to detail, understood in terms of their internal patterns and forms, should be used to develop theoretical ideas about social processes and cultural forms that have relevance *beyond these data themselves*. (1996: 163, my emphasis)

SUMMARY

You should never write a summary as your concluding chapter. Instead, your final chapter must help the reader to decide what to make of your dissertation. This should explain: the relation between the work done, the original research questions, previous work discussed in the literature review chapter

253

and any new work appearing since the study began; anything you would do differently now; any implications for policy and practice; further research that might follow from your findings, methods or concepts used; and the limitations of your own study.

Above all, your final chapter should stimulate your readers. One effective way to do that is to show how theories have helped you think.

Further reading

Estelle Phillips and Derek Pugh's *How To Get a PhD* (2nd edn, Open University Press, 1994), Chapter 6 is the best British account of the practical issues involved in concluding a research dissertation.

On using theory to develop your conclusions, see: Pertti Alasuutari, *Researching Culture: Qualitative Method and Cultural Studies* (Sage, 1995), Chapter 13; Anselm Strauss and Juliet Corbin, *Basics of Qualitative Research* (Sage, 1990), Chapters 1–4; Jennifer Mason, *Qualitative Researching* (Sage, 1996), Chapter 7; and Amanda Coffey and Paul Atkinson, *Making Sense of Qualitative Data* (Sage, 1996), Chapter 6.

Exercise 21.1

Get into the habit of keeping files on each of the following issues (taken from Table 21.1):

- the relation between your present work and your original research questions
- anything you would do differently now
- implications for policy and practice
- further research that might follow from your findings, methods or concepts
- the limitations of your own study.

At regular intervals, attempt to write a summary of what you can currently say about each of these issues.

Exercise 21.2

As this chapter has argued: 'Data are there to think with and to think about
. . . [this means] that methods of data collection and data analysis do not
make sense when treated in an intellectual vacuum and divorced from more
general and fundamental disciplinary frameworks' (Coffey and Atkinson,
1996: 153).

Find one or two recent journal articles which you think are important
and show why your dissertation adds to what they say.

22

Surviving an Oral Examination

When you have finished a BA or MA thesis, your task is done. Your research paper will now be marked but its grading will be out of your hands. However, if you are working for a PhD, one further task awaits you – your oral examination or 'viva'. Here you will be expected to 'defend' your dissertation and your performance will have an impact on the outcome. For instance, in Britain, your dissertation may pass but you may be required to retake your viva if your performance is weak.

How this viva is conducted will vary between different universities and countries. In Britain, a specialist external examiner will be appointed from outside your university and will take the lead in questioning you. Further questions will come from an internal examiner who may be rather less of a specialist in your area.

In other countries, many more academics may be able to question you. In the Nordic countries, for instance, an 'opponent' will be appointed from outside your university to interrogate you. The viva will be a public affair with members of the audience able to ask questions.

In Scandinavia, your faculty committee are usually passive observers of the dialogue between opponent and candidate. By contrast, in North America, you will face a faculty committee all of whom may ask you questions. The character of this dialogue can vary considerably, as an American text points out:

> The defense ranges from a congenial ritual in which the student publicly presents his or her findings to an assemblage of receptive 'colleagues', to a more excruciating examination of the quality of the dissertation and grilling of the candidate by an unsympathetic faculty committee. (Rudestam and Newton, 1992: 142)

PREPARING FOR YOUR ORAL

Examiners need time to read your dissertation. They also have busy diaries. So you will probably have one to three months between submission of your dissertation and your oral examination. How should you spend this time?

In the immediate weeks after submission, with the viva some way away, you deserve some time off after your exertions – although a break is usually an unavailable luxury to students in full-time employment. However, as your viva approaches, some preparation is very useful.

This preparation can take a number of forms, set out in Table 22.1.

First, Phillips and Pugh suggest that summarizing in a sentence each page of your finished thesis can be a very effective way of revising your thesis so that you will be fully in touch with it on the big day. You should then use this summary as a basis for deciding which points you want to try to get across at the examination.

Second, now is a good time to research your examiners' own work. Reading their latest papers may well inform you about the likely slant of their questions and, perhaps, allow you to look for any links between your work and theirs – although you should first consult your supervisor about whether this is appropriate.

Finally, try to find some fellow students or some friendly faculty members prepared to simulate an oral examination.

DOING THE ORAL

Remember that, as a result of your research, you are now a specialist. This probably means that you now know more about your topic than your examiners. As Kjell Rudestam and Rae Newton put it:

> In the best of cases, the oral defense is an opportunity to think about and articulate the implications of your study [for] your own discipline and to be challenged by your committee to claim your right to sit among them as an acknowledged expert in your field of study. (1992: 142)

Being 'an acknowledged expert' is not a licence to wallow in jargon. By contrast, part of one's expertise is the ability to explain your work in a straightforward way and to make links with the work of others.

TABLE 22.1 **Preparing for your PhD oral examination**

- Revise your thesis
- Prepare a list of points you want to get across
- Find out about your external/internal examiners' work
- Practise with others in a mock viva

Source: adapted, in part, from Phillips and Pugh, 1994: 140; Cryer, 1996: 190–8

So, at the viva, be ready to summarize your main research problem, the contribution of your research and how you would do anything differently. Remember that the oral examination is not a test of memory. So you will be allowed to refer to the text of your thesis as necessary.

In order to add more substance to these points, in the final section of this chapter I have given some details of a Swedish PhD dissertation that I examined in September 1998. While the questions I asked as opponent were, of course, tied to that particular dissertation, I believe that they give you some flavour of the kind of concerns, both specific and general, that examiners raise at PhD vivas.

As Clive Seale (personal correspondence) has pointed out, the skills you need at an oral examination are not dissimilar to those you need at a job interview (see Chapter 25). In both situations, it helps to be fairly assertive while respecting the knowledge and experience of your interviewer. Table 22.2 offers some tips for your oral along these lines.

OUTCOMES

In most British universities, the possible outcomes of a PhD viva are as follows (see also Phillips and Pugh, 1994: 142–5):

- The immediate award of the PhD – often subject to certain minor corrections or amendments.
- The requirement that you put right some weaknesses identified in writing by the examiners (the 'yes, but . . .' result, as Phillips and Pugh, 1994: 143, put it) and a given period (up to two years) to do this.
- A pass on the dissertation but a fail on the viva, with an opportunity to resit the latter after a period of up to a year.
- The examiners deem your dissertation inadequate and cannot see any way in which it can be successfully revised, but offer you the lower award of an MPhil degree.
- An outright fail with no possibility of resubmission and no offer of any lower degree.

TABLE 22.2 **Tips for the oral examination**

- Always say if you have not understood a question; if so, ask for more clarification
- Avoid one-word or one-sentence answers even if the question is a 'closed' one. Use the questions as opportunities to get your point across by making links between the questions and the things you want to say
- Avoid overlong answers which drift very far from the original question
- Refer to the list of points you want to get across when your examiners ask whether there is anything they have not covered
- Ask your supervisor to make notes of questions and answers. This will be of considerable use if you have to revise your thesis and/or intend to publish any of it

Source: adapted in part from Seale, personal correspondence

Despite your worse fears, an outright fail is rare. This is less to do with the goodwill of your examiners than with the fact that your supervisor(s) are unlikely to recommend submission unless they believe that your work has a reasonable chance of passing – although the recent punitive policy of the British Economic and Social Research Council on departments whose funded students take more than four years to submit may change this.

If you are passed, remember to ask for advice about what parts of your thesis might be publishable, how you should revise or shorten them, and which journals might be the best place to submit them. Now go out and celebrate!

REVISING YOUR THESIS AFTER THE ORAL

In Britain, it is common practice for examiners to require some rewriting of your thesis before they will pass it. After discussion with your supervisor, they will allow you a certain period to undertake such revision – normally between six and eighteen months.

Following Seale (personal correspondence), I suggest some tips to follow when you are revising a thesis for re-examination:

- Make a list of the main criticisms.
- Make sure your revisions address all of these criticisms.
- Resubmit your thesis together with a separate sheet of paper identifying what you understand the criticisms to have been, how you have addressed them, and the page numbers where this has been done.

A CASE STUDY: AN EXAMPLE OF A PhD ORAL EXAMINATION

Vesa Leppanen is a Swedish citizen of Finnish origins. He completed his PhD at the Department of Sociology at Lund University in Sweden. I was appointed his opponent because Vesa's work was related to mine analytically (we both use conversation analysis – CA) and substantively (we both had studied communication between health care professionals and patients).

Summary of the dissertation

Vesa had researched encounters between Swedish district nurses and their elderly patients. These encounters may take place in the patient's home or at a clinic. Their primary clinical purpose is to perform routine tasks like measuring blood pressure or giving injections. Naturally, in the course of these encounters, other matters arise – from the patient raising a problem to the nurse giving advice. A sample of 32 consultations provided just over ten hours of videotaped and transcribed nurse–patient interaction – half at primary care centres, half in patients' homes. Standard CA notation was used on the audio. Non-verbal activities were reported by descriptions placed immediately above the place in the transcript where they occurred.

Four principal topics were studied:

- the interactional achievement of tests and treatments
- patients' presentations of their concerns
- the delivery of test results to patients
- advice giving about health behaviours.

The dissertation concludes with a summary of the research findings, a practical recommendation that such data are highly appropriate in training nurses (and many other practitioners) and some general implications for future research. Its call for the study of apparently non-problematic research settings and data is a useful reminder of Harvey Sacks's (1992) call, three decades ago, to discover the extraordinary in the ordinary.

My questions

What do you see as the main contribution of your research?

Would you do anything differently now?

Chapter 4 on tests and treatments reads as very 'descriptive' based on one extended case. Would you agree?

On p. 88, you explain that this chapter serves as a background to the other three data chapters. But can you say anything more, e.g. do you ever meet resistance to tests? Do nurses ever have to work at getting permission?

(Several detailed questions on the data analysis follow. Now come some more general points.)

Your data are drawn equally from home and clinic. Why did you decide not to systematically compare these different environments? Don't clinic and home provide very different resources? (I mention one of my past PhDs, by Maura Hunt, who had looked at the problems that community nurses may face in beginning their work in the patient's home, as well as the work of Anssi Peräkylä on doctors' use of X-rays and scans in the clinic to 'prove' diagnoses to patients.)

Your use of the video material. I remember us talking about your video data on nurses touching patients when I visited Lund in March 1996. Yet the only detailed treatment is on pp. 213–18 where you use the video to show how the nurse underlines advice by abandoning other tasks, gazing at the patient and waving a pill bottle. Why is there relatively little use of the video data elsewhere?

(I discuss various possible uses of the video data that might have strengthened the dissertation.)

Have you never given feedback to the nurses you studied? Why not?

Your only practical conclusion is about the relevance of this kind of detailed research for professional training. I entirely agree about this, but isn't there more that you can say?

Your discussion of the analytic implications of your research is not very specific. How does your work advance other well-known (named) studies and findings?

My concluding remarks

This is a fascinating, detailed and orderly study of great analytic interest. I learned a lot from reading it. It is also an exemplary case from which nurses and beginning researchers could learn a great deal about the value of the analytic mentality of CA.

The highlights for me were:

1   Various parts of Chapter 5. First, the most detailed treatment on institutional data about the positioning and functioning of the question: 'how are you?' Second the discussion about how patients achieve recipiency for the statement of their concerns.
2   Parts of Chapter 7. In particular, nurses finding the right position to deliver advice.
3   An unusually lively methods (or procedures) chapter. This provides a nice natural history of your research and a lovely account of the ethnographic work that preceded it.
4   Throughout, I liked your non-partisan spirit and open-mindedness, particularly towards the judicious combination of CA and ethnography (e.g. p. 44).

Of course, as you show, bad news is usually delayed. So in this case too. But I really have only two reservations. The first is your somewhat limited use of your video data. The second is your underplaying of the practical relevance of your research.

But, in the context of such a well-crafted dissertation, these are quibbles. I eagerly encourage you to turn parts of the thesis into journal articles. In particular:

• Your excellent summary and critique of much nursing research (pp. 21–7) is highly relevant in a field riddled by crude positivism and romanticism.
• Your account of patients' skills in positioning their statement of their concerns is highly original and publishable (pp. 110–28). Perhaps it could be combined with your comparison (pp. 130–1) with Jefferson on everyday trouble-telling, or perhaps the latter could be a separate article.
• Parts of Chapter 7 where you compare your findings with other (named) research on advice giving and advice reception are also highly publishable.

The outcome

I am pleased to say Vesa was awarded his PhD by his local committee. Dr Leppanen has a teaching position at a Swedish university and his supervisor, Professor Ann-Mari Sellerberg, has obtained a substantial research grant for the two of them to study telephone counselling by community nurses.

General implications

1 My two first questions are pretty standard for PhD vivas, namely:

'What do you see as the main contribution of your research?'
'Would you do anything differently now?'

It pays to prepare your answers to such questions!

2 Prepare for constructive criticism of your analysis, e.g.:

'Chapter 4 on tests and treatments reads as very "descriptive" based on one extended case. Would you agree?'

This is a nice example of a question where a one-word answer would have been inappropriate. The right strategy here might be to agree in part but point to counter-evidence elsewhere.

3 Prepare to defend your methods and selection of cases, e.g.:

'Your data are drawn equally from home and clinic. Why did you decide not to systematically compare these different environments?'

If possible, explain the advantages of not making such a comparison.

4 Be ready to discuss further the contribution of your research to your discipline and (where relevant) to practitioners and policy-makers.

5 Expect your examiners to offer advice about which parts of your thesis may be publishable (see my concluding remarks).

SUMMARY

Use your revision period to prepare a list of points you want to get across at the examination. Now is also the time to find out about your examiners' own published work. In addition, try to get some practice with others in a mock viva.

At the oral examination, always say if you have not understood a question and, if so, ask for more clarification. Avoid one-word or one-sentence answers even if the question is a 'closed' one. Use the questions as opportunities to get your point across by making links between the questions and the things you want to say. But avoid overlong answers which drift very far from the original question. Finally, refer to the list of points you want to get across when your examiners ask whether there is anything they have not covered.

It is also a good idea to ask your supervisor to make notes of questions and answers. This will be of considerable use if you have to revise your thesis and/or intend to publish any of it.

Further reading

The most useful guides to preparing for oral examinations are: Pat Cryer's *The Research Student's Guide to Success* (Open University Press, 1996), Chapter 19; and Estelle Phillips and Derek Pugh's *How To Get a PhD* (2nd edn, Open University Press, 1994), Chapter 10.
For an American guide, see Kjell Rudestam and Rae Newton's *Surviving Your Dissertation* (Sage, 1992), Chapter 8.

Exercise 22.1

To find out about your examiners' own published work, read at least one book or journal article by each of them. As you read, make notes about the following points:

1 What 'model' of social research (see Chapter 6) is being used? How far does it differ or complement your own? What useful lessons can you learn from these differences or similarities?
2 Are there any theoretical developments, methodological innovations or substantive findings that relate to your own work? If so, how can you bring these out in the oral? If not, how can you demonstrate respect for your examiners' approach while standing up for your own?
3 Examine the writing style in the material. How different is it from your own? What can you learn from these differences (or similarities)? For example, do these simply reflect the differing demands of (say) a scholarly journal and a research dissertation, or are there basic differences of temperament and outlook?

Exercise 22.2

When you have completed your revision, ask your supervisor or a couple of your fellow students who are familiar with your research to give you a mock oral examination. Following Table 22.2 and using your prepared list of points that you want to get across, try out your skills in answering their questions.

23

Getting Published

'Publish or perish' has, for many years, been the injunction that rings in the ears of most academics. But at least such people have already succeeded in climbing the greasy pole. If you aspire to a university career as a teacher or researcher, you still need to work out how to clamber onto the foot of that pole.

The most discouraging news is that, in these competitive times, it is unlikely that an MA or even a PhD will get you a university post. Certainly, a good reference from your supervisor and other examiners will help. And any teaching experience you have gained is also a plus mark if you are seeking a regular academic post. However, if you have not yet made it into print, faced with people with PhDs and several publications, you may not even make it on to the shortlist – at least at prestigious institutions.

To remedy this situation you may have plans to publish your PhD as a book. But don't count on it! PhDs can be written for a tiny audience – effectively composed of your supervisor, committee and examiners. Before a publisher will even consider publication, they will usually want to know how you plan to revise your thesis to reach a wider audience.

The other thing is that publishers in the new millennium are not actually standing in line to publish (even revised) PhDs. Unless you discover a kind university press, you will find that publishers are driven by the commercial need to find books that will sell upwards of 5000 copies. And the sad fact is that even a good research monograph will be unlikely to sell more than 1000 – an amount that probably will mean that its publisher will actually lose money.

In 1990, it was this situation that made Harry Wolcott (1990) write about how difficult it can be to get your PhD published in entirety. A decade later, things are still tougher. Most social science publishers will now only rarely publish research monographs – even by established scholars. So be realistic! Pick out a promising data chapter and rewrite it for a journal.

The moral of this story is to plan ahead. So, if your supervisor likes, say, one of your data chapters, discuss with her whether it might not be worth sending it to a journal. Once it is submitted, don't be discouraged by a rejection. Most journal articles are rejected or returned with a request for substantial revision. So treat the outcome as a learning experience.

The great thing is that, in return for a submission, you are very likely to get a set of (often detailed) referees' comments. Treat these as gold dust.

However biased you might think they are, they inform you, in practical detail, of the external audience outside (what may be) your cosy relationship with your supervisor. So now you can see what might be required to make your way in the academic world. If your resubmission is not much better received, you probably have only yourself to blame.

Of course, it is important to find the journal which is likely to be most sympathetic to what you have to say because its audience shares your interests and its editorial policy is favourable to your kind of ideas and/or data.

For example, qualitative researchers should be cautious about journals that expect papers to be written in the standard form of introduction, methods, results and discussion. As Pertti Alasuutari (1995: 180–1) points out, this format is likely to be inappropriate to non-quantitative, inductive studies. Again, not all qualitative journals have the same policy about legitimate approaches and/or adequate datasets. For instance, a paper submitted by one of my students was unexpectedly turned down on the grounds that 'it did not have a big enough dataset'.

So find the right journal. Seek guidance from established academics and look at recent editions of journals they mention.

Above all, bear in mind that journal articles (at around 6000 words) are often much shorter than data chapters of PhD. This can make things very difficult for you since, in a shorter space, you must fill in your audience about the overall orientation of your research. So, in writing a journal article, you must, at one and the same time, be highly focused but also provide a proper context.

There are three solutions to this dilemma. First, select a topic which will be the most intriguing to readers of this journal. Second, ensure that this topic can be handled with a limited amount of data extracts. Third, provide the appropriate context for your work: for instance, your audience will not need to be reminded about the basic assumptions of research in their area.

REVIEWERS' COMMENTS

It is also useful to have advance warning of the kind of criticisms that reviewers make about the submissions they see. Since other people may be quite sensitive about showing you the critical reviews they have received, I have set out below extracts from some of my (usually anonymous) reviews during the past few years. Naturally, I've tried to delete any references that might identify the paper or the author. No doubt I am still going to make myself very unpopular by giving these examples!

To help you follow these comments, I have grouped them as 'good news' and 'bad news'. Each section contains portions of comments about many papers.

Good news

A fascinating topic with some nice data.

This is an interesting paper, using theoretically generated analysis on a practically relevant topic.

This paper deals with an important issue. As presently written, it is highly accessible to practitioners and patients.

The paper is based on an apparently well-transcribed piece of data.

The data chosen are very manageable.

This is a carefully done study and brings out some important practical issues.

This is a highly ambitious methodological paper. Its claim to originality, I take it, is that several different methods can be combined to shed more light on a text than any one alone. There is considerable insight in the way in which these methods are used.

This paper discusses some potentially interesting data. It uses an approach which, I presume, will be relatively unfamiliar to readers of the journal. Quite correctly, therefore, the author(s) take up a fair bit of space explaining the approach used.

Bad news

I have grouped these 'bad news' comments under several headings.

I hope that my present readers will not be intimidated by the comments. Please treat them as providing guidance about practices best avoided.

However, I try never to be merely negative. In the following section are some suggestions I have made to authors.

OVER-AMBITION

I think it currently tries to do too much.

Unfortunately, the abstract promises much more than is ever delivered.

There are so many issues that are raised that it is difficult for any to be developed properly. Each would make a separate paper. Given so many issues, it is not surprising that the data analysis is rather thin and not really linked to the literature review.

OVER-GENERALITY

The broad-brush approach adopted here I found frustrating. There is no attempt to ground the argument in data.

UNANALYTIC

For the most part, the observations on the data strike me as commonsensical. To develop this paper further, much more use needs to be made of the vast literature on this subject based on transcripts of this kind.

The final sentence of the abstract is trite and unnewsworthy. The analysis of data only begins more than halfway through the paper and is very thin.

It hardly analyses its data at all and should be rejected. The paper works by assertion. For instance, it simply isn't always the case that [X follows Y].

Unfortunately, the data analysis is very thin indeed, barely rising above descriptions which are sometimes banal.

INCONSISTENCY
Methodologically, the approach does not fit the issues that the author wants to address.

METHODOLOGICAL FAILINGS
I found the citation of 'cases' less than convincing. While space constraints always limit the number of data extracts one can use, the paper fails to give any sense that deviant cases were analysed and that prior assumptions were in any way tested by the data.

LACK OF ORIGINALITY
The paper discusses a contentious methodological issue. It is also an issue that has been discussed in a mountain of publications over the last ten years. Therefore, it is particularly hard to say anything fresh about the topic.

LACK OF CLARITY
I am unclear about the relevance of the approach used; the presence of several traditional assumptions which sit uneasily with it; and the issue of practical relevance.

I don't understand the first sentence of the abstract.

LACK OF RECIPIENT DESIGN
The section on theory is, I feel, inappropriate. Readers who know about this already will be bored, and readers who do not will not want to cope with a theoretical discussion before they get to the data. Much better, then, to introduce the required elements of theory in the course of the data analysis.

You may lose your international audience by going straight into issues relating to one small country.

Suggestions

I would like the paper to be revised to become sharper in focus and to take account of other relevant work.

You need an introduction setting out the *general* themes. Then an early data extract would whet the reader's appetite.

I suggest that you submit your revised draft to a native English speaker. Currently, there are multiple infelicities.

If space allowed, the analysis would also benefit from comparison with one more case.

The present conclusion combines analytic *descriptions* of the findings and practical recommendations. Instead, I would like to see the practical conclusions separated and the paper's analytic *contribution* clarified.

Implications

It may be the case that my own reviewing methods are idiosyncratic and even unfair! If so, I hope you never come across me as a reviewer. To give more balance, therefore, my summary below draws upon a wider range of experienced reviewers. As you will see, this summary has the same thrust as my comments above.

SUMMARY

There are five ways of improving your chances of getting your paper accepted by a journal:

1 *Find a focus* 'Decide on what you wish to focus. What is your theoretical story?' (Strauss and Corbin, 1990: 246).
2 *Avoid too much detail* Ask yourself: 'Do I need this detail in order to maximize the clarity of the analytic discussion, and/or to achieve maximum substantive understanding?' (1990: 247).
3 *Redefine your audience* Remember that your audience is both bigger than and very different from the small audience for your thesis. So ruthlessly strip out inappropriate references and material and recontext your work. As Harry Wolcott (1990: 51) puts it, when writing a journal article 'dedissertationalize' your work.
4 *Expect an initial rejection* Don't expect to get your paper accepted as is. Make use of the referees' comments as helpful encouragements to rewrite a better article!
5 *Make a compelling case* Jay Gubrium (personal communication) has suggested that many qualitative data are 'inherently' interesting. Take advantage of this and use the interest that the reader may have in your material to your advantage. Tease, entice and puzzle your readers.

Further reading

The three best sources on this topic are: Harry Wolcott's *Writing Up Qualitative Research* (Sage, 1990), Chapter 6; Anselm Strauss and Juliet Corbin's *Basics of Qualitative Research* (Sage, 1990), Chapter 13; and Nigel Gilbert's chapter 'Writing about social research', in N. Gilbert (ed.), *Researching Social Life* (Sage, 1993), pp. 328–44.

Exercise 23.1

Nigel Gilbert (1993a) suggests choosing a journal article written by someone else and writing a review of it as if you were the referee. If you need guidance on what to look for, use some of the 'good news' and 'bad news' lines of approach found in this chapter.

Now ask your supervisor to read your review. Use the feedback you get:

1 to think critically about how you might publish your own work
2 to invite your supervisor to ask book review editors to send books to you for review in journals (this is one way to get a first step on the publications ladder!).

24

Audiences

As I suggested in the previous chapter, getting published is all about designing your writing for a particular audience. In this way, we attempt to tailor our writing for the likely sense-making priorities of our audience.

As Amanda Coffey and Paul Atkinson put it:

> Reading is an active process, and no text can have a completely fixed meaning . . . when we write – and hence inscribe certain preferred interpretations in our books, dissertations and papers – we do so with an implied audience of readers. (1996: 118)

In this sense, fellow academics are only one of several potential audiences; others include policy-makers, practitioners and lay audiences. Each group will only want to hear about your work if it relates to their needs. These four audiences and their likely expectations are set out in Table 24.1.

The expectations of academic audiences about both written work and oral presentations have already been discussed at length in this book. However, the range of other audiences, shown in Table 24.1, may tend to induce despair about the amount of work required to meet their separate expectations and needs. However, it contains a simple, easy to follow message: good communication requires focus and yet more focus.

The trick is to combine a recognition of the expectations and needs of such audiences with our own active shaping of our materials. The good news is

TABLE 24.1 **Audiences and their expectations**

Audience	Expectation
Academic colleagues	Theoretical, factual or methodological insights
Policy-makers	Practical information relevant to current policy issues
Practitioners	A theoretical framework for understanding clients better; factual information; practical suggestions for better procedures; reform of existing practices
Lay audiences	New facts; ideas for reform of current practices or policies; guidelines for how to manage better or get better service from practitioners or institutions; assurances that others share their own experience of particular problems in life

Source: adapted from Strauss and Corbin, 1990: 242–3

that a little practice may make you adept at working the same material in a range of different ways. In this context, Gary Marx's concept of 'leverage' is very useful. As he puts it:

> Try to leverage your work. The sociological equivalent of a bases-loaded homerun is to take material prepared for a class lecture, deliver it at a professional meeting, publish it in a refereed journal, have it reprinted in an edited collection, use it in a book you write, publish foreign versions and a more popular version and have the work inform a documentary. (Marx, 1997: 115)

Marx reminds us of the range of audiences that await the qualitative researcher. Below, I consider the three non-academic audiences listed in Table 24.1: policy-makers, practitioners and lay audiences. How do you fashion what Marx calls 'a popular version' for such audiences?

THE POLICY-MAKING AUDIENCE

The idea that social research might influence public policy provides an inspiration for many young social scientists. In most English-speaking countries, the sad truth is that things have never worked in this way.

Qualitative research has rarely had much appeal to civil servants and administrators geared to focus on numbers and the 'bottom line'. The one possible exception, Erving Goffman's (1961) account of the dehumanizing consequences of 'total institutions' in his book *Asylums*, appears merely to have legitimated the cost-cutting frenzy known as 'community care'.

Moreover, it is arguable that number-crunching researchers have fared little better. As Roger Hadley (1987: 100) has pointed out, 'not being heard' is the common experience of Anglo-American social researchers who attempt to influence public policy.

Among the reasons for this, Hadley cites:

- Research is often commissioned to buy time in the face of public scandal or criticism. This means that: 'the customer's motives for commissioning a research project may not necessarily be directly related to an interest in the topic concerned' (1987: 101).
- The time lag between commissioning a study and receiving a report may mean that the customer's interests have shifted (see my discussion in Chapter 15 of the failure of the funding body to implement my findings about HIV counselling).
- Academic researchers who produce unpalatable conclusions can be written off as 'unrealistic' (1987: 102).

Of course, fashions change. At the time of writing, there is some evidence that public bodies may be starting to take qualitative research more seriously. Focus groups in particular seem to be 'the flavour of the month', mainly, I think, because they are relatively cheap and quick and give nice 'sound-bites' for politicians and advertisers. However, such changes in fashion do little to affect the natural tendency of policy-makers to redefine the meaning of research 'findings'.

However, as Bloor (1997) has noted, the policy community is not the sole audience for social research.

THE PRACTITIONER AUDIENCE

> The real opportunities for sociological influence lie closer to the coalface than they do to head office . . . [they] lie in relations with practitioners, not with the managers of practice. (Bloor, 1997: 234)

Taking the example of the sociology of health and illness, Michael Bloor argues that practitioners rather than policy-makers are the most reliable and eager audience for social research:

> Sociologists who have conducted research on sociological aspects of health and medicine . . . have long been aware that there is a role for sociologists as partici-pants in debates on public policy, but that there are also other audiences for social research, notably audiences of patients and practitioners (clinicians, nurses and other professionals). (1997: 223)

Bloor suggests that qualitative social researchers have a twofold advantage in influencing practitioners. First, they can build upon their research relation-ships with practitioners in order to discuss practical implications. As he puts it:

> In respect of practitioners who are research subjects, qualitative researchers can call upon their pre-existing research relationships with their research subjects as a resource for ensuring an attentive and even sympathetic response to their research findings. A close personal and working relationship, based on lengthy social contact and built up over weeks and months, is likely to ensure that not only will practitioner research subjects have a particular interest in the findings (because of the identity of the researcher as much as a particular interest in the research topic), but also practitioner research subjects may be willing to devote an unusual amount of time and effort to discussions of the findings. (1997: 236)

Second, even if you have no research relationship with them, the detail and transparency of some qualitative data has an appeal to many practitioners:

> the qualitative researcher has the advantage that the research methods allow rich descriptions of everyday practice which allow practitioner audiences imagina-tively to juxtapose their own everyday practices with the research description. There is therefore an opportunity for practitioners to make evaluative judgments about their own practices and experiment with the adoption of new approaches described in the research findings. (1997: 236)

Bloor's argument resonates with my own recent experience with AIDS counsellors. For further discussion of how to approach such practitioner audiences, please refer back to Chapter 15, especially Table 15.3.

THE LAY AUDIENCE

There are at least four reasons why qualitative researchers may become involved in reporting back to lay audiences:

1 to answer questions asked by your respondents
2 to 'check' provisional findings
3 to provide 'feedback' to organizations and relevant groups
4 to provide information for the media.

Points 1 and 2 have been considered in Chapter 15. In particular, you should refer to the section on settings and access for point 1 and the section on feedback as a validation exercise for point 2.

Feedback to lay audiences is usually set up because of your own desire to 'give something back' to the general public. The format should vary according to whether your audience are members of an established organization or simply just a group of people with similar interests or concerns.

As an example, following my own research on hospital clinics for children, I gave a talk to the parents' association at one of the hospitals I had studied. In this talk, following Table 24.1, I discussed new facts from my research about doctor–parent communication. I also examined the implications of my findings for reform of current hospital practices. Subsequently, I was invited to write a short piece on my research for the newsletter of a British organization called the Patients' Association. In this article, I covered much the same ground as well as adding guidelines for how to manage better or get better service from hospitals that treat sick children. Finally, I spoke at a meeting of parents of children with diabetes. My aim here was to stress what my research had revealed about the painful dilemmas experienced by such parents. In this way, I sought to assure them that others share their own experience and that there is no need for them to reproach themselves.

It is most unlikely, however, that you will be able to reach a general audience through the mass media. Nearly all social science goes unreported by such media. Needless to say, this is even more true of student research.

However, perhaps your research has provided you with a story that you want to tell to the general public. How should you go about this?

Perhaps a journalist approaches you after a talk you have given. More likely, a media contact will begin after you have studied the kind of topics covered by broadcast programmes and by particular journalists and approached the 'right' person.

For example, when my book on communication in hospital clinics was published (Silverman, 1987), I rang the medical correspondent of a national newspaper. He was very interested in some of my findings and, by the next day, I had a reporter at my house.

At this point, I panicked! I started to worry that the reporter might sensationalize my research and thereby upset the medical staff who had supported it. To try to avoid this, I got the reporter to agree for me to tape-record her interview and for me to have a sight of her copy before it was published.

My cautiousness had an unforeseen and unfortunate consequence. The 'story' that followed ended up being so bland that it was never printed.

This experience highlights the dilemma that researchers have in seeking to get their work more widely known. The cautious way in which researchers are taught to write about their findings runs up against the media's need to pull in audiences with sensational stories. So it is always a question of balance between the media's sense of what is 'newsworthy' and your own desire for an accurate, unsensationalized account of your research.

CONCLUSIONS

It is appropriate that towards the end of this book we are reflecting on 'audiences'. Too often, qualitative research is written up in an intellectual and social vacuum in which one writes for just oneself or, at best, for one's supervisor. Sometimes, this poor approach can succeed in getting you the degree you require. More frequently, in the absence of actual or imagined audiences, it will lead to writer's block and consequent failure to complete.

In the final analysis, if you want to succeed in your research and beyond, you will have to be responsive to the various audiences who might be prepared to listen to what you have to say. As in so many other aspects of life, people who complain about the 'cruel world' are often the very people who disdain the occasionally difficult but generally rewarding business of listening to what others are saying.

SUMMARY

Communication should always be designed for a particular audience. Academic colleagues will expect theoretical, factual or methodological insights. Policy-makers will want practical information relevant to current policy issues. Practitioners will expect a theoretical framework for understanding clients better; factual information; and practical suggestions for better procedures and the reform of existing practices. Finally, the general public wants new facts; ideas for reform of current practices or policies; guidelines for how to manage better or get better service from practitioners or institutions; and assurances that others share their own experience of particular problems in life.

If you want to communicate effectively, you must decide what your audience wants and recipient design your output accordingly.

Further reading

Anselm Strauss and Juliet Corbin's *Basics of Qualitative Research* (Sage, 1990), Chapter 13 covers both written and oral presentations of your research for different audiences. Gary Marx's paper 'Of methods and manners for aspiring sociologists: 37 moral imperatives' (*The American Sociologist*, Spring 1997, 102–25) is a lively and extremely helpful guide for the apprentice researcher desiring to make links with a range of audiences. Roger Hadley's chapter 'Publish and be ignored: proselytise and be damnned', in G.C. Wenger (ed.), *The Research Relationship: Practice and Politics in Social Policy Research* (Allen and Unwin, 1987), pp. 98–110 is a lively account of the pitfalls of trying to reach a policy audience. Practitioner audiences are very well discussed in Michael Bloor's chapter 'Addressing social problems through qualitative research', in D. Silverman (ed.), *Qualitative Research: Theory, Method and Practice*, (Sage, 1997), pp. 221–38.

Exercise 24.1

Refer back to Gary Marx's comments, cited in this chapter, about 'leveraging' your work. Now take any chapter of your dissertation and outline how you might write it up for as many as possible of the following audiences:

1 a specialist academic journal
2 a non-specialist social science audience
3 policy-makers
4 practitioners
5 the general public.

Now try out these different versions with their intended audiences.

25
Finding a Job

Another, more forbidding, audience awaits most of us – the employer. There are three stages in the process of getting a job:

1 learning about appropriate vacancies
2 getting on a shortlist
3 succeeding at a job interview.

I will deal with each stage in turn.

LEARNING ABOUT VACANCIES

There are two main information channels about jobs: formal and informal. The formal channels consist of job advertisements in the general press and in more specialist, professional publications, as well as the job markets that may be set up at career fairs and meetings of professional associations. For instance, the annual meetings of the American Sociological Association provide a venue for university employers to meet potential recruits.

The informal channels work through the guidance and information you can get from people on 'the inside'. Here the most likely contacts will be your supervisor(s) and, perhaps, the academics who examined your thesis.

Whatever channels you use, it is worth making an inventory of the skills you possess and then relating them to the skills demanded by likely employers. This should be done well before you complete your degree so that you can seek to give yourself the best chances on the job market.

Your research should have given you the useful qualities of being able to express yourself clearly, to work independently and to meet deadlines. It will also have probably provided you with substantive knowledge of a particular area relevant to university and non-university employers.

Other kinds of marketable skills that you can pick up during your university courses are:

- information technology skills
- knowledge of basic statistical packages
- teaching experience

- administrative skills (for instance, gained by serving as a student representative).

So plan for the future: find out where the job openings are and gain the skills that will be most likely to fit you for them.

GETTING ON A SHORTLIST

Of course, before you get a job interview, you have to be shortlisted. My experience as candidate and selector tells me that there are several things that may tilt the balance in your favour. For instance:

- Write a curriculum vitae that embodies the capacity for logical, organized thought that your employer will be looking for. Spelling mistakes and hasty corrections are complete 'no-nos'! Don't undersell yourself. Recipient design your CV. for different employers, having worked out which features are most likely to interest a particular employer.
- Choose referees that cover the different aspects of your life in which a particular employer is likely to be interested. Try to ensure that you are getting the 'right kind' of references. At interview, try to elicit information about how helpful your references were and/or ask referees if you can have sight of an old reference they wrote for you. If a possible referee does not seem highly enthusiastic about agreeing to write a reference for you, find somebody else.
- Always write an accompanying letter with your CV in which you explain why your experience is right for this job and your provisional thoughts on what fresh ideas you can bring to the tasks involved.

Shortlisting committees will generally assess your application in terms of agreed criteria. For instance, many years ago, I was asked to write a report for a university making a senior academic appointment in the field of medical sociology. I used the following criteria in my assessment of the candidates:

1 breadth of interests
2 quality of published work
3 research productivity
4 international research contacts
5 overall standing as a sociologist.

I then attached a letter grade to these criteria for each candidate.

This gives you an idea of some of the criteria that selectors may use when they scan your CV. Of course, how they will use these criteria is an open question. As my own research on selection interviews suggests, such criteria generally operate to rationalize decisions that are already made rather than to cause these decisions (Silverman and Jones, 1976).

THE INTERVIEW

Job selection interviews are one of the most intimidating experiences that we have to go through. Part of the reason for this is that we know that employers will treat our answers as a way of evaluating our qualities. This is, of course, very different from question–answer sequences in ordinary conversation where no such hidden agenda may be present.

For instance, as Graham Button (1992) points out, in ordinary conversation, where an answerer seems to have misunderstood a question, the questioner will repair the understanding. This is shown in Extract 25.1:

Extract 25.1 (OEI; Button, 1992)
1 Mandy: There should be 'bout twuny or so people
2 Tina: I hope- will Chris be coming?
3 Mandy: If she can: [: get
4 Tina: [No you ninny Christo*pher*

Button compares this extract with data from a job interview for the post of head of an arts faculty in an English school. Extract 25.2 occurs during this interview:

Extract 25.2 (RMI 0077 and 0078; IV = interviewer, IE = interviewee; Button, 1992)
1 IV: Huhrm (.) What sort of sty:: le do you see (.) yourself as-
2   as a le:: ader of- of (.) a- a team of teach*e*rs.
3   (0.5)
4 IE: D'you mean how w'd I get other people to do it.
5   (1.5)
6 IE: Well er:: (0.5).mpt I think there are two ways of approaching
7   tea:: m teaching

Although, as Button suggests, IV's question is hearable as about person management, IE chooses to hear it as about a teaching style ('team teaching'). Later the selectors noted that the candidate's answer 'does not answer the question'.

As Button points out, unlike the Mandy–Tina extract, where Tina corrected Mandy's understanding of her question:

> the interviewers never undertook this sort of correction on occasions where understanding problems may have been possibly relevant. Interviewers not only did not start to speak at first possible places where a transfer of speakership could be co-ordinated [e.g. line in Extract 25.2 – but note that IV might have nodded at this point], they neither, without request from the candidate, intervened in the course of an answer. (1992: 217)

Button's data make clear that you can expect few favours at job interviews. As at your university oral examination, this is the time to sell yourself while respecting the knowledge and experience of your assessors. So refer back to Table 22.2 and follow the tips there about self-presentation.

CONCLUDING REMARKS

As with policy-makers, selection committees have their own agendas. For instance, in the shortlisting example discussed earlier, the appointing committee chose not to follow my advice.

Nonetheless, this is a game that has to be played and which can be played well or badly. So go to it!

SUMMARY

There are two main information channels about jobs:

- formal channels (job advertisements and job markets)
- informal channels which work through the guidance and information you can get from people on 'the inside'.

Whatever channels you use, make an inventory of the skills you possess and then relate them to the skills demanded by likely employers.

To improve your chances of getting a job, you should:

- Write a curriculum vitae showing logical, organized thought.
- Redesign your CV for the needs of different employers.
- Choose referees that cover the different aspects of your life in which a particular employer is likely to be interested.
- Try to ensure that you are getting the 'right kind' of references.
- Always write an accompanying letter with your CV geared to what you can bring to this particular opening.

Further reading

For research on job selection interviews, see David Silverman and Jill Jones, *Organizational Work: The Language of Grading/The Grading of Language* (Collier-Macmillan: 1976); and Graham Button's chapter 'Answers as interactional products: two sequential practices used in job interviews', in P. Drew and J.C. Heritage (eds), *Talk at Work* (Cambridge University Press, 1992), pp. 212–34.

Exercise 25.1

Collect job advertisements for positions that interest you. Now make a list of the skills you possess and then relate them to the skills demanded by likely employers.

26

The Contested Character of Qualitative Research

As I have implied throughout this book, neither quality nor choice of method is ever purely a technical matter. Our theoretical orientation, whether explicit or implicit, is what drives our research.

As we have seen, qualitative research depends on a variety of theoretical positions with very different implications. Given the contested nature of the field, any account of qualitative research cannot claim to *describe* all such research. Instead, it has to be somewhat prescriptive.

I offer here a summary statement of my prejudices for two reasons. First, your teachers and colleagues will have prejudices of their own and it is sensible to ask them, like me, 'where they are coming from'. Second, prejudices are properly relevant to research if they can help us to establish a clear set of criteria through which to evaluate our own and other's work.

Here are some of my prejudices about qualitative research:

- Qualitative research is best viewed not as a set of free-standing techniques but as based on some analytically defined perspective or 'model' (see Chapter 6).
- From my perspective, the particular strength of qualitative research, for both researchers and practitioners, is its ability to focus on actual practice *in situ*, looking at how social interactions are routinely *enacted*.
- The fashionable identification of qualitative method with an analysis of how people 'see things' ignores the importance of how people 'do things'. This means that the apparent identification of non-quantitative social science with the open-ended interview needs to be re-examined. This does *not* mean that we should never interview but means that, as a minimum, we should first think through the alternatives (see Chapter 3).
- Qualitative researchers ought to question the conventional wisdom that their kind of research can only be 'exploratory' or 'anecdotal'. Case study

methods can be applied to large datasets and standard issues of 'reliability' can, in part, be addressed by systematic transcription of data.

Like all of us, I like to think that my assumptions and prejudices, while not everybody's cup of tea, can at least be argued through rather than just asserted. To that end, I will now offer you some examples of published qualitative research articles to see how far I can convince you about my sense of how to assess the quality of qualitative research.

I limit the discussion to the four aspects of quality set out in Table 26.1.

QUALITY IN FOUR RESEARCH STUDIES

For convenience, I have simply selected the four articles reporting research studies in the last two 1996 issues of the US journal *Qualitative Health Research* (QHR). The Editor of QHR, Janice Morse, has a nursing background and many of its contributors are in university nursing departments. This nursing focus distinguishes QHR from other journals like *Sociology of Health and Illness* and *Social Science and Medicine*, although its explicit concern with practice has a parallel with *Social Sciences in Health*.

The contents of these papers can, therefore, only offer a taste of the kind of work that counts as qualitative health research, let alone qualitative research in general. Furthermore, such a 'taste' does not allow inspection of the deviant cases that I recommend below as a feature of good research practice. However, these papers allow me to develop a coherent focus with implications which extend well beyond health research.

Women's process of recovery from depression

Schreiber (1996) describes an interview study with a snowball sample of 21 women who identified themselves as having recovered from depression. She sets out to establish an account of the depression experience which, she claims, is 'grounded in the real world of the participant' (1996: 471). This real world, we are told, contains six phases of (re)defining the self, each with between three and five properties or dimensions.

TABLE 26.1 **Criteria for assessing research quality**

1 How far can we demonstrate that our research has mobilized the conceptual apparatus of our social science disciplines and, thereby, helped to build useful social theories?

2 How far can our data, methods and findings satisfy the criteria of reliability and validity or, put more crudely, counter the cynic who comments 'Sez you'?

3 To what extent do our preferred research methods reflect careful weighing of the alternatives or simple responses to time and resource constraints or even an unthinking adoption of the current fashions?

4 How can valid, reliable and conceptually defined qualitative studies contribute to practice and policy by revealing something new to practitioners, clients and/or policy-makers?

Schreiber's discussion of her methodology shows some concern for the quality of her research. Like many researchers with an academic appointment in nursing, she holds up Glaser and Strauss's (1967) account of 'grounded theory' as a *sine qua non* of good qualitative research (see Chapter 8). Indeed, three of the four papers I am considering here mentioned grounded theory at some point – usually as a central reference.

Following the logic of 'grounded theory', Schreiber searched her data for subjects' categories and only stopped when her analysis became 'saturated' because no new information about the emerging theory was forthcoming (1996: 472). These findings were then fed back to the participants and revised accordingly.

However, in my view, a number of problems remain with what we are told about this research and I set these out as follows:

1 This was a retrospective study. This problem is recognized by the researcher who comments that the first phase ('my self before') 'is only seen upon reflection' (1996: 474). Such recognition might have led her to abandon her claim to 'access the depression experience'.[1] But instead Schreiber is satisfied with the rather glib assertion that 'there is merit in hearing the women's understandings of the people they were at the time' (1996: 474). What merit, we might ask? Moreover, despite the fragile status of her data, she has no hesitation in setting out to search for external causes of these accounts (1996: 489).

2 Schreiber presents extracts from her data. But, in place of analysis, we are simply presented with a common-sense precis of what each respondent said followed by an apparently arbitrary label. This gives the paper an anecdotal feel and makes this reviewer wonder why one needs social science skills to write this kind of report.

3 Of course, it is not difficult to find instances that fit a given set of categories. Despite this, this paper does not report deviant cases although such reporting and subsequent analysis are a central feature of grounded theory.

4 I am uncertain from where Schreiber is claiming her categories (phases and dimensions) derive. It is unclear whether these are the women's categories ('the recovery process was described by the women in this study as . . .'; (1996: 473) or the researcher's. If the latter, the author gives no hint of the relevant social science theories from which her categories might derive (e.g. a theory of self-definition). If the former, then one wonders at the lack of analytic nerve which treats research as simply reporting what respondents tell you (see my comments in Chapter 3 on 'going beyond a list'; and see Gilbert and Mulkay, 1983).

Urban healers

Engebretson (1996) reports a participant observation and interview study of three groups of healers who 'heal' through the laying on of hands. She locates her findings in terms of three 'dimensions' (setting, interaction and cognitive process) and finds, unsurprisingly, that such healing differed from biomedicine on each of these dimensions.

Although she mentions no explicit theory and, unlike Schreiber, has no explicit quality controls, Engebretson does strengthen the reliability of her account by detailed ethnographic description. Through it, we learn about the setting, how healing was organized and how the sessions were opened and closed. All of this description has at least the potential to suggest practical relevance. However, three problems remain with the observational data presented:

1   No data extracts are given (presumably what occurred was not taped, and for some reason the researcher's fieldnotes are not made available). This means that the reader has no basis to contest the researcher's account.
2   No mention is made of the system used for recording fieldnotes and its impact on the reliability of her data (see Chapter 13).
3   Like Schreiber's study, the account of the data is presented just as a simple description. Without a discussion of the analytic basis for the researcher's account, her report once more can only have a journalistic status.[2]

Again, like Schreiber, Engebretson groups her interview respondents' accounts into a number of categories (in this case, physical sensations, emotional experiences and visual images). But there is nothing to suggest that these are anything but *ad hoc* labels without a clear analytical basis. Again the chosen extracts simply illustrate her argument and no deviant cases are provided or explored.

Quality care in the hospital

Irurita (1996) describes semi-structured interviews with a sample of ten patients (one to two weeks after discharge) and ten nurses from the same hospital wards. Respondents were asked about what they saw as the nature and causes of 'quality care'.

According to the author, patients saw themselves as 'vulnerable' and described what they and the nurses did to preserve patient 'integrity'. Nurses described the time and resource constraints which limited them providing such care.

Like Schreiber, Irurita locates her research within the approach of 'grounded theory', particularly through her attempt at the constant comparative method. Like many interview researchers, she reports the use of a qualitative software program (in her case ETHNOGRAPH). Moreover, she argues that an important quality control was the separation of the studies of nurses and patients and because theory was built as 'an ongoing process' (1996: 346).

Nonetheless, in my view, three serious quality problems remain:

1   Is 'quality care' a normative or a participants' category? Irurita's account of her research findings is unclear about this but her abstract implies that she accepts a normative category without question.[3]
2   The interview protocol is not provided and, unlike Schreiber, no extracts from the interviews are given. Hence the reader is in no position to know how 'quality care' was investigated or how the researchers analysed data.
3   No analytic basis behind the researcher's selection of categories is given (e.g. 'preserving integrity' is presented as a simple description of what respondents said – not, for instance, in relation to Goffman's, 1961, account of identity in total institutions). Hence the findings appear, once more, to be journalistic.

Perinatal cocaine crack users

Pursley-Crotteau and Stern (1996) report a longitudinal interview study with nine female crack users during and after their pregnancies. The longitudinal research design allows a solution to the problem of retrospective accounts not found in Schreiber's study.

Moreover, these researchers make a real attempt to establish an analytic framework (based upon 'four dimensions of temperance') with which to make sense of how such women struggle with addiction.[4] Thus, unlike the other three studies, this paper does not simply offer lists of (common-sense) categories but combines them into an analytic scheme which holds out the possibility of generating formal theories of the kind that Glaser and Strauss (1967) recommend and which may well have practical relevance.

Unfortunately, Pursley-Crotteau and Stern (1996) do not, in my view, avoid some of the defects of the other studies. In particular:

1   Data extracts are treated as having a self-evident meaning and no deviant cases are discussed (see Chapter 13).
2   The questions which provoked the interviewee's response are not given.
3   An atheoretical reading of grounded theory is offered. For instance, the researchers suggest that grounded theory 'is used to discover the problem from the point of view of the actors' (1996: 352). But if this is all that research does, how is it different from 'human interest' journalism or indeed Oprah Winfrey?

Obviously, from my own perspective, I have found many defects, as well as some good points, in these examples of qualitative research. Table 26.2 summarizes my criticisms.

Having given these examples of the failings (and successes) of several qualitative research studies, the rest of this chapter will contain some positive proposals about each of the four 'quality' issues identified in Table 26.1.

TABLE 26.2 **Some defects in selected qualitative research studies**

Atheoretical
- Categories are usually participants' own or are *ad hoc* and commonsensical, i.e. journalistic
- Normative concepts are sometimes accepted unproblematically

Unreliable data
- Only tidied-up data extracts are given: no interviewers' questions; no indication of how far a particular answer had to be extracted from a respondent, e.g. after a pause or a monosyllabic initial response
- Data extracts are sometimes replaced by researchers' 'summaries'

Doubtful validity of analysis
- No deviant cases
- Some accounts are retrospective

FOUR 'QUALITY' ISSUES

Analytic depth

> How far can we demonstrate that our research has mobilized the conceptual apparatus of our social science disciplines and, thereby, helped to build useful social theories?

A continuing theme of my critiques above was that these researchers tended to describe their data in terms of sets of categories which either reproduced participants' categories or put a common-sense gloss upon them. Although it is arguable that this is a proper first-stage procedure within 'grounded theory', Glaser and Strauss (1967) make clear that such description cannot itself build theories. To do so, we need to move beyond *ad hoc* labels and re-define our data within a well-articulated analytic scheme.

As we saw above, one of the strengths of Pursley-Crotteau and Stern's (1996) account of pregnant crack users is precisely that it attempts to establish an analytic framework (based upon 'four dimensions of temperance') with which to make sense of how such women struggle with addiction. In this way, categories are combined into an analytic scheme in order to generate what Glaser and Strauss (1967) would call a 'formal' theory.

As I argue in Chapter 6, a theory is best understood as a set of concepts used to define and/or explain some phenomenon. A criterion for adopting a theory is its usefulness.

The following examples illustrate this sense of theory in sociology and anthropology:

- Using an 'interactionist' theory concerned with 'labelling', awareness of dying is related to a set of 'awareness contexts' (Glaser and Strauss, 1968).
- Using a 'structuralist' theory of the nature of binary oppositions, an African tribe's favourable response to an anteater is used to build a theory about the relation between perceived 'anomalies' and the experience of crossing boundaries (Douglas, 1975).
- Using a 'discourse analytic' theory of the active use of language,

scientists' accounts of their work are shown to function in local contexts (Gilbert and Mulkay, 1983).

- Using an 'ethnomethodological' theory of accounting practices, the 'cause' of 'suicide' is to be found in the common-sense judgements of coroners (Atkinson, 1978).

Without the active employment of these and other theories, we are bound to lapse into *ad hoc* use of common-sense interpretations and may, like Irurita's (1996) appeal to the label 'quality care', even smuggle normative concepts into our data analysis. However, like many other people researching issues that affect our daily lives, health researchers may have two particular difficulties in thinking theoretically. First, their preference for the study of 'people' rather than, say, 'variables' may lead to the pursuit of a kind of 'empathy' which does not permit sufficient distance. Second, if you research an area like health, which generates so many pressing social problems, it may sometimes be difficult to look beyond what your common-sense knowledge tells you about the 'meaning' of social situations.

How, then, can we aid our sluggish imaginations to think theoretically about data? In Chapter 5, I discussed how social science theory building can benefit from four types of sensitivity: historical, cultural, political and contextual.

I shall return to the question of whether such theoretically guided research can have a greater practical relevance as well as building a better social science. For the moment, I will turn to my second 'quality' issue.

Why should we believe qualitative research?

> How far can our data, methods and findings satisfy the criteria of reliability and validity or, put more crudely, counter the cynic who comments 'Sez you'?

If we argue for the pre-eminence of analytic issues in research, the implication might follow that the sole requirement for any research study is analytic integrity. This would mean that the validity of a piece of qualitative research could be settled simply by asserting its pristine, theoretical roots.

Along these lines, it is sometimes suggested that the assessment of the quality of qualitative data should transcend the conventional methodological approaches. The quality of qualitative research, it is argued:

> cannot be determined by following prescribed formulas. Rather its quality lies in the power of its language to display a picture of the world in which we discover something about ourselves and our common humanity. (Buchanan, 1992: 133)

If Buchanan is saying that the main question in field research is the quality of the analysis rather than the recruitment of the sample or, say, the format of the interview, then I would agree (see Mitchell, 1983). However, Buchanan's opposition to 'prescribed formulas' can amount to something which might be called 'methodological anarchy' (see Clavarino et al., 1995).

I resist the 'anarchic' position on two grounds. First, it simply makes no sense to argue that all knowledge and feelings are of equal weight and value. Even in everyday life, we readily sort 'fact' from 'fancy'. Why, therefore, should science be any different? Second, methodological anarchy offers a clearly negative message to research funding agencies, namely: don't fund qualitative research because even its proponents have given up claims to reliability and validity. Moreover, in such an environment, can we wonder that qualitative research's potential audiences (e.g. the medical professions, corporations, trade unions) take its 'findings' less than seriously?

The reliability of our data should be a central concern of any research. Attempts to bypass this issue by appealing to the different ontological position of qualitative research (e.g. Marshall and Rossman, 1989) are unconvincing. As others have recently pointed out:

> Qualitative researchers can no longer afford to beg the issue of reliability. While the forte of field research will always lie in its capability to sort out the validity of propositions, its results will (reasonably) go ignored minus attention to reliability. For reliability to be calculated, it is incumbent on the scientific investigator to document his or her procedure. (Kirk and Miller, 1986: 72)

In Chapter 13, I examined in detail methods for improving the validity, reliability and generalizability of qualitative research. I now turn to my third 'quality' issue.

Only interviews?

> To what extent do our preferred research methods reflect careful weighing of the alternatives or simple responses to time and resource constraints or even an unthinking adoption of the current fashions?

In 1996, while writing a paper for a methodology conference, I did a crude survey of recent published research-based articles which used qualitative methods. In my own sub-speciality, the sociology of health, the preference for the open-ended interview was overwhelming. Table 26.3 is based on recent articles in *Qualitative Health Research*.

Table 26.3 is consistent with the four non-randomly selected health

TABLE 26.3 **Type of research method (Qualitative Health Research)**

	Articles	
	Number	**%**
Qualitative interviews	65	71
Other methods	26	29

Source: qualitative data articles in *Qualitative Health Research*, 1991–6: n = 91

research articles discussed earlier, all of which used interviews as their sole (or main) method. The skewing towards qualitative interviews in *Qualitative Health Research* probably reflects the fact, already noted, that many of the authors are in nursing where the open-ended interview is regarded as both an appropriate research technique and a preferred model of communicating with the patient.

Of course, we should not make too much of findings based on such a tiny and perhaps unrepresentative dataset. Nonetheless, Table 26.3 may not be strikingly out of line with the preference for interview-based qualitative research found in the articles published in the more mainstream journals.

To test out this hypothesis, I turned to the journal of the British Sociological Association called *Sociology*. My findings are set out in Table 26.4.

Table 26.4 shows a preference for the use of the interview method in recent qualitative papers published in *Sociology*. Although the proportion is only 55/45, given that the category 'other methods' lumps together every other non-interview-based qualitative method, the interview method clearly predominates as the single most preferred method.

Other social sciences may vary in the extent of use made of the interview method. Anthropologists, for instance, may pay relatively more attention to observational methods. However, I suspect that the choice of the open-ended interview as the gold standard of qualitative research is pretty widely spread. For example, information systems (IS) is a discipline which studies the human consequences of information technology. In preparing a recent talk to an IS conference, I surveyed the methodologies chosen in research articles published in a number of recent IS journals. Of the six qualitative research articles, five were derived from interviews.

I have discussed elsewhere the possible cultural roots of this phenomenon in the context of an 'interview society' (Atkinson and Silverman, 1997). At the present, I am more concerned with its methodological impact.

In interviews, as Heritage puts it, the mistake is to treat the verbal formulations of subjects 'as an appropriate substitute for the observation of actual behaviour' (1984: 236).

Drew and Heritage (1992) show how this has a direct impact on the kind of data we think are relevant. Most qualitative researchers use such data as interviews, focus groups and diaries. They thus attempt 'to get inside the

TABLE 26.4 **Type of research method (*Sociology*)**

	Articles	
	Number	**%**
Qualitative interviews	27	55
Other methods	22	45

Source: qualitative data articles in *Sociology*, 1991–6: n = 49

"black box" of social institutions to gain access to their interior processes and practices' (1992: 5). However, such studies may suffer from two problems:

- the assumption of a stable reality or context (e.g. the 'organization') to which people respond
- the gap between beliefs and action and between what people say and what they do (Webb and Stimson, 1976; Gilbert and Mulkay, 1983).

Qualitative researchers' preference for interview studies ironically respects a division of labour preferred by quantitative researchers. According to this division, while quantitative research focuses on objective structures, it falls to qualitative researchers to give 'insight' into people's subjective states.

The unfortunate consequence of this division of labour is that *both* approaches neglect a great deal about how people interact. Put more strongly, both kinds of research are fundamentally concerned with the environment around the phenomenon rather than the phenomenon itself.

Moreover, we need to question the argument that observational or other naturally occurring data are 'unavailable' in the supposedly 'private' sphere of human interaction (e.g. in domestic life). As Gubrium and Holstein have noted:

> The formulations of domestic order that we hear outside households are treated as authentic as are those heard within them . . . As a practical matter, this means that the analyst would treat *private* and *public* as experiential categories – constructed and oriented to by interacting persons – not actual geographic or social locations . . . [This implies that] methodologically, we should not take for granted that privacy implies privileged access – that those occupying the private sphere are taken to be experts on its description, the final arbiters of its meaning. (1995: 205)

Such a situation suggests that we need to look twice at the unthinking identification of the open-ended interview as the 'gold standard' of qualitative research. Note that this is not to reject each and every interview study. I merely suggest that the choice of any research instrument needs to be defended and that the pursuit of people's 'experience' by no means constitutes an adequate defence for the use of the open-ended interview.

I now turn to my final 'quality' point.

Research and practitioners

How can valid, reliable and conceptually defined qualitative studies contribute to practice and policy by revealing something new to practitioners, clients and/or policy-makers?

Research instruments, like interviews, focus groups and questionnaires, which ask respondents to provide facts, attitudes or experiences, have an important part to play in areas like health which affect us all. In particular, they can give policy-makers a reasonable sense of how, at one moment of time, their clients are responding to a particular service (see Chapters 15 and 24). Moreover, unlike observational or conversation analytic studies, interview studies can be completed relatively quickly and, in this sense, can give rapid 'answers'.

Unfortunately, as I have already suggested, some qualitative interview studies may lack the analytic imagination to provide anything more than anecdotal 'insights'. When there are also legitimate doubts about the rigour of the data analysis, then I suggest that policy-makers and practitioners should doubt the quality of the 'answers' such research provides.

One response might be to return to purely quantitative research, given the serious attention it usually pays to issues of reliability and validity. Indeed, if the only alternative was *impressionistic* qualitative research, I would certainly always back quantitative studies such as well-designed questionnaires or randomized control trials.

However, this is not the only alternative. As already suggested, both the 'in-depth' accounts apparently provided by the 'open-ended' interview and the seemingly unequivocal measures of information retention, attitude and behaviour that we obtain via laboratory or questionnaire methods have a tenuous basis in what people may be saying and doing in everyday health contexts.

Take the case of general practice consultations. In an interview study of patients involved in 50 British GP consultations, Webb and Stimson (1976) noted how doctors were routinely portrayed as acting insensitively or with poor judgement. By contrast, patients presented themselves as having acted rationally and sensibly.

As Webb and Stimson (1976) imply, we only get into difficulties if we treat patients' responses as standing in a one-to-one account with what happened in the actual consultation. This is not to suggest that these patients were lying. Rather, by telling 'atrocity stories', Webb and Stimson suggest that patients were able to give vent to thoughts which had gone unvoiced at the time of the consultation, to redress a real or perceived inequality between doctor and patient and to highlight the teller's own rationality. Equally, atrocity stories have a dramatic form which captures the hearer's attention – a point of which qualitative researchers become aware when asked to give brief accounts of their findings.

As I have commented elsewhere:

> Stimson and Webb are rejecting the assumption that lay accounts can do the work of sociological explanations. [They do not] want to take the actor's point of view as an explanation because this would be to equate commonsense with sociology – a recipe for the lazy field researcher. Only when such a researcher moves beyond the gaze of the tourist, bemused with a sense of bizarre cultural practices ('Goodness, you do things differently here'), do the interesting analytic questions begin. (Silverman, 1993: 200)

To underline my earlier point, this is not to suggest that interview studies of patient satisfaction have *no* place in health research. Rather it implies that such studies must be supplemented by data on what actually happens in the consultation itself. Fortunately, from the pioneering work of Byrne and Long (1976) through to Heath's (1997) precise analysis of videos of the consultation, this is what we now possess. Because of this work, practitioners and clients can be informed of interactional skills they did not know they possessed and of communication dilemmas of which they may have been unaware (see also Silverman, 1987: Ch. 8). Moreover, policy-makers can make decisions on far fuller evidence than provided by simple records of respondents' 'opinions' or 'attitudes'.

A further bonus of studying communication *in situ* is that both findings and raw data can be valuable resources in training practitioners. Like the teaching of communication skills to doctors, the training of counsellors may achieve little if based simply on sets of 'dos and don'ts' supported by invented examples. Purely normative versions of counselling are limited because of the varying contexts of practice. In this respect, Feltham has suggested that:

> training courses will need to pay more attention to these issues, for example by challenging the idea of pure, core, theoretical models and by taking research and critiques of counselling more seriously. (1995: 163)

Following Feltham, based on a study of HIV and AIDS counselling, I have argued that in teaching such skills through normative instruction or role-plays, one can easily miss some of the complexities of actual counselling practice – both the problems that counsellors encounter and the practical solutions they find in the constraints of routine counselling practice (Silverman, 1997a: 223).

As my workshops with AIDS counsellors show, professionals respond to research which seeks to document the fine detail of their practice, while acknowledging the structural constraints to which they must respond (see Chapter 16). Put in another way, this means that we should aim to identify the interactional skills of the participants rather than their failings. Although the researcher cannot tell practitioners how they should behave, understanding the intended and unintended consequences of actions can provide the basis for a fruitful dialogue.

CONCLUDING REMARKS

As I remarked at the outset, I do not expect my biases to be supported in every quarter. However, even if you do not agree with me at every point, I hope that I have at least made out a case that there is a serious imbalance in qualitative research in favour of the open-ended interview and towards a somewhat simplistic reading of 'grounded theory'. When this is wedded to a less than thorough attention to the reasonable demands of reliability and validity and a somewhat limited analytical imagination, practitioners and policy-makers may, rightfully, become uneasy about what they are buying.

Correcting this imbalance will not be easy. Qualitative researchers may have to forgo a proportion of their pleasant hot baths in 'empathic' exchanges with interview respondents and to think critically about the siren calls of 'humanity' and 'authenticity'.[5] Equally, funding bodies will have to think again about whether a limited 'quick fix' is really more useful than a longer, more expensive but more detailed study.

Of course, in writing a research dissertation, a 'quick fix' may be just what you need! As we saw in Chapters 5 and 7, your choice of research problem and research design often reflects practical contingencies as much as conscious planning.

So the message of this book is *not* that you should never use open-ended interviews. Rather I am saying that your choice of method should never be unreflective. Indeed, there is nothing wrong in choosing an interview-based study providing that the method is chosen after reflection because it is relevant to your research problem and theoretical approach.

SUMMARY

In this final chapter, I have critically assessed four published qualitative research articles using four criteria of 'quality':

- How far can we demonstrate that our research has mobilized the conceptual apparatus of our social science disciplines and, thereby, helped to build useful social theories?
- How far can our data, methods and findings satisfy the criteria of reliability and validity or, put more crudely, counter the cynic who comments 'Sez you'?
- To what extent do our preferred research methods reflect careful weighing of the alternatives or simple responses to time and resource constraints or even an unthinking adoption of the current fashions?
- How can valid, reliable and conceptually defined qualitative studies contribute to practice and policy by revealing something new to practitioners, clients and/or policy-makers?

The second half of this chapter develops these criteria, showing how we can:

- think theoretically through data
- develop empirically sound findings
- use interviews only when demonstrably appropriate to our research problem
- contribute to practice and policy.

NOTES

This chapter is a revised version of my paper 'The quality of qualitative health research', *Social Sciences in Health*, 1998, 8 (1), 104–18.

1 Abandoning the claim that interview accounts directly represent 'experience' need not be disastrous to interview research, as I show elsewhere (Silverman, 1993: 106–14). As Gubrium and Holstein (1997) point out, we can say analytically and practically interesting things about interviews analysed as locally structured narrative forms.
2 This is not to criticize journalism which, at its best, can be highly illuminating. It is simply intended to distinguish between journalism and social science.
3 Note how 'quality care' gets defined and is not treated as problematic in the following sentence: 'The delivery of quality care, although acknowledged as being vital to health care systems, is a complex, poorly understood phenomenon' (Irurita, 1996: 331).
4 The four dimensions of temperance are framed as follows (adapted from Pursley-Crotteau and Stern, 1996: 360):

| | | Having desire | |
		+	−
Having structure	+	Holding onto the lifeline	Messin' up
	−	Goin' it alone	Dancin' with the devil

5 See Gubrium and Holstein's (1997) analysis of what they call 'emotionalism' and Atkinson and Silverman's (1997) discussion of the cultural roots of what they call 'romanticism'.

Further reading

This chapter develops some ideas that first appeared in David Silverman, *Interpreting Qualitative Data* (Sage, 1993).

State of the art accounts of qualitative research which fit the criteria discussed in this chapter are to be found in David Silverman (ed.), *Qualitative Research: Theory, Method and Practice* (Sage, 1997).

Good treatments of theoretically inspired but rigorous qualitative research are: Pertti Alasuutari, *Researching Culture: Qualitative Method and Cultural Studies* (Sage, 1995); Jennifer Mason, *Qualitative Researching* (Sage, 1996); Amanda Coffey and Paul Atkinson, *Making Sense of Qualitative Data* (Sage, 1996); and Anselm Strauss and Juliet Corbin, *Basics of Qualitative Research* (Sage, 1990).

The various theoretical traditions that comprise qualitative research are skilfully dissected in Jaber Gubrium and James Holstein's *The New Language of Qualitative Method* (Oxford, 1997).

Gary Marx's paper 'Of methods and manners for aspiring sociologists: 37 moral imperatives' (*The American Sociologist*, Spring 1997, 102–25) is a lively and extremely helpful short guide for the apprentice researcher.

Exercise 26.1

Select a qualitative research study in your own area. Now go through the following steps:

1 Review the study in terms of the four quality criteria set out in Table 26.1.
2 If the study fails to satisfy all these criteria, consider how it could have been improved to satisfy them.
3 Consider to what extent these criteria are appropriate to your area. Are there additional or different criteria which you would choose?

Appendix: Transcript conventions

[	C2:	quite a	[while	Left brackets indicate
	Mo:		[yea	the point at which a current speakers talk is overlapped by another's talk.

=	W:	that I'm aware of =	Equal signs, one at the end of a line and one at the beginning, indicate no gap between the two lines.
	C:	= Yes. Would you confirm that?	

(.4)	Yes (.2) yeah	Numbers in parentheses indicate elapsed time in silence in tenths of a second.

(.)	to get (.) treatment	A dot in parentheses indicates a tiny gap, probably no more than one-tenth of a second.

———	What's <u>up</u>?	Underscoring indicates some form of stress, via pitch and/or amplitude.

: :	O:<u>kay</u>?	Colons indicate prolongation of the immediately prior sound. The length of the row of colons indicates the length of the prolongation.

WORD	I've got ENOUGH TO WORRY ABOUT	Capitals, except at the beginnings of lines, indicate especially loud sounds relative to the surrounding talk.
.hhhh	I feel that (.2) .hhh	A row of h's prefixed by a dot indicates an inbreath; without a dot, an outbreath. The length of the row of h's indicates the length of the in- or outbreath.
( )	future risks and ( ) and life ( )	Empty parentheses indicate the transcribers inability to hear what was said.
(word)	Would you see (there) anything positive	Parenthesized words are possible hearings.
(( ))	confirm that ((continues))	Double parentheses contain author's descriptions rather than transcriptions.
. , ?	What do you think?	Indicate speaker's intonation (. = falling intonation; , = flat or slightly rising intonation)
>	>What do you think?	Indicates data later discussed

Glossary

CAQDAS	Computer-assisted analysis of qualitative data
Concept	An idea deriving from from a given model (e.g. 'stimulus–response', 'oppression')
Conversation analysis (CA)	The study of talk-in-interaction in order to discover how we produce an orderly social world
Discourse analysis (DA)	The study of 'the way versions of the world, of society, events, and inner psychological worlds are produced in discourse' (Potter, 1997: 146). The Foucaultian discourse analytic approach is concerned with the construction of subjects within various forms of power/knowledge
Ethnography	Observational work in particular social settings. The initial thrust in favour of ethnography was anthropological
Generalizability	Generalizing from particular cases to populations
Hypothesis	A testable proposition
Methodology	A general approach to studying research topics which relates theories to methods
Method	A specific research technique
Model	An overall framework for looking at reality (e.g. behaviouralism, feminism)
Macrostructure	How you craft your overall argument in the data chapters of a research report (Alasuutari, 1995: 179)
Microstructure	How you write up your analysis of particular sets of data in your research report (Alasuutari, 1995: 179)
Positivism	The search for laws of social behaviour

Reliability	The degree of consistency with which instances are assigned to the same category by different observers or by the same observer on different occasions (Hammersley, 1992: 67)
Science	A critical sifting of data, leading to cumulative generalizations which can always be later refuted
Text	A way of defining data consisting of words and images which have become recorded without the intervention of a researcher
Theory	A set of concepts used to define and/or explain some phenomenon
Triangulation	The attempt to get a 'true' fix on a situation by combining different ways of looking at it or different findings
Validity	The extent to which an account accurately represents the social phenomena to which it refers (Hammersley, 1990: 57)

References

Abrams, P. (1984) 'Evaluating soft findings: some problems of measuring informal care', *Research Policy and Planning*, 2 (2), 1–8.

Acourt, P. (1997) *'Progress, utopia and intellectual practice: arguments for the resurrection of the future'*, unpublished PhD thesis, University of London, Goldsmiths College.

Agar, M. (1986) *Speaking of Ethnography*, Qualitative Research Methods Series, Vol. 2, London: Sage.

Alasuutari, P. (1995) *Researching Culture: Qualitative Method and Cultural Studies*, London: Sage.

Antaki, C. and Rapley, M. (1996) ' "Quality of life" talk: the liberal paradox of psychological testing', *Discourse and Society*, 7 (3), 293–316.

Arber, S. (1993) 'The research process', in N. Gilbert (ed.), *Researching Social Life*, London: Sage, 32–50.

Armstrong, D., Gosling, A., Weinman, J. and Marteau, T. (1997) 'The place of inter-rater reliability in qualitative research: an empirical study', *Sociology*, 31 (3), 597–606.

Atkinson, J.M. (1978) *Discovering Suicide*, London: Macmillan.

Atkinson, J.M. and Heritage, J.C. (eds) (1984) *Structures of Social Action*, Cambridge: Cambridge University Press.

Atkinson, P. (1992) 'The ethnography of a medical setting: reading, writing and rhetoric', *Qualitative Health Research*, 2 (4), 451–74.

Atkinson, P. and Coffey, A. (1997) 'Analysing documentary realities', in D. Silverman (ed.), *Qualitative Research*, London: Sage, 45–62.

Atkinson, P. and Silverman, D. (1997) 'Kundera's *Immortality*: the interview society and the invention of self', *Qualitative Inquiry*, 3 (3), 324–45.

Barthes, R. (1973) *Mythologies*, London: Paladin.

Baruch, G. (1981) 'Moral tales: parents' stories of encounters with the health profession', *Social Health and Illness*, 3 (3), 275–96.

Baruch, G. (1982) 'Moral tales: interviewing parents of congenitally ill children', unpublished PhD thesis, University of London, Goldsmiths' College.

Baszanger, I. and Dodier, N. (1997) 'Ethnography: relating the part to the whole', in D. Silverman (ed.), *Qualitative Research: Theory, Method and Practice*, London: Sage, 8–23.

Becker, H. (1998) *Tricks of the Trade: How to Think about Your Research while Doing It*, Chicago and London: University of Chicago Press.

Becker, H. and Geer, B. (1960) 'Participant observation: the analysis of qualitative field data', in R. Adams and J. Preiss (eds), *Human Organization Research: Field Relations and Techniques*, Homewood, IL: Dorsey.

Bell, J. (1993) *Doing Your Research Project*, 2nd edn, Buckingham: Open University Press.

Berelson, B. (1952) *Content Analysis in Communicative Research*, New York: Free Press.

Bergmann, J. (1992) 'Veiled morality: notes on discretion in psychiatry', in P. Drew and J. Heritage (eds), *Talk at Work*, Cambridge: Cambridge University Press, 137–62.

Blaikie, N. (1993) *Approaches to Social Enquiry*, Cambridge: Polity.

Blau, P. and Schoenherr, R. (1971) *The Structure of Organizations*, New York: Basic Books.

Bloor, M. (1978) 'On the analysis of observational data: a discussion of the worth and uses of inductive techniques and respondent validation', *Sociology*, 12 (3), 545–57.

Bloor, M. (1983) 'Notes on member validation', in R. Emerson (ed.), *Contemporary Field Research: a Collection of Readings*, Boston: Little, Brown.

Bloor, M. (1997) 'Addressing social problems through qualitative research', in D. Silverman (ed.), *Qualitative Research: Theory, Method and Practice*, London: Sage, 221–38.

Blumer, H. (1956) 'Sociological analysis and the "variable"', *American Sociological Review*, 21, 633–60.

British Research Councils (1996) *Priorities News*, Spring, Swindon: ESRC, http://www.pparc.ac.uk/work/supervis/intro.ht

Brown, P. and Levinson, S. (1987) *Politeness: Some Universals in Language Usage*, Cambridge: Cambridge University Press.

Bryman, A. (1988) *Quantity and Quality in Social Research*, London: Unwin Hyman.

Buchanan, D.R. (1992) 'An uneasy alliance: combining qualitative and quantitative research methods', *Health Education Quarterly*, 117–35.

Bulmer, M. (1984) *The Chicago School of Sociology*, Chicago: Chicago University Press.

Button, G. (1992) 'Answers as interactional products: two sequential practices used in job interviews', in P. Drew and J.C. Heritage (eds), *Talk at Work*, Cambridge: Cambridge University Press, 212–34.

Byrne, P. and Long, B. (1976) *Doctors Talking to Patients*, London: HMSO.

Chapman, G. (1987) 'Talk, text and discourse: nurses' talk in a therapeutic community', PhD thesis, Goldsmiths College, University of London.

Cicourel, A. (1964) *Method and Measurement in Sociology*, New York: Free Press.

Cicourel, A. (1968) *The Social Organization of Juvenile Justice*, New York: Wiley.

Clavarino, A., Najman, J. and Silverman, D. (1995) 'Assessing the quality of qualitative data', *Qualitative Inquiry*, 1 (2), 223–42.

Coffey, A. and Atkinson, P. (1996) *Making Sense of Qualitative Data*, London: Sage.

Coffey, A., Holbrook, B. and Atkinson, P. (1996) 'Qualitative data analysis: technologies and representations', *Sociological Research Online*, 1 (1). http://www.soc.surrey.ac.uk/socresonline/1/1/4.html

Cornwell, J. (1981) *Hard Earned Lives*, London: Tavistock.

Cryer, P. (1996) *The Research Student's Guide to Success*, Buckingham: Open University Press.

Davidson, J. (1984) 'Subsequent versions of invitations, offers, requests, and proposals dealing with potential or actual rejection', in J.M. Atkinson and J.C. Heritage (eds), *Structures of Social Action*, Cambridge: Cambridge University Press, 102–28.

Denzin, N. (1970) *The Research Act in Sociology*, London: Butterworth.

Denzin, N. (1997) *Interpretive Ethnography: Ethnographic Practices for the 21st Century*, Thousand Oaks, CA: Sage.

Denzin, N. and Lincoln, Y. (eds) (1994) *Handbook of Qualitative Research*, Thousand Oaks, CA: Sage.

Dey, I. (1993) *Qualitative Data Analysis: a User-Friendly Guide for Social Scientists*, London: Routledge.

Dingwall, R. and Murray, T. (1983) 'Categorization in accident departments: "good" patients, "bad" patients and children', *Sociology of Health and Illness*, 5 (12), 121–48.

Douglas, M. (1975) 'Self-evidence', in M. Douglas, *Implicit Meanings*, London: Routledge.

Drew, P. and Heritage, J.C. (1992) 'Analysing talk at work: an introduction', in P. Drew and J.C. Heritage (eds), *Talk at Work*, Cambridge: Cambridge University Press, 3–65.

Durkheim, E. (1951) *Suicide*, New York: Free Press.

Durkin, T. (1997) 'Using computers in strategic qualitative research', in G. Miller and R. Dingwall (eds), *Context and Method in Qualitative Research*, London: Sage, 92–105.

Edwards, G., Williamson, V., Hawker, A., Hensman, C., Postoyan (now Waller), S. (1968) 'Census of a reception centre', *British Journal of Psychiatry*, 114, 1031–9.

Emerson, R.M., Fretz, R.I. and Shaw, L.L. (1995) *Writing Ethnographic Fieldnotes*, Chicago: University of Chicago Press.

Engebretson, J. (1996) 'Urban healers: an experiential description of American healing touch groups', *Qualitative Health Research*, 6 (4), 526–41.

Feltham, C. (1995) *What is Counselling?*, London: Sage.

Fielding, N. (1982) 'Observational research on the National Front', in M. Bulmer (ed.), *Social Research Ethics: an Examination of the Merits of Covert Participant Observation*, London: Macmillan.

Fielding, N. and Fielding, J. (1986) *Linking Data*, London: Sage.

Fielding, N. and Lee, R. (eds) (1991) *Using Computers in Qualitative Research*, Newbury Park, CA: Sage.

Filmer, P., Phillipson, M., Silverman, D. and Walsh, D. (1972) *New Directions in Sociological Theory*, London: Collier-Macmillan.

Fisher, M. (1997) 'Qualitative computing: using software for qualitative data analysis', Cardiff Papers in Qualitative Research, Aldershot: Ashgate.

Foucault, M. (1977) *Discipline and Punish*, Harmondsworth: Penguin.

Foucault, M. (1979) *The History of Sexuality*: Vol. 1, Harmondsworth: Penguin.

Frake, C. (1964) 'Notes on queries in ethnography', *American Anthropologist*, 66, 132–45.

Fraser, M. (1995) 'The history of the child: 1905–1989', PhD thesis, Goldsmiths College, University of London.

Garfinkel, H. (1967) *Studies in Ethnomethodology*, Englewood Cliffs, NJ: Prentice-Hall.

Gilbert, N. (1993a) 'Writing about social research', in N. Gilbert (ed.), *Researching Social Life*, London: Sage, 328–44.

Gilbert, N. (ed.) (1993b), *Researching Social Life*, London: Sage.

Gilbert, N. and Mulkay, M. (1983) 'In search of the action', in N. Gilbert and P. Abell (eds), *Accounts and Action*, Aldershot: Gower.

Glaser, B. and Strauss, A. (1964) 'The social loss of dying patients', *American Journal of Nursing*, 64 (6), 119–21.

Glaser, B. and Strauss, A. (1967) *The Discovery of Grounded Theory*, Chicago: Aldine.

Glaser, B. and Strauss, A. (1968) *Time for Dying*, Chicago: Aldine.

Glassner, B. and Loughlin, J. (1987) *Drugs in Adolescent Worlds: Burnouts to Straights*, New York: St Martin's Press.

Goffman, E. (1959) *The Presentation of Self in Everyday Life*, New York: Doubleday Anchor.

Goffman, E. (1961) *Asylums*, New York: Doubleday Anchor.

Goffman, E. (1974) *Frame Analysis*, New York: Harper and Row.

Gouldner, A. (1954) *Patterns of Industrial Bureaucracy*, Glencoe, IL: Free Press.

Guba, E. and Lincoln, Y. (1994) 'Competing paradigms in qualitative research', in N.

Denzin and Y. Lincoln (eds), *Handbook of Qualitative Research*, Thousand Oaks, CA: Sage, 105–17.

Gubrium, J. (1988) *Analyzing Field Reality*, Newbury Park, CA: Sage.

Gubrium, J. (1992) *Out of Control: Family Therapy and Domestic Disorder*, London: Sage.

Gubrium, J. (1997) *Living and Dying in Murray Manor*, Charlottesville, VA: University Press of Virginia.

Gubrium, J. and Buckholdt, D. (1982) *Describing Care: Image and Practice in Rehabilitation*, Cambridge, MA: Oelschlager, Gunn and Hain.

Gubrium, J. and Holstein, J. (1995) 'Qualitative inquiry and the deprivatization of experience', *Qualitative Inquiry*, 1 (2), 204–22.

Gubrium, J. and Holstein, J. (1997) *The New Language of Qualitative Method*, New York: Oxford University Press.

Hadley, R. (1987) 'Publish and be ignored: proselytise and be damned', in G.C. Wenger (ed.), *The Research Relationship: Practice and Politics in Social Policy Research*, London: Allen and Unwin, 98–110.

Halfpenny, P. (1979) 'The analysis of qualitative data', *Sociological Review*, 27 (4), 799–825.

Hammersley, M. (1990) *Reading Ethnographic Research: a Critical Guide*, London: Longmans.

Hammersley, M. (1992) *What's Wrong with Ethnography? Methodological Explorations*, London: Routledge.

Hammersley, M. and Atkinson, P. (1983) *Ethnography: Principles in Practice*, London: Tavistock.

Hart, C. (1998) *Doing a Literature Review: Releasing the Social Science Imagination*, London: Sage.

Heath, C. (1997) 'Using video: analysing activities in face to face interaction', in D. Silverman (ed.), *Qualitative Research: Theory, Method and Practice*, London: Sage, 221–38.

Heaton, J.M. (1979) 'Theory in psychotherapy', in N. Bolton (ed.), *Philosophical Problems in Psychology*, London: Methuen, 179–98.

Heise, D. (1988) 'Computer analysis of cultural structures', *Social Science Computer Review*, 6, 183–96.

Heritage, J. (1984) *Garfinkel and Ethnomethodology*, Cambridge: Polity.

Heritage, J. and Sefi, S. (1992) 'Dilemmas of advice: aspects of the delivery and reception of advice in interactions between health visitors and first time mothers', in P. Drew and J. Heritage (eds), *Talk at Work*, Cambridge: Cambridge University Press, 359–417.

Hesse-Biber, S. and Dupuis, P. (1995) 'Hypothesis testing in computer-aided qualitative data analysis', in U. Kelle (ed.), *Computer Aided Qualitative Data Analysis: Theory, Methods and Practice*, London: Sage, 129–35.

Hill, C.E. (1989) *Therapist Techniques and Client Outcomes: Eight Cases of Brief Psychotherapy*, London: Sage.

Hindess, B. (1973) *The Use of Official Statistics in Sociology*, London: Macmillan.

Holstein, J. and Gubrium, J. (1995) *The Active Interview*, Thousand Oaks, CA: Sage.

Hornsby-Smith, M. (1993) 'Gaining access', in N. Gilbert (ed.), *Researching Social Life*, London: Sage, 52–67.

Houtkoop-Steenstra, H. (1991) 'Opening sequences in Dutch telephone conversations', in D. Boden and D.H. Zimmerman (eds), *Talk and Social Structure: Studies in Ethnomethodology and Conversation Analysis*, Cambridge: Polity, 232–50.

Huber, G.L. and Garcia, C.M. (1991) 'Computer assistance for testing hypotheses about qualitative data: the software package AQUAD 3.0', *Qualitative Sociology*, 14 (4), 325–48.

Huberman, A.M. and Miles, M.B. (1994) 'Data management and analysis methods', in N. Denzin and Y. Lincoln (eds), *Handbook of Qualitative Research*, Thousand Oaks, CA: Sage, 413–27.

Irurita, V. (1996) 'Hidden dimensions revealed: progressive grounded theory study of quality care in the hospital', *Qualitative Health Research*, 6 (3), 331–49.

Jeffery, R. (1979) 'Normal rubbish: deviant patients in casualty departments', *Sociology of Health and Illness*, 1 (1), 90–107.

Kafka, F. (1961) 'Investigations of a dog', in *Metamorphosis and Other Stories*, Harmondsworth: Penguin.

Kelle, U. (ed.) (1995) *Computer Aided Qualitative Data Analysis: Theory, Methods and Practice*, London: Sage.

Kelle, U. (1997) 'Theory building in qualitative research and computer programs for the management of textual data', *Sociological Research Online*, 2 (2), http://www.socresonline.org.uk/socresonline/2/2/1.html

Kelle, U. and Laurie, H. (1995) 'Computer use in qualitative research and issues of validity', in U. Kelle (ed.), *Computer Aided Qualitative Data Analysis: Theory, Methods and Practice*, London: Sage, 19–28.

Kelly, M. (1998) 'Writing a research proposal', in C. Seale (ed.), *Researching Society and Culture*, London: Sage, 111–22.

Kendall, G. and Wickham, G. (1998) *Using Foucault's Methods*, London: Sage.

Kent, G. (1996) 'Informed consent', in 'The principled researcher', unpublished manuscript, Social Science Division, The Graduate School, University of Sheffield, 18–24.

Kirk, J. and Miller, M. (1986) *Reliability and Validity in Qualitative Research*, London: Sage.

Kuhn, T.S. (1970) *The Structure of Scientific Revolutions*, 2nd edn, Chicago: University of Chicago Press.

Lee, R.M. and Fielding, N.G. (1995) 'Users' experiences of qualitative data analysis software', in U. Kelle (ed.), *Computer Aided Qualitative Data Analysis: Theory, Methods and Practice*, London: Sage, 29–140.

Lepper, G. (1995) 'Making trouble: the uses of "formal organization" as an institutional resource', *Studies in Cultures, Organizations and Societies*, 1, 189–207.

Lindström, A. (1994) 'Identification and recognition in Swedish telephone conversation openings', *Language in Society*, 23 (2), 231–52.

Lipset, S.M., Trow, M. and Coleman, J. (1962) *Union Democracy*, Garden City, NY: Anchor Doubleday.

Livingston, E. (1987) *Making Sense of Ethnomethodology*, London: Routledge.

Lynch, M. (1984) *Art and Artifact in Laboratory Science*, London: Routledge.

Malinowski, B. (1922) *Argonauts of the Western Pacific*, London: Routledge.

Marsh, C. (1982) *The Survey Method*, London: Allen and Unwin.

Marshall, C. and Rossman, G. (1989) *Designing Qualitative Research*, London: Sage.

Marx, G. (1997) 'Of methods and manners for aspiring sociologists: 37 moral imperatives', *The American Sociologist*, Spring, 102–25.

Mason, J. (1996) *Qualitative Researching*, London: Sage.

Maynard, D.W. (1991) 'Interaction and asymmetry in clinical discourse', *American Journal of Sociology*, 97 (2), 448–95.

Maynard, D.W. (1992) 'On clinicians co-implicating recipients' perspective in the delivery of diagnostic news', in P. Drew and J.C. Heritage (eds), *Talk at Work*, Cambridge: Cambridge University Press, 331–58.

McKeganey, N. and Bloor, M. (1991) 'Spotting the invisible man: the influence of male gender on fieldwork relations', *British Journal of Sociology*, 42 (2), 195–210.

McLeod, J. (1994) *Doing Counselling Research*, London: Sage.

Mehan, H. (1979) *Learning Lessons: Social Organization in the Classroom*, Cambridge, MA: Harvard University Press.

Mercer, K. (1990) 'Powellism as a political discourse', PhD thesis, Goldsmiths College, University of London.

Mergenthaler, E. (1996) 'Emotion-abstraction patterns in verbatim protocols: a new way of describing psychotherapeutic process', *Journal of Consulting and Clinical Psychology*, 64 (6), 1306–15.

Miall, D.S. (ed.) (1990) *Humanities and the Computer: New Directions*, Oxford: Clarendon.

Miles, M. and Huberman, A. (1984) *Qualitative Data Analysis*, London: Sage.

Miles, M. and Weitzman, E. (1995) *Computer Programs for Qualitative Data Analysis*, Beverly Hills, CA: Sage.

Miller, G. and Silverman, D. (1995) 'Troubles talk and counseling discourse: a comparative study', *The Sociological Quarterly*, 36 (4), 725–47.

Miller, J. (1996) 'Female gang involvement in the Midwest: a two-city comparison', doctoral dissertation, Department of Sociology, University of Southern California.

Miller, J. and Glassner, B. (1997) 'The "Inside" and the "Outside": finding realities in interviews', in D. Silverman (ed.), *Qualitative Research*, 99–112.

Miller, R. and Bor, R. (1988) *AIDS: a Guide to Clinical Counselling*, London: Science Press.

Mills, C.W. (1959) *The Sociological Imagination*, New York: Oxford University Press.

Mitchell, J.C. (1983) 'Case and situational analysis', *Sociological Review*, 31 (2), 187–211.

Moerman, M. (1974) 'Accomplishing ethnicity', in R. Turner (ed.), *Ethnomethodology*, Harmondsworth: Penguin, 34–68.

Morse, J.M. (1994) 'Designing funded qualitative research', in N. Denzin and Y. Lincoln (eds), *Handbook of Qualitative Research*, Thousand Oaks, CA: Sage, 220–35.

Mulkay, M. (1984) 'The ultimate compliment: a sociological analysis of ceremonial discourse', *Sociology*, 18, 531–49.

Murcott, A. (1997) 'The PhD: some informal notes', unpublished paper, School of Health and Social Care, South Bank University, London.

O'Brien, M. (1993) 'Social research and sociology', in N. Gilbert (ed.), *Researching Social Life*, London: Sage, 1–17.

Oboler, R. (1986) 'For better or for worse: anthropologists and husbands in the field', in T. Whitehead and M. Conway (eds), *Self, Sex and Gender in Cross-Cultural Fieldwork*, Urbana, IL: University of Illinois Press, 28–51.

Orford, J., Waller, S. and Peto, J. (1974) 'Drinking behaviour and attitudes and their correlates among university students in England', *Quarterly Journal of Studies on Alcohol*, 35, 1316–74.

Peräkylä, A. (1989) 'Appealing to the experience of the patient in the care of the dying', *Sociology of Health and Illness*, 11 (2), 117–34.

Peräkylä, A. (1995) *AIDS Counselling*. Cambridge: Cambridge University Press.

Peräkylä, A. (1997) 'Reliability and validity in research based upon transcripts', in D. Silverman (ed.), *Qualitative Research*, London: Sage, 201–19.

Phillips, D. (1973) *Abandoning Method*. San Francisco and London: Jossey Bass.

Phillips, E. and Pugh, D. (1994) *How To Get a PhD*, 2nd edn, Buckingham: Open University Press.

Pomerantz, A. (1984) 'Agreeing and disagreeing with assessments: some features of preferred/dispreferred turn shapes, in J.M. Atkinson and J.C. Heritage (eds), *Structures of Social Action*, Cambridge: Cambridge University Press, 57–101.

Popper, K. (1959) *The Logic of Scientific Discovery*, New York: Basic Books.

Potter, J. (1997) 'Discourse analysis as a way of analysing naturally-occurring talk', in D. Silverman (ed.), *Qualitative Research: Theory, Method and Practice*, London: Sage, 144–60.

Potter, J. and Wetherell, M. (1987) *Discourse and Social Psychology: Beyond Attitudes and Behaviour*, London: Sage.

Potter, J. and Wetherell, M. (1994) 'Analysing discourse', in A. Bryman and R.G. Burgess (eds), *Analysing Qualitative Data*, London: Routledge, 47–66.

Prior, L. (1987) 'Policing the dead: a sociology of the mortuary', *Sociology*, 21 (3), 355–76.

Procter, M. (1993) 'Analysing survey data', in N. Gilbert (ed.), *Researching Social Life*, London: Sage.

Propp, V.I. (1968) *Morphology of the Folktale*, 2nd rev. edn, ed. L.A. Wagner, Austin and London: University of Texas Press.

Punch, M. (1986) *The Politics and Ethics of Fieldwork*, Beverly Hills, CA: Sage.

Punch, M. (1994) 'Politics and ethics in fieldwork', in N. Denzin and Y. Lincoln (eds), *Handbook of Qualitative Research*, Thousand Oaks, CA: Sage, 83–97.

Pursley-Crotteau, S. and Stern, P. (1996) 'Creating a new life: dimensions of temperance in perinatal cocaine crack users', *Qualitative Health Research*, 6 (3), 350–67.

Radcliffe-Brown, A.R. (1948) *The Andaman Islanders*, Glencoe, IL: Free Press.

Rayner, G. and Stimson, G. (1979) 'Medicine, superstructure and micropolitics: a response', *Social Science and Medicine*, 13A, 611–12.

Reason, P. and Rowan, J. (1981) *Human Inquiry: a Sourcebook of New Paradigm Research*, Chichester: Wiley.

Reid, A.O. (1992) 'Computer management strategies for text data', in B.F. Crabtree and W.L. Miller (eds), *Doing Qualitative Research*, Newbury Park, CA: Sage, 125–45.

Richards, L. and Richards, T. (1994) 'Using computers in qualitative analysis', in N. Denzin and Y. Lincoln (eds), *Handbook of Qualitative Research*, Thousand Oaks, CA: Sage, 445–62.

Richardson, L. (1990) *Writing Strategies: Reaching Diverse Audiences*, Newbury Park, CA: Sage.

Richardson, L. (1994) 'Writing: a method of inquiry', in N. Denzin and Y. Lincoln (eds), *Handbook of Qualitative Research*, Thousand Oaks, CA: Sage, 516–29.

Riessman, C.K. (1993) *Narrative Analysis*, Newbury Park, CA: Sage.

Rudestam, K. and Newton, R. (1992) *Surviving Your Dissertation*, Newbury Park, CA: Sage.

Sacks, H. (1974) 'On the analysability of stories by children', in R. Turner (ed.), *Ethnomethodology*, Harmondsworth: Penguin.

Sacks, H. (1984) 'On doing "being ordinary" ', in J.M. Atkinson and J. Heritage (eds), *Structures of Social Action: Studies in Conversation Analysis*, Cambridge: Cambridge University Press, 513–29.

Sacks, H. (1992) *Lectures on Conversation*, Vols 1 and 2, ed. Gail Jefferson with introduction by Emmanuel Schegloff, Oxford: Blackwell.

Sacks, H., Schegloff, E.A. and Jefferson, G. (1974) 'A simplest systematics for the organization of turn-taking in conversation', *Language*, 50 (4), 696–735.

Schegloff, E. (1986) 'The routine as achievement', *Human Studies*, 9, 111–51.

Schegloff, E. (1991) 'Reflections on talk and social structure', in D. Boden and D.

Zimmerman (eds), *Talk and Social Structure: Studies in Ethnomethodology and Conversation Analysis*, Cambridge: Polity, 44–70.

Schreiber, R. (1996) '(Re)defining my self: women's process of recovery from depression', *Qualitative Health Research*, 6 (4), 469–91.

Schwartz, H. and Jacobs, J. (1979) *Qualitative Sociology: a Method to the Madness*, New York: Free Press.

Seale, C. (1996) 'Living alone towards the end of life', *Ageing and Society*, 16, 75–91.

Seale, C. (ed.) (1998) *Researching Society and Culture*, London: Sage.

Seale, C. (1999) *The Quality of Qualitative Research*, London: Sage.

Selltiz, C., Jahoda, M., Deutsch, M. and Cook, S. (1964) *Research Methods in Social Relations*, New York: Holt, Rinehart and Winston.

Silverman, D. (1975) 'Accounts of organizations: organizational structures and the accounting process', in J. McKinlay (ed.), *Processing People: Cases in Organizational Behaviour*, London: Holt, Rinehart and Winston.

Silverman, D. (1981) 'The child as a social object: Down's syndrome children in a paediatric cardiology clinic', *Sociology of Health and Illness*, 3 (3), 254–74.

Silverman, D. (1983) 'The clinical subject: adolescents in a cleft palate clinic', *Sociology of Health and Illness*, (5) 3, 253–74.

Silverman, D. (1984) 'Going private: ceremonial forms in a private oncology clinic', *Sociology*, 18, 191–202.

Silverman, D. (1985) *Qualitative Methodology and Sociology: Describing the Social World*, Aldershot: Gower.

Silverman D. (1987) *Communication and Medical Practice: Social Relations in the Clinic*, London: Sage.

Silverman, D. (1989) 'Making sense of a precipice: constituting identity in an HIV clinic', in P. Aggleton, G. Hart and P. Davies (eds), *AIDS: Social Representations, Social Practices*, Lewes: Falmer.

Silverman, D. (1990) 'The social organization of HIV counselling', in P. Aggleton, G. Hart and P. Davies (eds), *AIDS: Individual, Cultural and Policy Perspectives*, Lewes: Falmer, 191–211.

Silverman, D. (1993) *Interpreting Qualitative Data: Methods for Analysing Talk, Text and Interaction*, London: Sage.

Silverman, D. (ed.) (1997a) *Qualitative Research: Theory, Method and Practice*, London: Sage.

Silverman, D. (1997b) *Discourses of Counselling: HIV Counselling as Social Interaction*, London: Sage.

Silverman, D. (1998a) *Harvey Sacks: Social Science and Conversation Analysis*, Cambridge: Polity, New York: Oxford University Press.

Silverman, D. (1998b) 'Analysing conversation', in C. Seale (ed.), *Researching Society and Culture*, London: Sage, 261–74.

Silverman, D. and Bloor, M. (1989) 'Patient-centred medicine: some sociological observations on its constitution, penetration and cultural assonance', in G.L. Albrecht (ed.), *Advances in Medical Sociology*, Greenwich, CT: JAI Press, 3–26.

Silverman, D. and Gubrium, J. (1994) 'Competing strategies for analyzing the contexts of social interaction', *Sociological Inquiry*, 64 (2), 179–98.

Silverman, D. and Jones, J. (1976) *Organizational Work: the Language of Grading/the Grading of Language*, London: Collier-Macmillan.

Silverman, D., Baker, C. and Keogh, J. (1997) 'Advice-giving and advice-reception in parent–teacher interviews', in I. Hutchby and J. Moran-Ellis (eds), *Children and Social Competence*, London: Falmer, 220–40.

REFERENCES

Singleton, R., Straits, B., Straits, M. and McAllister, R. (1988) *Approaches to Social Research*, Oxford: Oxford University Press.

Smith, J.K. and Heshusius, L. (1986) 'Closing down the conversation: the end of the qualitative–quantitative debate among educational enquirers', *Educational Researcher*, 15, 4–12.

Sontag, S. (1979) *Illness as Metaphor*, Harmondsworth: Penguin.

Spradley, J.P. (1979) *The Ethnographic Interview*, New York: Holt, Rinehart and Winston.

Stake, R. (1994) 'Case studies', in N. Denzin and Y. Lincoln (eds), *Handbook of Qualitative Research*, Thousand Oaks, CA: Sage, 236–47.

Stimson, G. (1986) 'Place and space in sociological fieldwork', *Sociological Review*, 34 (3), 641–56.

Strauss, A. and Corbin, J. (1990) *Basics of Qualitative Research*, Thousand Oaks, CA: Sage.

Strauss, A. and Corbin, J. (1994) 'Grounded theory methodology: an overview', in N. Denzin and Y. Lincoln (eds), *Handbook of Qualitative Research*, Thousand Oaks, CA: Sage, 262–72.

Strong, P. (1979) *The Ceremonial Order of the Clinic*, London: Routledge.

Suchman, L. (1987) *Plans and Situated Actions: the Problem of Human–Machine Communication*, Cambridge: Cambridge University Press.

Sudnow, D. (1968a) *Passing On: the Social Organization of Dying*, Englewood Cliffs, NJ: Prentice-Hall.

Sudnow, D. (1968b) 'Normal crimes', in E. Rubington and M. Weinberg (eds), *Deviance: the Interactionist Perspective*, New York: Macmillan.

Taylor, V. (1994) 'Preference organization in anxiety/phobia counselling: preserving social solidarity', *Counselling Psychology Quarterly*, 7 (2), 143–66.

ten Have, P. (1998) *Doing Conversation Analysis: a Practical Guide*, London: Sage.

Thomas, W. and Znaniecki, F. (1927) *The Polish Peasant in Europe and America*, New York: Alfred Knopf.

Tyler, S.A. (1986) 'Post-modern ethnography: from document of the occult to occult document', in J. Clifford and G. Marcus (eds), *Writing Culture: the Poetics and Politics of Ethnography*, Los Angeles: University of California Press, 122–40.

Waitzkin, H. (1979) 'Medicine, superstructure and micropolitics', *Social Science and Medicine*, 13A, 601–9.

Walsh, D. (1998) 'Doing ethnography', in C. Seale (ed.), *Researching Society and Culture*, London: Sage, 217–32.

Warren, A. (1988) *Gender Issues in Field Research*, Newbury Park, CA: Sage.

Warren, A. and Rasmussen, P. (1977) 'Sex and gender in fieldwork research', *Urban Life*, 6, 359–69.

Webb, B. and Stimson, G. (1976) 'People's accounts of medical encounters', in M. Wadsworth (ed.), *Everyday Medical Life*, London: Martin Robertson.

Weber, M. (1946) 'Science as a vocation', in H. Gerth and C.W. Mills (eds), *From Max Weber*, New York: Oxford University Press.

Weber, M. (1949) *Methodology of the Social Sciences*, New York: Free Press.

Whyte, W.F. (1949) 'The social structure of the restaurant', *American Journal of Sociology*, 54, 302–10.

Wolcott, H. (1990) *Writing Up Qualitative Research*, Newbury Park, CA: Sage.

Author index

Subject index

ethics 200–2, 204
ethnicity 46–7
ETHNO 163, 165
ETHNOGRAPH 163, 166–8, 171, 286
ethnography 1, 37–9, 141, 143, 148–9,
    186–7, 194–5, 197, 241
ethnomethodology 8, 19, 35, 77–8, 197,
    289
experiments 3, 7, 8

face 182, 184
families 123, 136, 292
fashions 71
feedback 211
feminism 8, 77, 197
fieldnotes 10, 126–8, 140–3, 144,
    147–50
fieldwork
    access 119–21, 198–200, 203
    contract 200
    feedback 199–200, 202–3, 205–6, 218
    informed consent in 201–2
    relations 197–209
    settings 198
Finland 31, 40, 45, 108, 205
flow charts 67–8
focus groups 294
frames 126–8
functionalism 77

gangs 123–5
gender 33, 47–50, 75, 106, 206–8
generalizations 83–5, 102–11
grand theory 64–5, 71
grounded theory 62–3, 84, 144–5, 148,
    152, 161, 168–72, 252–3, 285, 287–8

health promotion 14, 21, 92
history 41, 65
HYPERSOFT 171
hypothesis-testing 7–8, 77–83, 86, 145,
    170–1, 192

induction 8, 21, 61–3, 150, 168, 267
information studies 32, 38
instrumentation 88
interactionism 8, 77, 99, 288
Internet 39, 45, 121, 227
interviews 8, 11, 19, 32–7, 88, 90–7, 99,
    122–5, 158, 186, 283–8, 290–5

Japan 40
jobs 278–81

laboratories 176
linguistics 15, 42, 44, 109, 147
literature reviews 191–2, 226–31

mass media 14, 41, 47–8
meanings 8, 19, 32, 35–6, 89
medicine 10, 20, 38, 41, 43–4, 49–50, 66,
    70, 91–2, 126–8, 133–5, 138–41,
    144–7, 179, 185, 202–3, 206, 260–3,
    275, 286
membership categorization devices
    (MCDs) 16, 35, 41–3, 129–30, 241
methods 32, 77–83, 86, 88–100
models 77–83, 86, 283
mothers 45–6, 171
multiple methods 48–51, 98–9

narratives 19–20, 32, 34–6, 123–5, 163–4
naturalism 78, 197
natural sciences 176
navy pilot story 129–30
newspapers 41, 276
NUD•IST 159–61, 166–7, 170
nursing 58, 168, 260–3, 284, 286, 291

objectivity 11
observation 3, 7, 10, 34, 88, 90, 92, 140–3,
    143, 195, 202, 285
oral examination 257–64
organizations 5–6
originality 54–9

positivism 5, 8, 10, 188
postmodernism 8, 78, 156, 170–1, 197
preference organization 182–4
psychiatry 34, 49–50
psychology 75, 93, 127
psychotherapy 156
publishing 31, 266–70
puzzles 68–9, 131, 132, 135, 213, 270

quantitative research 1–7, 9, 18, 80, 88–9,
    93–6, 102–3, 110, 128, 143, 176, 178,
    180–1, 184, 186–7, 234–5, 242

realism 122, 124
reductionism 69–70, 72